Armstrong's Handbook of Management and Leadership

THIRD EDITION

Armstrong's Handbook of Management and Leadership

Developing effective people skills for better leadership and management

Michael Armstrong

KoganPage

LONDON PHILADELPHIA NEW DELHI

First published in Great Britain and the United States in 2005 by Kogan Page Limited
Second edition 2009
Third edition 2012

120 Pentonville Road
London N1 9JN
United Kingdom
www.koganpage.com

1518 Walnut Street, Suite 1100
Philadelphia PA 19102
USA

4737/23 Ansari Road
Daryaganj
New Delhi 110002
India

© Michael Armstrong and Tina Stephens, 2005
© Michael Armstrong 2009, 2012

ISBN   978 0 7494 6552 0
E-ISBN   978 0 7494 6553 7

British Library Cataloguing-in-Publication Data

A CIP record for this book is available from the British Library.

Library of Congress Cataloging-in-Publication Data

Armstrong, Michael, 1928-
   Armstrong's handbook of management and leadership : developing effective people skills for better leadership and management / Michael Armstrong. – 3rd ed.
      p. cm.
   ISBN 978-0-7494-6552-0 – ISBN 978-0-7494-6553-7   1. Management–Handbooks, manuals, etc.
2. Leadership–Handbooks, manuals, etc. I. Title.
   HD38.15.A76 2012
   658.4'092–dc23
                                                                            2011041045

Typeset by Cenveo Publisher Services
Printed and bound in India by Replika Press Pvt Ltd

CONTENTS

LIST OF FIGURES

LIST OF TABLES

FOREWORD

The aim of this book is to explore the key concepts of leadership, management and development as they affect the work of everyone involved in management but with special reference to those concerned with human resource management. The book takes account of the learning objective stated by the CIPD in its description of its Leadership, Management and Development module. This is to help those studying the subject to 'become effective managers as well as effective HR specialists, managing others fairly and effectively and increasing levels of engagement, commitment, motivation and performance'.

A recurring theme in the first three parts of the book is that in order to make an effective contribution, HR specialists have to be good at management, leadership and developing themselves and others, but in addition they need to be aware of the management and business considerations that affect their work. They function alongside line managers as part of the management of the organization and can only do that well if they understand what managers do, the leadership and development activities managers carry out and how they, as HR professionals, provide guidance, support and services to managers in the performance of the latters' roles. However, although the business dimension of management, leadership and development is important, there is also an ethical dimension. This too is emphasized throughout the book.

The final part of the book is concerned with enhancing HR skills for business leadership. It concentrates on people management skills and the aim, in the words of the CIPD module, is to 'develop and improve a range of definable skills that are pivotal to successful management practice and to effective leadership. These include thinking and decision-making skills, the management of financial information, managing budgets, a range of team working and interpersonal skills and others associated with developing personal effectiveness and credibility at work.'

The CIPD states that its module for Leadership, Management and Development 'seeks to familiarise learners with major contemporary research evidence on employment and effective approaches to human resource (HR) and learning and development (L&D) practice. Research focusing on the links between people management practices and positive organisational outcomes is covered, as is research that highlights major contemporary changes and developments in practice.' References to research are made frequently in the main parts of this book but in addition, summaries of the main findings from a number of recent research studies are provided in the web-based supporting material.

The Appendix provides cross references between the main provisions of the two CIPD modules referred to above and the relevant sections of this book.

PART ONE
Leading, managing and developing fundamentals

Leading people

Key concepts and terms

- *Authentic leaders*
- *Charismatic leaders*
- *Contingent leadership*
- *Distributed leadership*
- *Emotional intelligence*
- *Leader–member exchange theory*
- *Leadership*
- *Leadership development*
- *Path–goal model*
- *Situational leadership*
- *Social exchange theory*
- *Trait*
- *Transactional leaders*
- *Transformational leaders*
- *Visionary leaders*

LEARNING OUTCOMES

On completing this chapter you should be able to define these key concepts. You should also know about:

- The meaning of leadership
- The main leadership theories
- What leaders do
- The main leadership styles
- The qualities of a good leader
- The process of leadership development
- What makes an effective leader

Introduction

To lead people is to inspire, influence and guide. The significance of leadership in achieving results was established in research conducted by the consulting firm Hay McBer as reported by Goleman (2000). This study of 3,871 executives, selected from a database of more than 20,000 executives worldwide, found that leadership had a direct impact on organizational climate, and that climate in turn accounted for nearly one-third of the financial results of organizations. The conclusion from research conducted by Higgs (2006) was that leadership behaviour is responsible for almost 50 per cent of the difference between change success and failure. Research by Northouse (2006) into 167 US firms in 13 industries established that over a 20-year period, leadership was the cause of more variations in performance than any other variable.

This chapter starts with basic definitions of leadership. However, even if the essence of leadership can be defined quite simply, it has to be recognized that in practice it is a complex affair which takes place in all sorts of ways. To understand it fully it is necessary to know more about:

- the underpinning theories which explain the process of leadership;
- what leaders do;
- how they do it;
- the different types of leaders;
- the various styles that leaders can adopt;
- the qualities that good leaders possess;
- approaches to leading people.

These aspects of leadership are considered in turn in this chapter, which ends with a summary of what constitutes effective leadership.

Leadership defined

Leadership can be described as the ability to persuade others willingly to behave differently. It is the process of influencing people – getting them to do their best to achieve a desired result. It involves developing and communicating a vision for the future, motivating people and securing their engagement. Other definitions (there are many) include:

- Bennis and Nanus (1985: 17) Leadership is: 'the capacity to translate intentions into reality and sustain it'.
- Dixon (1994: 214) 'Leadership is no more than exercising such an influence upon others that they tend to act in concert towards achieving a goal which they might not have achieved so readily had they been left to their own devices.'

- Buchanan and Huczynski (2007: 696) Leadership is: 'the process of influencing the activities of an organized group in its efforts toward goal setting and goal achievement'.
- Goleman (2000: 78) 'A leader's singular job is to get results.'

Leadership theories

Leadership is a complicated notion and a number of theories have been produced to explain it. These theories, as summarized below and described more fully later in this section, have developed over the years and explore a number of different facets of leadership and leadership behaviour. In many ways they complement one another and together they help to gain a comprehensive understanding of what the process of leadership is about.

Trait theory, which explains leadership by reference to the qualities leaders have, is the basic – and to many people, the most familiar – theory. But it has its limitations, as explained later, and pragmatic research was carried out to identify what types of behaviour characterized leadership rather than focusing on the personalities of leaders. The key leadership behaviour studies conducted by the Universities of Michigan and Ohio State led respectively to the identification of employee as distinct from job-centred behaviour and the processes of consideration and initiating structure.

The next step in the development of leadership theory was the recognition by researchers that what leaders did and how they did it were dependent or contingent on the situation they were in. Different traits became important, different behaviours or styles of leadership had to be used to achieve effectiveness in different situations. These studies resulted in the theories of contingent and situational leadership.

But the evolution of thinking about leadership still had some way to go. Researchers began to dig more deeply into what went on when people exercised leadership. This led to the path–goal and leader–member exchange theories. At the same time it was recognized that leaders could not exist or succeed without followers and that the role of the latter therefore deserved consideration. Next, trait theory was in effect revived by Goleman (2001) in the notion of emotional intelligence as a necessary attribute of leaders. Most recently, Dave Ulrich put his oar in alongside that of his colleague, Norman Smallwood (2007), with the notion of the leadership brand as a comprehensive approach to leadership by organizations.

Trait theory

Trait theory, which defines leadership in terms of the traits (enduring characteristics of behaviour) that all leaders are said to possess, was amongst the earliest approaches to describing leaders and leadership. In its initial form it provided an easy explanation for the complex set of individual characteristics that together form a leader. As a way of describing the qualities required of leaders, it still persists in some quarters. However, its limitations were exposed long ago by Stogdill (1948: 64), whose research found that a person does not become a leader by virtue of the possession of some combination of traits,

Trait theorists have generated dozens of lists. The research by Stogdill (1948) revealed 79 unique traits but only four (extroversion, humour, intelligence and initiative) appeared in five or more studies. Research conducted by Perren and Burgoyne (2001) identified over 1,000 traits distilled to 83 more or less distinct attributes.

The following list of qualities produced by Adair (1973) is fairly typical:

- enthusiasm – to get things done, which they can communicate to other people;
- confidence – belief in themselves, which again people can sense (but this must not be overconfidence, which leads to arrogance);
- toughness – resilient, tenacious and demanding high standards, seeking respect but not necessarily popularity;
- integrity – being true to oneself: personal wholeness, soundness and honesty, which inspire trust;
- warmth – in personal relationships, caring for people and being considerate;
- humility – willingness to listen and take the blame; not being arrogant and overbearing.

Yet, as Levine (2008: 165) observed: 'It is clear that traits alone are not sufficient to explain or to give rise to successful leadership... More importantly, there is no agreement about what mix of traits really distinguishes leaders from others.' Adair (1973: 13) argued earlier that the study of leadership in terms of the qualities that one person has to a greater degree than his or her fellows is still relevant, but it is far from being the whole story. The later leadership theories discussed below showed this to be the case.

Leadership behaviour studies

The conclusion that trait theory was too vague, inconsistent and generalized to help in understanding the process of leadership (and therefore the identification, selection and training of leaders) led to a shift of focus by researchers to how leaders behaved and the leadership styles they adopted. The studies at the Survey Research Center in Michigan (Katz et al, 1950) identified two dimensions of leadership behaviour:

- employee-centred behaviour, focusing on relationships and employee needs;
- job centred-behaviour, focusing on getting the job done.

Similar results were obtained by the Ohio State University research (Stog-dill, 1950) which revealed two categories of leadership behaviour: consid-eration (concern for people) and initiating structure (getting the job done). In both cases, the researchers stressed that the two types of behaviour did not represent the extremes of a continuum. A leader can emphasize one or other of them or both to different degrees.

The problem with the leadership behaviour approach is that it did not take sufficient account of the effect of the situation in which leadership took place. This gap was filled by the contingent and situational theories described below.

Contingent leadership

The theory of contingent leadership developed by Fiedler (1967) states that the type of leadership exercised depends to a large extent on the situation and the ability of the leader to understand it and act accordingly. Fiedler wrote (ibid: 261):

> Leadership performance... depends as much on the organization as on the leader's own attributes. Except perhaps for the unusual case, it is simply not meaningful to speak of an effective leader or an ineffective leader. We can only speak of a leader who tends to be effective in one situation and ineffective in another.

The performance of a group, as Fiedler pointed out, is related both to the leadership style and the degree to which the situation provides the leader with the opportunity to exert influence. He referred to the leadership be-haviour studies of Ohio State and established through his research that an initiating structure approach worked best for leaders in conditions where the leader has power, formal backing and a relatively well-structured task. Considerate leaders do better in unstructured or ambiguous situations or where their power as a leader is restricted.

Situational leadership

The notion of situational leadership is an extension of contingency theory. As described by Hersey and Blanchard (1974), leaders move between four different styles – directing, coaching, supporting and delegating – depending on the situation in terms of the development level of the subordinate and their own competence and commitment. A later version of the model (Hersey et al, 2001) identified the four main styles as telling, selling, partici-pating and delegating. This is an intuitively appealing approach which has been popular with practitioners.

The path–goal model

Based on expectancy theory (see Chapter 10), the path–goal model devel-oped by House (1971) states that leaders are there to define the path that should be followed by their team in order to achieve its goals. A leader's behaviour is acceptable to subordinates when viewed as a source of satisfaction, and it is motivational when need satisfaction is contingent on performance, and the leader facilitates, coaches and rewards effective performance. Leaders have to engage in different types of behaviour depending on the nature and the demands of a particular situation. It is the leader's job to assist followers in attaining goals and to provide the direction and support needed to ensure that their goals are compatible with the organization's goals. Path–goal theory identifies four leadership styles: achievement-orientated, directive, participative, and supportive.

Leader–member exchange theory

The leader–member exchange (LMX) theory of leadership as formulated by Graen (1976) focuses on the two-way relationship between supervisors and subordinates. It is linked to social exchange theory, which explains social change and stability as a process of negotiated exchanges between parties. Leaders usually have special relationships with an inner circle of assistants and advisors, who are often given high levels of responsibility and access to resources. This is called the 'in-group', and their position can come with a price. These employees work harder, have to be more committed to task objectives and share more administrative duties. They are also expected to be totally committed and loyal to their leader. Conversely, subordinates in the 'out-group' are given low levels of choice or influence and put constraints on the leader.

Leaders/followers theory

Ultimately, leaders depend on the followers they lead. The originator of leader/follower theory, Kelley (1988: 142), argued that: 'Leaders matter greatly. But in searching so zealously for better leaders we tend to lose sight of the people these people will lead... Organizations stand or fall partly on the basis of how well their leaders lead, but partly also on the basis of how well their followers follow.' He suggested that the role of the follower should be studied as carefully as that of the leader. Dixon (1994: 215) observed that: 'Leadership depends upon a proper understanding of the needs and opinions of those one hopes to lead.' And Hesketh and Hird (2010: 104) emphasized that: 'Leadership is not reducible simply to what leaders do, or, in fact, who they are or even the capabilities they possess. We should focus instead on whom leaders do leadership with, and how they achieve together what they cannot achieve alone.'

Leaders need effective followers. Successful leaders depend on followers who want to feel that they are being led in the right direction. Followers need to know where they stand, where they are going and what is in it for them. They want to feel that it is all worth while. Grint (2005) observed that what leaders have to do is to develop followers who can privately resolve the problems leaders have caused or cannot resolve. Leaders need to learn what the role of their followers is and how to enable them to perform that role effectively.

A report on the poet Robert Graves by his CO in the First World War said that 'The men will follow this young officer if only to know where he is going.' This is a good start but it is not enough. Followers have three requirements of their leaders:

- Leaders must fit their followers' expectations – they are more likely to gain the respect and cooperation of their followers if they behave in ways that people expect from their leaders. These expectations will vary according to the group and the context but will often include being straight, fair and firm; as a 19th-century schoolboy once said of his headmaster: 'He's a beast but a just beast.' They also appreciate leaders who are considerate, friendly and approachable but don't want them to get too close – leaders who take too much time courting popularity are not liked.

- Leaders must be perceived as the 'best of us' – they have to demonstrate that they are experts in the overall task facing the group. They need not necessarily have more expertise than any members of their group in particular aspects of the task, but they must demonstrate that they can get the group working purposefully together and direct and harness the expertise shared by group members to obtain results.

- Leaders must be perceived as 'the most of us' – they must incorporate the norms and values which are central to the group. They can influence these values by visionary powers but they will fail if they move too far away from them.

Leadership and emotional intelligence

According to Goleman (2001), emotional intelligence (the capacity of leaders to understand the emotional makeup of people in order to relate to them effectively), is a critical ingredient in leadership. He claimed that good leaders are alike in one crucial way: they have a high degree of emotional intelligence which plays an increasingly important part at higher levels in organizations where differences in technical skills are of negligible importance.

Leadership brand

Ulrich and Smallwood (2007) stressed that businesses are responsible for establishing a leadership brand as an organizational capability by introducing and maintaining processes that help leaders to grow and develop. Leadership brand is pervasive through all levels of leadership in the organization.

Every leader must contribute to the creation of this leadership brand, which defines their identity as leaders, translates customer expectations into employee behaviours and outlasts them.

The problem with leadership theories

In spite of all the research and theorizing, the concept of leadership is still problematic. As Meindl et al (1985: 78) commented: 'It has become apparent that, after years of trying, we have been unable to generate an understanding of leadership that is both intellectually compelling and emotionally satisfying. The concept of leadership remains elusive and enigmatic.'

These problems may arise because, as a notion, leadership is difficult to pin down. There are many different types of situations in which leaders operate, many different types of leaders and many different leadership styles. Producing one theory which covers all these variables is difficult if not impossible. All that can be done is to draw on the various theories that exist to explain different facets of leadership without necessarily relying on any one of them for a comprehensive explanation of what is involved. Perhaps leadership is best defined by considering what leaders do and how they do it (the different styles they adopt), examining what sort of leaders carry out these activities and practise these styles, and looking at any empirical evidence available on what makes them good leaders. These are all covered in the next four sections of this chapter.

What leaders do

The most convincing analysis of what leaders do was produced by John Adair (1973). He explained that the three essential roles of leaders are to:

- Define the task – they make it quite clear what the group is expected to do.
- Achieve the task – that is why the group exists. Leaders ensure that the group's purpose is fulfilled. If it is not, the result is frustration, disharmony, criticism and, eventually perhaps, disintegration of the group.
- Maintain effective relationships – between themselves and the members of the group, and between the people within the group. These relationships are effective if they contribute to achieving the task. They can be divided into those concerned with the team and its morale and sense of common purpose, and those concerned with individuals and how they are motivated.

He suggested that demands on leaders are best expressed as three areas of need which they must satisfy. These are: (1) task needs – to get the job done; (2) individual needs – to harmonize the needs of the individual with

FIGURE 1.1 John Adair's model of leadership

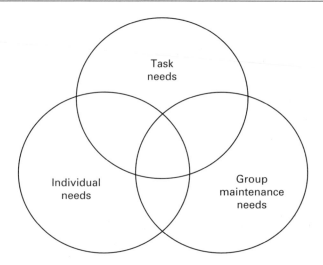

the needs of the task and the group; and (3) group maintenance needs – to build and maintain team spirit. As shown in Figure 1.1, he modelled these demands as three interlocking circles.

This model indicates that the task, individual and group needs are interdependent. Satisfying task needs will also satisfy group and individual needs. Task needs, however, cannot be met unless attention is paid to individual and group needs, and looking after individual needs will also contribute to satisfying group needs and vice versa. There is a risk of becoming so task orientated that leaders ignore individual and group or team needs. It is just as dangerous to be too people orientated, focusing on meeting individual or group needs at the expense of the task. Unsuccessful leaders are those who fail to keep these three needs satisfied and in balance according to the demands of the situation.

Leadership styles

Leadership style is the approach managers use in exercising leadership when they are relating to their team members. It is sometimes called management style. There are many styles of leadership and no one style is necessarily better than the other in any situation. To greater or lesser degrees, leaders can be autocratic or democratic, controlling or enabling, task orientated or people centred. The Hay McBer research reported by Goleman (2000) identified the following six styles and indicated when they might be used:

- Coercive – demands compliance (use in a crisis or with problem people).
- Authoritative – mobilizes people (use when new vision and direction are needed).

- Affiliative – creates harmony (use to heal wounds and to motivate people under stress).
- Democratic – forges consensus (use to build agreement and get contributions).
- Pacesetting – sets high standards (use to get fast results from a motivated team).
- Coaching – develops people (to improve performance and develop strengths).

In line with contingency and situational theories, it should not be assumed that any one style is right in any circumstance. There is no such thing as an ideal leadership style. It all depends. The factors affecting the degree to which a style is appropriate will be the type of organization, the nature of the task, the characteristics of the individuals in the leader's team (the followers) and of the group as a whole and, importantly, the personality of the leader.

Effective leaders are capable of flexing their style to meet the demands of the situation. Normally democratic leaders may have to shift into more of a directive mode when faced with a crisis, but they make clear what they are doing and why. Poor leaders change their style arbitrarily so that their team members are confused and do not know what to expect next.

Good leaders may also flex their style when dealing with individual team members according to their characteristics. Some people need more positive directions than others. Others respond best if they are involved in decision making with their boss. But there is a limit to the degree of flexibility that should be used. It is unwise to differentiate too much between the ways in which individuals are treated or to be inconsistent in one's approach.

Types of leaders

To understand the process of leadership (and, incidentally, provide a basis for leadership development programmes), it is useful not only to analyse the styles that leaders can adopt but also to classify the different types of leaders that apply those styles. As described below, leaders can be charismatic, visionary, transformational, transactional or 'authentic'. However, typical leaders may exhibit any or even all of these characteristics either consistently or in response to the situation in which they find themselves.

Leadership may be exercised by a few selected authoritative individuals and many studies focus on top managers as 'charismatic' or 'visionary' leaders. But it may and indeed should take the form of distributed leadership which is spread through the organization amongst people working together by processes of influence and interdependencies. As Huczynski and Buchanan (2007: 720) commented: 'leadership is a widely distributed phenomenon. Leadership functions are best carried out by those who have the interest, knowledge, skills and motivation to perform them effectively.' The possibility that people who become managers may not have these qualities to a desirable extent creates a need for systematic leadership development programmes as considered later.

Charismatic leaders

Charismatic leaders rely on their personality, their inspirational qualities and their 'aura' to get people to follow them. Burns (1978), who coined the term, suggested that charismatic leaders were set apart from ordinary people and treated as being endowed with exceptional powers or qualities which inspire followers.

Conger and Kanungo (1998) described charismatic leadership as a process of formulating an inspiring vision of the future and then demonstrating the importance of the articulated vision. This may involve unconventional behaviour which conveys important goals that are part of the vision and demonstrates means to achieve these goals. Charismatic leaders also take risks and motivate followers by setting a personal example. In this sense, charismatic leaders operate as visionary and transformational leaders as described below.

But Carey (1992: 232) charged that 'when the gifts of charisma, inspiration, consideration and intellectual strength are abused for the self-interest of the leader, the effect on followers ceases to be liberating and moral and becomes instead oppressive and ideological'. And Bennis (2010: 4) commented that: 'the ability to inspire trust, not charisma, is what enables leaders to recruit others to a cause'.

Visionary leaders

Visionary leaders are inspired by a clear vision of an exciting future and inspire their followers by successfully conveying that vision to them. Bennis and Nanus (1985: 89) defined a vision as 'a target that beckons'. Their notion of visionary leadership was explained as follows (ibid: 89):

> To choose a direction, a leader must first have developed a mental image of a possible and desirable future state of the organization. This image, which we call a vision, may be as vague as a dream or as precise as a goal or mission statement. The critical point is that a vision articulates a view of a realistic, credible and attractive future for the organization, a condition that is important in some important ways from one that now exists.

Kouzes and Posner (2003: 112) claimed that: 'One of the most important practices of leadership is giving life and work a sense of meaning and purpose by offering an exciting vision.'

Transformational leaders

Transformational leaders are able by their force of personality to make significant changes in the behaviour of their followers in order to achieve the leader's vision or goals. As described by Burns (1978), what he called transforming leadership involves motivating people to strive for higher-level goals. He believed that good leadership implies a moral responsibility to respond to the values and needs of people in a way that is conducive to the highest form of human relations. As he put it: 'The ultimate test of moral leadership is its capacity to transcend the claims of the multiplicity of every-day needs, wants and expectations' (ibid: 46).

Another researcher, Bass (1985), extended the work of Burns (1978) by explaining the psychological mechanisms that underlie transforming leadership. He pointed out that the extent to which leaders are transformational is measured by their influence on the leader's followers in terms of the degree to which they feel trust, admiration, loyalty and respect for the leader and are willing to work harder than originally expected. According to Bass, this occurs because the leader transforms and motivates through an inspiring mission and vision and gives them an identity. Tichy and Devanna (1986) concluded that the transformational leader has three main roles: recognizing the need for revitalization, creating a new vision and institutionalizing change.

Yukl (1999) advised transformational leaders to:

- develop a challenging and attractive vision together with employees;
- tie the vision to a strategy for its achievement;
- develop the vision, specify and translate it to actions;
- express confidence, decisiveness and optimism about the vision and its implementation;
- realize the vision through small planned steps and small successes in the path for its full implementation.

Transactional leaders

Transactional leaders trade money, jobs and security for compliance. As Burns (1978: 19) noted: 'Such leadership occurs when a person takes the initiative in making contact with others for the purpose of an exchange of valued things'. Tavanti (2008: 169) stated that: 'Transactional leaders exhibit specific leadership skills usually associated with the ability to obtain results, to control through structures and processes, to solve problems, to plan and organize, and work within the structures and boundaries of the organization.' Put like this, a transactional leader conforms to the stereotype of the manager rather than the leader(the distinction between them is discussed in Chapter 2). Bass (1985) argued that leaders can display both transformational and transactional characteristics. Tavanti (2008) observed that transactional leadership behaviour is used to one degree or another by most leaders but that: 'Particular instances of transactional leadership are motivated simply by people's wants and preferences. This form of leadership uncritically responds to our preferences, that is, even when they are grounded in base motivations or an undeveloped moral sense' (ibid: 171).

Authentic leaders

The authentic leader was originally defined by George (2003: 12) as follows:

> Authentic leaders genuinely desire to serve others through their leadership. They are more interested in empowering the people they lead to make a difference than they are in power, money or prestige for themselves. They lead with purpose, meaning and values. They build enduring relationships with them. Others follow them because they know where they stand. They are consistent and self-disciplined.

Authenticity was defined by Harter (2002: 382) as 'owning one's personal experiences, be they thoughts, emotions, needs, preferences, or beliefs, processes captured by the injunction to know oneself and behaving in accordance with the true self'. Authentic leadership is based on a positive moral perspective characterized by high ethical standards that guide decision making and behaviour (May et al, 2003). As Avolio et al (2004) explained, authentic leaders act in accordance with deep personal values and convictions to build credibility and win the respect and trust of followers. By encouraging diverse viewpoints and building networks of collaborative relationships with followers, they lead in a manner that followers perceive and describe as authentic.

George et al (2007: 129) set out the basis of authentic leadership as follows:

> We all have the capacity to inspire and empower others. But we must first be willing to devote ourselves to our personal growth and development as leaders ... No one can be authentic by trying to imitate someone else. You can learn from others' experiences, but there is no way you can be successful when you are trying to be like them. People trust you when you are genuine and authentic, not a replica of someone else.

Authentic leadership is in essence ethical leadership. Walumbwa et al (2008) claimed that it can lead to enhanced trust, job satisfaction and performance.

The reality of leadership

The reality of leadership is that many first-line managers and supervisors are appointed or promoted to their posts with some idea, possibly, of what their managerial or supervisory duties are, but with no appreciation of the leadership skills they need. They see their role as being to tell people what to do and then seeing that they do it. They may tend to adopt a transactional approach, focusing on getting the job done and neglecting everything else. They are unlikely to be charismatic, visionary or transformational leaders because even if they have the latent qualities required, their situation does not seem to require or encourage any of these approaches.

However, the better ones will rely on their know-how (authority goes to the person who knows), their quiet confidence and their cool, analytical approach to dealing with problems. Any newly appointed leader or individual who is progressing to a higher level of leadership will benefit from a leadership development programme that will help them to understand and apply the skills they need.

The qualities of a good leader

As mentioned earlier, the trait theory of leadership has its limitations but there is still some value in studying the qualities required by good leaders. It is generally accepted that one of the key skills a leader or manager needs is an ability to analyse and read situations and to establish order and clarity in situations of ambiguity. Gold et al (2010: 6) stated that: 'Leadership demands a sense of purpose, and an ability to influence others, interpret situations, negotiate and express their views, often in the face of opposition.'

Research conducted by the Work Foundation (Tamkin et al, 2010), involving 260 in-depth interviews conducted with 77 business leaders from six high-profile organizations, found that outstanding leaders:

- view things as a whole rather than compartmentalizing them;
- connect the parts through a guiding sense of purpose;
- are highly motivated to achieve excellence and are focused on organizational outcomes, vision and purpose;
- understand they cannot create performance themselves but are conduits for performance through their influence on others;
- watch themselves carefully and act consistently to achieve excellence through their interactions and their embodiment of the leadership role.

Leadership development

It is sometimes said that leaders are born, not made. This is a rather discouraging statement for those who are not leaders by birthright. It may be true to the extent that some exceptional people seem to be visionaries, have built-in charisma and a natural ability to impose their personality on others. However, even they probably have to develop and hone these qualities when confronted with a situation demanding leadership. Ordinary mortals need not despair. They too can build on their natural capacities and develop their leadership abilities.

This can be helped by leadership development programmes which prepare people for leadership roles and situations beyond their current experience. As defined by Burgoyne (2010: 43): 'Leadership development in the widest sense involves the acquisition, development and utilization of leadership capability or the potential for it.' He identified the following leadership development activities (ibid: 44):

- job/work placements with leadership capability development as one of the purposes;
- education, training and development of individuals, including the 'context-sensitive' methods of coaching, mentoring and action learning and more formal education – training and development programmes;
- 'soft' organization development processes, including culture change, team building and 'hearts and minds' collective mission/values creating initiatives.

Yukl (2006) proposed the following conditions for successful leadership development:

- clear learning objectives;
- clear, meaningful content;
- appropriate sequencing of content;
- appropriate mix of training methods;
- opportunity for active practice;
- relevant, timely feedback;
- high trainee confidence;
- appropriate follow-up activities.

But it is not all about subjecting leaders to development programmes. The organization has to play its part in ensuring that leaders are provided with the support and the working conditions they need to carry out their role properly. As Fiedler (1967: 276) emphasized: 'If we wish to increase organizational and group effectiveness we must learn not only to train leaders more effectively but also to build an organizational environment in which the leaders can perform well.'

Effective leaders

Effective leaders are confident and know where they want to go and what they want to do. They have the ability to take charge, convey their vision to their team, get their team members into action and ensure that they achieve their agreed goals. They are trustworthy, effective at influencing people and earn the respect of their team. They are aware of their own strengths and weaknesses and are skilled at understanding what will motivate their team members. They appreciate the advantages of consulting and involving people in decision making. They can switch flexibly from one leadership style to another to meet the demands of different situations and people. They have to answer the following questions about the individuals in the group and the group itself:

- Individuals in the group:
    - What are their strengths and weaknesses?
    - What are their needs, attitudes, perspectives and preferences?
    - What are likely to be the best ways of motivating them?
    - What tasks are they best at doing?
    - Is there scope to increase flexibility by developing new skills?
    - How well do they perform in achieving targets and performance standards?
    - To what extent can they manage their own performance and development?
    - Are there any areas where there is a need to develop skill or competence?
    - How can I provide them with the sort of support and guidance which will improve their performance?
    - What can be done to improve the performance of any individuals in the group by coaching or mentoring?

- The team:
    - How well is the team organized?
    - Is the team clear about what is expected of it?
    - Do the members of the team work well together?
    - If there is any conflict between team members, how can I resolve it?
    - How can the commitment and motivation of the team be achieved?
    - Are team members flexible – capable of carrying out different tasks?
    - To what extent can the team manage its own performance?
    - Is there scope to empower the team so that it can take on greater responsibility for setting standards, monitoring performance and taking corrective action?
    - Can the team be encouraged to work together to produce ideas for improving performance?
    - What is the team good and not so good at doing?
    - What can I do to improve the performance of the team through coaching and mentoring?

KEY LEARNING POINTS

Leadership defined

Leadership is the process of influencing the behaviour of others to achieve results.

Leadership theories

The main leadership theories are trait theory, leadership behaviour theory, contingent and situational theories, path–goal theory, leader–member exchange theory, emotional intelligence theory and the leadership brand.

What leaders do

John Adair (1973) explained that the three essential roles of leaders are to define the task, achieve the task and maintain effective relationships. They have to satisfy interdependent task, individual and group needs.

Types of leaders

Leaders can be charismatic, visionary, transformational, transactional or 'authentic'.

The qualities of a good leader

Leaders need the ability to analyse and read situations and to establish order and clarity in situations of ambiguity.

Leadership demands a sense of purpose, and an ability to influence others, interpret situations, negotiate and express views, often in the face of opposition. (Gold et al, 2010: 6)

The reality of leadership is that many first-line managers and supervisors are appointed or promoted to their posts with some idea, possibly, of what their managerial or supervisory duties are, but with no appreciation of the leadership skills they need to get the results they want with the help of their team.

Leadership development

Leadership development programmes prepare people for leadership roles and situations beyond their current experience.

'Leadership development in the widest sense involves the acquisition, development and utilization of leadership capability or the potential for it' (Burgoyne, 2010: 43)

References

Adair, J (1973) *The Action Centred Leader*, London, McGrawHill

Avolio, B J, Gardner, W L, Walumbwa, F O, Luthans, F and May, D R (2004) Unlocking the mask: A look at the process by which authentic leaders impact follower attitudes and behaviours, *Leadership Quarterly*, **15**, pp 801–23

Bass, B M (1985) *Leadership and Performance*, New York, Free Press

Bennis, W (2010) We need leaders, *Leadership Excellence*, **27** (12), p 4

Bennis, W G and Nanus, B (1985) *Leadership: The strategies for taking charge*, New York, Harper & Row

Buchanan, D and Huczynski, A (2007) *Organizational Behaviour*, Harlow, FT Prentice-Hall

Burgoyne J (2010) Craftting a leadership and management development strategy 1, in J Gold, R Thorpe and A Mumford (eds) *Gower Handbook of Leadership and Management Development*, Farnham, Gower, pp 42–55

Burns, J M (1978) *Leadership*, New York, Harper & Row

Carey, M R (1992) Transformational leadership and the fundamental option for self-trandescence, *Leadership Quarterly*, **3**, pp 217–36

Conger, J A and Kanungo, R N (1998) *Charismatic Leadership in Organizations*, Thousand Oaks CA, Sage

Dixon, N F (1994) *On the Psychology of Military Incompetence*, London, Pimlico

Fiedler, F E (1967) *A Theory of Leadership Effectiveness*, New York, McGraw-Hill

George, B (2003) *Authentic Leadership*, San Francisco, Jossey-Bass

George, B, Sims, P, McLean, A N and Mayer D (2007) Discovering your authentic leadership, *Harvard Business Review*, February, pp 129–38

Gold, J, Thorpe, R and Mumford, A (eds) (2010) *Gower Handbook of Leadership and Management Development*, Farnham, Gower

Goleman, D (2000) Leadership that gets results, *Harvard Business Review*, March/April, pp 78–90

Goleman, D (2001) *What Makes a Leader*, Boston MA, Harvard Business School Press

Graen, G (1976) Role-making processes within complex organizations, in M D Dunnette (ed) *Handbook of Industrial and Organizational Psychology*, Chicago IL, Rand-McNally

Grint, K (2005) *Leadership: Limits and Possibilities*, Basingstoke, Palgrave Macmillan

Harter, S (2002) Authenticity, in C R Snyder and S J Lopez (eds) *Handbook of Positive Psychology*, Oxford, Oxford University Press, pp 382–94

Hersey, P and Blanchard, K H (1974) So you want to know your leadership style? *Training and Development Journal*, **28**, pp 22–37

Hersey, P, Blanchard, K H and Johnson, D (2001) *Management of Organizational Behaviour: Leading human resources*, 8th edn, London, Prentice Hall

Hesketh, A and Hird, M (2010) Using relationships between leaders to leverage more value from people: building a golden triangle, in P Sparrow, A Hesketh, M Hird, and C Cooper (eds) *Leading HR*, Basingstoke, Palgrave Macmillan, pp 103–21

Higgs, M (2006) *Change and Its Leadership*, Rowland, Fisher, Lennox Consulting, www.rflc.co.uk (accessed 5 March 2011)

House, R J (1971) A path–goal theory of leader effectiveness, *Administrative Science Quarterly*, **16**, pp 321–38

Huczynski, A A and Buchanan, D A (2007) *Organizational Behaviour*, 6th edn, Harlow, FT Prentice Hall

Katz, D, Maccoby, M and Morse, N C (1950) *Productivity, Supervision and Morale in and Office Situation*, Ann Arbor, University of Michigan Institute for Social Research

Kelley, R (1988) In praise of followers, *Harvard Business Review*, November/December, pp 142–48

Kouzes, J and Posner, B (2003) *The Leadership Challenge*, San Francisco, Jossey-Bass

Levine, K J (2008) Trait theory, in A Marturano and J Gosling (eds) *Leadership: The key concepts*, London, Routledge, pp 163–66

May, D R, Chan, A, Hodges, T and Avolio, B J (2003) Developing the moral component of authentic leadership, *Organizational Dynamics*, 32 (3), pp 247–60

Meindl, J R, Ehrlich, S B and Dukerich, J M (1985) The romance of leadership, *Administrative Science Quarterly*, 30 (1) 78–102

Northouse, P G (2006) *Leadership: Theory and Practice*, 4th edn, Thousand Oaks CA, Sage

Perren, L and Burgoyne, J (2001) *Management and Leadership Abilities: An analysis of texts, testimony and practice*, London, Council for Excellence in Leadership and Management

Stogdill, R M (1948) Personal factors associated with leadership: A survey of the literature, *Journal of Psychology*, 25, pp 35–71

Stogdill, R M (1950) Leaders, membership and organization, *Psychological Bulletin*, 25, pp 1–14

Tamkin, P, Pearson, G, Hirsh, W and Constable, S (2010) *Exceeding Expectation: The principles of outstanding leadership*, London, The Work Foundation

Tavanti, M (2008) Transactional leadership, in A Marturano and J Gosling (eds) *Leadership: The key concepts*, London, Routledge, pp 166–70

Tichy, N M and Devanna, M A (1986) *The Transformational Leader*, New York, Wiley

Ulrich, D and Smallwood, N (2007) *Leadership Brand: Developing customer-focused leaders to drive performance and build lasting value*, Boston MA, Harvard Business School Press

Walumbwa, F O, Avolio, B J, Gardner, W L, Wernsing, T S and Peterson, S J (2008) Authentic leadership: development and validation of a theory-based measure, *Journal of Management*, 34 (1), pp 89–126

Yukl, G (1999) An evaluation of conceptual weaknesses in transformational and charismatic leadership theories, *Leadership Quarterly*, 10, 285–305

Yukl, G (2006) *Leadership in Organizations*, 6th edn, Upper Saddle River NJ, Prentice-Hall

Questions

1 What is leadership?

2 What is the trait theory of leadership?

3 What are the two dimensions of leadership behaviour?

4 What is the contingent theory of leadership?

5 What is situational leadership?

6 What is a transactional leader?

7 What is a transformational leader?

8 What is a charismatic leader?

9 What is an authentic leader?

10 What do leaders do – their essential roles?

11 What are the three needs that leaders must satisfy as defined by John Adair?

12 What are the main types of leadership styles?

13 What are the path–goal leadership styles?

14 What are the leadership styles identified by Hay McBer?

15 What choice of style do leaders have?

16 What qualities do good leaders have?

17 What is emotional intelligence?

18 What is the significance of followers?

19 What are the characteristic activities in a leadership development programme?

20 What are the conditions required for successful leadership development?

Managing people

Introduction

Management is essentially about managing people. But, as covered in this chapter, managers are also responsible for generally controlling the business or their part of it by managing their other resources — finance, work systems and technology. Additionally, they have to manage time and themselves.

The word 'management' is derived from the Italian verb '*maneggiare*', which means 'to handle a horse'. This definition at least states that to manage is to have charge of or responsibility for something, but there is clearly more to it than that and this is what this chapter is about. Consideration is given initially to what the process of managing is and the role of the manager. Managing includes the vital process of strategic management and this is also examined in the chapter. Finally, the processes of management and leadership are compared.

Management defined

Management is the process of making things happen. Managers define goals, determine and obtain the resources required to achieve the goals, allocate those resources to opportunities and planned activities and ensure that those activities take place as planned in order to achieve predetermined objectives. Management can be described as getting things done through people by exercising leadership. This definition emphasizes the importance of the leadership role but it should be remembered that managers are also there to make effective use of the other resources available to them.

Purpose of management

The purpose of management is to satisfy a range of stakeholders. In the private sector, this means making a profit and creating value for shareholders, and producing and delivering valued products and services at a reasonable cost for customers. In the public sector, management is there to ensure that the services the community requires are delivered effectively. In the voluntary sector, management sees that the purposes of the charity are achieved and also keeps the faith of the community and donors. In all sectors management is about exercising social responsibility and providing rewarding employment and development opportunities for employees.

The role of the manager

Peter Drucker (1955: 1) stated that 'The manager is the dynamic, life-giving element in every business.'

Managers are there to get results by ensuring that their function, unit or department operates effectively. They manage people and their other resources, which include time and themselves. They are accountable for attaining goals, having been given authority over those working in their unit or department.

The traditional model of what managers do is that it is a logical and systematic process of planning, organizing, motivating and controlling. However, this is misleading. Managers often carry out their work on a day-to-day basis in conditions of variety, turbulence and unpredictability. Managers may have to be specialists in ambiguity, with the ability to cope with conflicting and unclear requirements.

Managers are doers. They deal with events as they occur. But they must also be concerned with where they are going. This requires strategic thinking, especially at higher levels. As strategic thinkers, managers develop a sense of purpose and frameworks for defining intentions and future directions. They are engaged in the process of strategic management as considered below.

Strategic management

Strategic management is an approach to management which involves taking a broad and longer-term view of where the business or part of the business is going and managing activities in ways which ensure that this strategic thrust is maintained. Boxall and Purcell (2003: 44) explained that: 'Strategic management is best defined as a process. It is a process of strategy making, of forming and, if the firm survives, reforming its strategy over time.' The purpose of strategic management was expressed by Rosabeth Moss Kanter (1984: 288) as being to 'elicit the present actions for the future' and become 'action vehicles – integrating and institutionalizing mechanisms for change' (ibid: 301).

The key strategic management activity as identified by Thompson and Strickland (1996: 3) is 'deciding what business the company will be in and forming a strategic vision of where the organization needs to be headed – in effect, infusing the organization with a sense of purpose, providing long-term direction, and establishing a clear mission to be accomplished'.

The focus is on identifying the organization's mission and strategies, but attention is also given to the resource base required to make it succeed. Strategic management involves the development and implementation of strategy (business, HRM and L&D) as described below. It also includes the important activity of business model innovation, which identifies opportunities to increase the competitiveness and prosperity of the business through a review of all the elements of its business model (a picture of an organization which explains how it achieves competitive advantage and makes money).

Strategic management involves the formulation of strategy and it has to take account of the concepts of core competences or capabilities, the resource-based view, strategic fit and strategic capability.

Strategy

Strategy is a declaration of intent which sets out the approach selected to achieve defined goals in the future. It was defined by Thompson and Strickland

(1996: 20) as: 'The pattern of actions managers employ to achieve organizational objectives.'

Strategy is forward looking. It is about deciding where you want to go and how you mean to get there. It is concerned with both ends and means. It states: 'This is what we want to do and this is how we intend to do it.' Strategies define longer-term goals but they also cover how those goals will be attained (strategic planning). They guide purposeful action to deliver the required result.

But strategy formulation is not such a deterministic, rational and continuous process as is often supposed. Sparrow et al (2010: 4) asserted succinctly that: 'Strategy is not rational and never has been.' It has been said (Bower, 1982: 631) that 'strategy is everything not well defined or understood'. This may be going too far, but in reality, strategy formulation can best be described as 'problem solving in unstructured situations' (Digman, 1990: 53) and strategies will always be formed under conditions of partial ignorance. Quinn (1980: 9) pointed out that a strategy may simply be 'a widely held understanding resulting from a stream of decisions'. He believed that strategy formulation takes place by means of 'logical incrementalism', ie it evolves in several steps rather than being conceived as a whole.

Mintzberg (1987) argued that in theory strategy is a systematic process: first we think, then we act: we formulate, then we implement. But we also act in order to think. In practice, 'a realized strategy can emerge in response to an evolving situation' and the strategic planner is often 'a pattern organizer, a learner if you like, who manages a process in which strategies and visions can emerge as well as be deliberately conceived' (ibid: 68). This concept of 'emergent strategy' conveys the essence of how in practice organizations develop their business and HR strategies.

Core competencies and distinctive capabilities

Core competencies or distinctive capabilities describe what the organization is specially or uniquely capable of doing. The concept of core competencies was originated by Pralahad and Hamel (1990), who described them as a company's critical resource which represented the collective learning in the organization. Distinctive capabilities can exist in such areas as technology, innovation, marketing, delivering quality and making good use of human and financial resources. Understanding distinctive capabilities – what they are and should become – is an essential task for those concerned with HRM and L&D in achieving their aim of enhancing the human resource capability of the organization.

The resource-based view

The resource-based view of strategy is that the firm is a bundle of distinctive resources that are the keys to developing competitive advantage – the strategic capability of a firm depends on its resource capability. It is based on the ideas of Penrose (1959: 24–25) who wrote that the firm is 'an administrative organization and a collection of productive resources' and saw resources as 'a bundle of potential services'. It was expanded by Wernerfelt (1984: 172), who explained that strategy 'is a balance between the exploitation of existing resources and the development of new ones'. Resources were defined by Hunt (1991: 322) as 'anything that has an enabling capacity'.

The concept was developed by Barney (1991: 102), who stated that 'a firm is said to have a competitive advantage when it is implementing a value-creating strategy which is not simultaneously being implemented by any current or potential competitors and when these other firms are unable to duplicate the benefits of this strategy'. This will happen if their resources are valuable, rare, inimitable and non-substitutable.

The resource-based view (RBV) provides a practical justification for key aspects of a firm's HRM and L&D policies and practices such as human capital management, talent management, knowledge management, and learning and development. Kamoche (1996) stated that the RBV builds on and provides a unifying framework for the field of strategic human resource management. Boxall (1996: 66) pointed out that: 'The resource-based view of the firm provides a conceptual basis, if we needed one, for asserting that key human resources are sources of competitive advantage.'

Strategic fit

Strategic fit is a way of achieving competitive advantage which means attaining and sustaining better results than business rivals, thus placing the firm in a strong competitive position. The focus is upon the organization and the world around it. To maximize competitive advantage a firm must match its capabilities and resources to the opportunities available in the external environment. As Hofer and Schendel (1986: 4) concluded:

> A critical aspect of top management's work today involves matching
> organizational competences (internal resources and skills) with the opportunities
> and risks created by environmental change in ways that will be both effective
> and efficient over the time such resources will be deployed.

Strategic capability

Strategic capability refers to the ability of an organization to develop and implement strategies which will achieve sustained competitive advantage. It is therefore about the capacity to select the most appropriate vision, to define realistic intentions, to match resources to opportunities and to prepare and implement strategic plans.

The strategic capability of an organization depends on the strategic capabilities of its managers. People who display high levels of strategic capability know where they are going and know how they are going to get there.

They recognize that although they must be successful now to succeed in the future, it is always necessary to create and sustain a sense of purpose and direction. Managers who think strategically will be aware that they are responsible first, for planning how to allocate resources to opportunities which contribute to the implementation of strategy, and secondly, for managing these opportunities in ways which will add value to the results achieved by the firm.

Leadership and management compared

Are leadership and management the same or different? Some commentators regard leadership as synonymous with management, others see them as distinct but closely linked and equally necessary activities, others consider management a subset of leadership, and yet others praise leadership and demonize management. Warren Bennis (1989) viewed managers as those who promote efficiency, follow the rules and accept the status quo, while leaders focus on challenging the rules and promoting effectiveness. John Kotter (1991) saw managers as being the ones who plan, budget, organize and control, while leaders set direction, manage change and motivate people. Hersey and Blanchard (1998) claimed that management merely consists of leadership applied to business situations; or in other words, management forms a subset of the broader process of leadership.

As Birkinshaw (2010: 23) commented: 'By dichotomizing the work of executives in this way, Kotter, Bennis and others squeezed out the essence of what managers do and basically left them with the boring work that leaders "don't want".' His view on the leadership-versus-management debate was that: 'Leadership is a process of social influence, concerned with the traits, styles and behaviours of individuals that causes others to follow them. Management is the act of getting people together to accomplish desired goals. To put it simply, we all need to be both leaders and managers' (ibid: 23). Earlier, Mintzberg (2004: 22) summed it all up (as he often did) when he wrote: 'Let's stop the dysfunctional separation of leadership from management. We all know that managers who don't lead are boring, dispiriting. Well, leaders who don't manage are distant, disconnected.'

The answer to the question posed at the beginning of this section is that management is different from leadership although they are closely associated. Management is the process of making effective use of all available resources in order to achieve goals while leadership focuses on the key resource which enables goals to be achieved, ie people. Management necessarily involves leadership and leadership necessarily involves management.

KEY LEARNING POINTS

Management

Management is the process of making things happen. Managers define goals, determine and obtain the resources required to achieve the goals, allocate those resources to opportunities and planned activities and ensure that those activities take place as planned in order to achieve predetermined objectives.

The purpose of management is to satisfy a range of stakeholders.

Strategic management

Strategic management is an approach to management which involves taking a broad and longer-term view of where the business or part of the business is going and managing activities in ways which ensure that this strategic thrust is maintained.

Business model innovation

Business model innovation is an approach to strategy which focuses on how the firm creates value. The aim is to change the ways in which companies view their business operations and to provide guidance on mapping their future strategy.

Strategy

Strategies define longer-term goals but they also cover how those goals will be attained (strategic planning). They guide purposeful action to deliver the required result.

Strategy formulation is not necessarily a deterministic, rational and continuous process.

Core competencies

Core competencies or distinctive capabilities describe what the organization is specially or uniquely capable of doing.

The resource-based view of strategy

A firm is a bundle of distinctive resources that are the keys to developing competitive advantage – the strategic capability of a firm depends on its resource capability. Boxall (1996) pointed out that: 'The resource-based view of the firm provides a conceptual basis, if we needed one, for asserting that key human resources are sources of competitive advantage.'

Strategic fit

To maximize competitive advantage, a firm must match its capabilities and resources to the opportunities available in the external environment.

Strategic capability

The ability of an organization to develop and implement strategies which will achieve sustained competitive advantage.

Leadership and management

Leadership is a process of social influence, concerned with the traits, styles and behaviours of individuals that causes others to follow them. Management is the act of getting people together to accomplish desired goals.

References

Barney, J (1991) Firm resources and sustained competitive advantage, *Journal of Management Studies*, **17** (1), pp 99–120

Bennis, W (1989) *On Becoming a Leader*, New York, Addison Wesley

Birkinshaw, J (2010) An experiment in reinvention, *People Management*, 15 July, pp 22–24

Bower, J L (1982) Business policy in the 1980s, *Academy of Management Review*, 7 (4), pp 630–38

Boxall, P F (1996) The strategic HRM debate and the resource-based view of the firm, *Human Resource Management Journal*, **6** (3), pp 59–75

Boxall, P F and Purcell, J (2003) *Strategy and Human Resource Management*, Basingstoke, Palgrave Macmillan

Digman, L A (1990) *Strategic Management – concepts, decisions, cases*, Georgetown, Ontario, Irwin

Drucker, P (1955) *The Practice of Management*, London, Heinemann

Hersey, P and Blanchard, K H (1998) *Management of Organizational Behavior*, Englewood Cliffs NJ, Prentice Hall

Hofer, C W and Schendel, D (1986) *Strategy Formulation: Analytical Concepts*, New York, West Publishing

Hunt, S (1991) The resource-advantage theory of competition, *Journal of Management Inquiry*, **4** (4), pp 317–22

Kamoche, K (1996) Strategic human resource management within a resource capability view of the firm, *Journal of Management Studies*, **33** (2), pp 213–33

Kanter, R M (1984) *The Change Masters*, London, Allen & Unwin

Kotter, J P (1991) Power, dependence and effective management, in J Gabarro (ed) *Managing People and Organizations*, Boston MA, Harvard Business School Publications

Mintzberg, H (1987) Crafting strategy, *Harvard Business Review*, July–August, pp 66–74

Mintzberg, H (2004) Enough leadership, *Harvard Business Review*, November, p 22

Penrose, E (1959) *The Theory of the Growth of the Firm*, Oxford, Blackwell

Prahalad, C K and Hamel, G (1990) The core competence of the organization, *Harvard Business Review*, May–June, pp 79–93

Quinn, J B (1980) *Strategies for Change: Logical Incrementalism*, Georgetown, Ontario, Irwin

Sparrow, P, Hesketh, A, Hird, M and Cooper, C (2010) Introduction: Performance-led HR, in P Sparrow, A Hesketh, M Hird and C Cooper (eds) *Leading HR*, Basingstoke, Palgrave Macmillan, pp 1–22

Thompson, A A and Strickland, A J (1996) *Strategic Management, Concepts and cases*, 9th edn, Chicago, Irwin

Wernerfelt, B (1984) A resource-based view of the firm, *Strategic Management Journal*, 5 (2), pp 171–80

Questions

1 How would you define management?

2 What is the purpose of management?

3 What is strategic management?

4 What is strategy?

5 How would you describe the process of strategy formulation?

6 What is a business model?

7 What is business model innovation?

8 What is a core competency?

9 What is the resource-based view?

10 What are the meaning and significance of strategic fit?

11 What is strategic capability?

12 What is the difference between management and leadership?

Developing
people

LEARNING OUTCOMES

On completing this chapter you should be able to define these key concepts. You should also understand:

- The meaning of learning and development
- Experiential learning
- Self-directed learning
- Personal development planning
- Coaching
- Mentoring
- Formal training and instruction
- Leadership and management development
- Blended learning

Introduction

Developing people is the process of providing them with learning opportunities which will enable them to acquire the knowledge and skills needed to carry out their current jobs effectively and prepare them to exercise wider or increased responsibilities. It involves growing and realizing a person's ability and potential by means of learning experiences and self-directed (self-managed) learning.

The aim is to achieve lifelong learning by the provision or use of both formal and informal learning opportunities throughout people's lives in order to foster the continuous development and improvement of the knowledge and skills needed for employment and personal fulfilment. This is achieved through learning and development processes and programmes as described in this chapter.

Learning and development defined

Learning and development processes aim to ensure that people in the organization acquire and develop the knowledge, skills and competencies they need to carry out their work effectively and advance their careers to their own benefit and that of the organization. Harrison (2009: 8) defined learning and development more broadly as follows:

> The primary purpose of learning and development as an organizational process is to aid collective progress through the collaborative, expert and ethical stimulation and facilitation of learning and knowledge that support business goals, develop individual potential, and respect and build on diversity.

The three elements of L&D are learning, training and development as described below.

Learning

Learning is the means by which a person acquires and develops new knowledge, skills, capabilities, behaviours and attitudes. As explained by Honey and Mumford (1996): 'Learning has happened when people can demonstrate that they know something that they did not know before (insights, realizations as well as facts) and when they can do something they could not do before (skills).'

Learning is a continuous process which not only enhances existing capabilities but also leads to the development of the skills, knowledge and attitudes which prepare people for enlarged or higher-level responsibilities in the future.

Development

Development is concerned with ensuring that a person's ability and potential are grown and realized through the provision of learning experiences or through self-directed (self-managed) learning. It is an unfolding process which enables people to progress from a present state of understanding and capability to a future state in which higher-level skills, knowledge and competencies are required.

Training

Training involves the application of formal processes of instruction and practice to impart knowledge and help people to acquire the skills necessary for them to perform their jobs satisfactorily.

Comparison of learning and training

Learning should be distinguished from training. 'Learning is the process by which a person constructs new knowledge, skills and capabilities, whereas training is one of several responses an organization can undertake to promote learning' (Reynolds et al, 2002).

The encouragement of learning makes use of a process model which is concerned with facilitating the learning activities of individuals and providing learning resources for them to use. Conversely, the provision of training involves the use of a content model which means deciding in advance the knowledge and skills that need to be enhanced by training, planning the programme, deciding on training methods and presenting the content in a logical sequence through various forms of instruction.

A distinction is made by Sloman (2003) between learning, which 'lies within the domain of the individual', and training, which 'lies within the domain of the organization'. Today the focus is on helping people to learn. There is much more to learning and development than simply laying on training courses.

The learning and development processes and activities described in the rest of this chapter are: experiential learning, self-directed learning, e-learning, personal development planning (together with learning contracts), coaching and mentoring, formal instruction through training interventions and leadership and management development programmes. These may be provided through 'blended learning'.

Experiential learning

Experiential learning is learning by doing and by reflecting on experience so that it can be understood and applied. It is largely an informal process, although line managers have an important part to play in facilitating it. But it can be planned in some circumstances.

Planned experience involves deciding on a sequence of experience which will enable people to obtain the knowledge and skills required in their jobs and prepare them to take on increased responsibilities. A programme is drawn up which sets down what people are expected to learn in each department or job in which they are given experience. This spells out what they are expected to discover for themselves. A suitable person (a mentor, who might well be a line manager) is available to see that people in a development programme are given the right experience and opportunity to learn, and arrangements should be made to check progress.

Self-directed learning

Self-directed or self-managed learning involves encouraging individuals to take responsibility for their own learning, either to improve performance in their present job or to develop their potential and satisfy their career aspirations. It can also be described as self-reflective learning, which is the kind of learning which involves encouraging individuals to develop new patterns of understanding, thinking and behaving.

Self-directed learning can be based on a process of recording achievement and action planning which involves individuals reviewing what they have learnt, what they have achieved, what their goals are, how they are going to achieve those goals and what new learning they need to acquire. The learning programme can be 'self-paced' in the sense that learners can decide for themselves up to a point the rate at which they work and are encouraged to measure their own progress and adjust the programme accordingly.

Self-directed learning is based on the principle that people learn and retain more if they find things out for themselves. But they still need to be given guidance on what to look for and help in finding it. Learners have to be encouraged to define, with whatever help they may require, what they need to know to perform their job effectively. They need advice on how to learn, where they can get the material or information which will help them to learn and how to make good use of it.

E-learning

E-learning was defined by Pollard and Hillage (2001) as 'the delivery and administration of learning opportunities and support via computer, networked and web-based technology to help individual performance and development'.

E-learning enhances learning by extending and supplementing face-to-face learning rather than replacing it. It enables learning to take place when it is most needed (just in time as distinct from just in case) and when it is most convenient. Learning can be provided in short segments or bites which focus on specific learning objectives. It is 'learner centric' in that it can be customized to suit an individual's learning needs – learners can choose different learning objects within an overall package. The main potential drawbacks are the degree of access to computers, the need for a reasonable degree of literacy, the need for learners to be self-motivated, and the time and effort required to develop and update e-learning programmes.

Coaching

Coaching is a personal (usually one-to-one) approach to helping people develop their skills and knowledge and improve their performance. The need for coaching may arise from formal or informal performance reviews but opportunities for coaching will emerge during everyday activities.

Coaching as part of the normal process of management consists of:

- making people aware of how well they are performing by, for example, asking them questions to establish the extent to which they have thought through what they are doing;
- controlled delegation – ensuring that individuals not only know what is expected of them but also understand what they need to know and be able to do to complete the task satisfactorily; this gives managers an opportunity to provide guidance at the outset, since guidance at a later stage may be seen as interference;
- using whatever situations which may arise as opportunities to promote learning;
- encouraging people to look at higher-level problems and how they would tackle them.

Mentoring

Mentoring is the process of using specially selected and trained individuals to provide guidance, pragmatic advice and continuing support which will help the person or persons allocated to them learn and develop. Mentors prepare individuals to perform better in the future and groom them for higher and greater things, ie career advancement.

Mentoring is a method of helping people to learn and develop as distinct from coaching, which is a relatively directive means of increasing people's competence. Mentoring promotes learning on the job, which is always the best way of acquiring the particular skills and knowledge the job holder needs. Mentoring also complements formal training by providing those who benefit from it with individual guidance from experienced managers who are 'wise in the ways of the organization'.

Personal development planning

Personal development planning is carried out by individuals with guidance, encouragement and help from their managers as required. A personal development plan sets out the actions people propose to take to learn and to develop themselves. They take responsibility for formulating and implementing the plan but they receive support from the organization and their managers in doing so. The plan can be expressed in the form of a learning contract as described below.

A learning contract is a formal agreement between the manager and the individual on what learning needs to take place, the objectives of such learning and what part the individual, the manager, the learning and development function or a mentor will play in ensuring that learning happens. The partners to the contract agree on how the objectives will be achieved and their respective roles. It will spell out learning programmes and indicate what coaching, mentoring and formal training activities should be carried out. It is, in effect, a blueprint for learning.

Formal training and instruction

Formal training involves the application of formal processes to impart knowledge and help people to acquire the skills necessary for them to perform their jobs satisfactorily. Instruction follows the sequence of explanation, demonstration, practice and follow-up:

- Explanation should be as simple and direct as possible: the trainer explains briefly the ground to be covered and what to look for.
- Demonstration of a 'doing' skill takes place in three steps: (1) the complete operation is shown at normal speed to show the trainee how the task should be carried out eventually; (2) the operation is demonstrated slowly and in correct sequence, element by element, to indicate clearly what is done and the order in which each task is carried out; and (3) the operation is demonstrated again slowly, at least two or three times, to stress the how, when and why of successive movements.
- Practice consists of the learner imitating the instructor and then repeating the operation under guidance.
- Follow-up continues during the training period for all the time required by the learner to reach a level of performance equal to that of the normal experienced worker in terms of quality, speed and attention to safety.

Leadership and management development

Leadership development as described in Chapter 1 consists of programmes or processes designed to improve the leadership ability of managers and supervisors.

Management development involves generally improving the performance of managers in their present roles and preparing them to take on greater responsibilities in the future. The following approaches can be used:

- coaching and mentoring;
- performance management processes to provide feedback and satisfy development needs;
- planned experience, which includes job rotation, job enlargement, taking part in project teams or task groups, 'action learning', and secondment outside the organization;
- formal training by means of internal or external courses;
- structured self-development following a self-directed learning programme set out in a personal development plan and agreed as a learning contract with the manager or a management development adviser;
- competency frameworks, which can be used as a means of identifying and expressing development needs and pointing the way to self-managed learning programmes or the provision of learning opportunities by the organization.

An important aspect of development programmes for line managers is to provide guidance on how they can enhance the skills and capabilities of their teams and their individual team members by providing them with learning opportunities as well as guidance, coaching and formal instruction.

Blended learning

Blended learning is the use of a combination of learning methods to increase the overall effectiveness of the learning process by providing for different parts of the learning mix to complement and support one another. A blended learning programme might be planned for an individual using a mix of self-directed learning activities defined in a personal development plan, e-learning facilities, group action learning activities, coaching or mentoring and instruction provided in an in-company course or externally. Generic training for groups of people might include e-learning, planned instruction programmes, planned experience and selected external courses. Within a training course a complementary mix of different training activities might take place, for example a skills development course for managers or team leaders might include some instruction on basic principles, but much more time would be spent on case studies, simulations, role playing and other exercises.

KEY LEARNING POINTS

Development

Development is an unfolding process which enables people to progress from a present state of understanding and capability to a future state in which higher-level skills, knowledge and competencies are required and exercised.

Learning and development defined

Learning and development processes aim to ensure that people in the organization acquire and develop the knowledge, skills and competencies they need to carry out their work effectively and advance their careers to their own benefit and that of the organization.

Learning

Learning is the means by which a person acquires and develops new knowledge, skills, capabilities, behaviours and attitudes.

Development

Development is concerned with ensuring that a person's ability and potential are grown and realized through the provision of learning experiences or through self-directed (self-managed) learning.

Training

Training involves the application of formal processes of instruction and practice to impart knowledge and help people to acquire the skills necessary for them to perform their jobs satisfactorily.

Experiential learning

Experiential learning is learning by doing and by reflecting on experience so that it can be understood and applied.

Self-directed learning

Self-directed or self-managed learning involves encouraging individuals to take responsibility for their own learning, either to improve performance in their present job or to develop their potential and satisfy their career aspirations.

E-learning

E-learning was defined by Pollard and Hillage (2001) as 'the delivery and administration of learning opportunities and support via computer, networked and web-based technology to help individual performance and development'.

Coaching

Coaching is a personal (usually one-to-one) approach to helping people develop their skills and knowledge and improve their performance.

Mentoring

Mentoring is the process of using specially selected and trained individuals to provide guidance, pragmatic advice and continuing support which will help the person or persons allocated to them to learn and develop.

Management development

Management development involves generally improving the performance of managers in their present roles and preparing them to take on greater responsibilities in the future.

Blended learning

Blended learning is the use of a combination of learning methods to increase the overall effectiveness of the learning process by providing for different parts of the learning mix to complement and support one another.

References

Harrison, R (2009) *Learning and Development*, 5th edn. London, CIPD

Honey, P and Mumford, A (1996) *The Manual of Learning Styles*, 3rd edn. Maidenhead, Honey Publications

Pollard, E and Hillage, J (2001) Explaining e-Learning, Report No 376, Institute for Employment Studies, Brighton

Reynolds, J, Caley, L and Mason, R (2002) *How Do People Learn?* London, CIPD

Sloman, M (2003) E-learning: Stepping up the learning curve, *Impact*, January, pp 16–17

Questions

1 What is involved in the process of developing people?

2 What are learning and development?

3 What is learning?

4   What is development?

5   What is training?

6   What is experiential learning?

7   What is self-directed learning?

8   What is e-learning?

9   What is involved in coaching?

10   What is involved in mentoring?

11   What are the four stages of instruction?

12   What is blended learning?

PART TWO
Approaches to HRM and L&D

The concept of human resource management

- *Commitment*
- *Competency*
- *Engagement*
- *Human relations*
- *Mutuality*
- *Personnel management*
- *Quality of working life*
- *Strategic human resource management*
- *Theory Y*

LEARNING OUTCOMES

On completing this chapter you should be able to define these key concepts. You should also understand:

- How the concept of HRM has developed
- The reservations made about HRM
- The meaning of HRM today

Introduction

As a concept, human resource management (HRM) can be defined as a strategic, integrated and coherent approach to the employment, development and well-being of the people working in organizations. Its characteristics are that it is diverse, strategic and commitment-orientated, adopts a unitary (the interests of management and employees coincide) rather than pluralist (the interests of management and employees differ) viewpoint, is founded on the belief that people should be treated as assets rather than costs, and is a management-driven activity.

However, the term as used now is often no more than a synonym for what used to be called personnel management. To provide a background to an analysis of the HRM concept, this chapter therefore starts with a brief history of personnel management. The chapter continues with a description of how the notion of HRM has evolved from its beginnings in the 1980s, covering first the concept as initially defined by the American pioneers, second how this concept was developed and questioned in the 1990s and third, what HRM looks like today.

The background to HRM

HRM grew out of the increasingly sophisticated approaches to personnel management, which started in the late 1930s and reached maturity in the 1960s and 1970s. Personnel management was rooted in the provision of welfare services and the development of labour management in the earlier years of the 20th century.

Welfare

The initial step in the long road to HRM was the provision of welfare services – looking after the personal interests of employees and providing them with facilities such as canteens and rest rooms. Welfare officers first appeared on the scene in any number in the munitions factories of the First World War and a focus on welfare work continued into the 1930s.

Labour management

Progressively during the 1920s and 1930s, basic welfare activities were extended to the provision of administrative support to management in such forms as recruitment, training, discipline, health and safety and works consultative committees. Labour managers in organizations such as ICI and Rowntree emerged in the later 1920s and became more common in the 1930s.

Personnel management, the developing phase

In the late 1930s the term 'personnel management' was imported to the UK from the United States (like many later developments in this field) and the British Institute of Labour Management changed its name to the Institute of Personnel Management in 1946. At this stage and during the 1950s, personnel management was often simply an administrative activity and the standard (American) textbook was *Personnel Administration* (Pigors, 1951). However, in some organizations personnel managers were becoming involved in industrial relations and payment systems as well as recruitment and training (the writer's first job was in what was called the wages research department at Rowntree & Co, York which developed and controlled wage systems and negotiated pay deals with trade unions).

Personnel management, the mature phase

Personnel management reached maturity in the 1960s and this phase continued into the 1980s. The services provided in the earlier stages were extended into such activities as systematic training (under the influence of the training boards), management development, salary administration, manpower planning, performance appraisal (management by objectives) and, in a few cases, OD (organization development). In some organizations, as trade union power and militancy grew, industrial relations became a major activity and the standing of personnel managers and the occasional personnel director was enhanced accordingly. Productivity bargaining came and went. Extended employment legislation meant that personnel specialists acquired extra responsibilities advising on legal considerations and dealing with cases. Behavioural science knowledge was applied to organization development activities and to job design (job enrichment) and motivation policies. The quality of working life (QWL) movement (Wilson, 1973) emphasized the role of organizations in providing work and working conditions that promote the well-being of employees.

The role of personnel management as a comprehensive approach to employment management was summed up in the following definition produced by Armstrong (1977: 13):

> Personnel management is concerned with obtaining, organizing and motivating the human resources required by the enterprise; with developing an organization climate and management style which will promote effective effort and trust between all the people working in it; and with helping the enterprise to meet its legal obligations and its social responsibilities towards its employee with regard to the conditions of work and quality of life provided for them.

Note that this definition mentioned 'human resources' (the phrase was just beginning to cross the Atlantic at the time) but made no reference to strategy or the role of personnel management in supporting the achievement of the organization's goals. These aspects became prominent in the first manifestations of HRM as described below.

Enter HRM

As conceived by the pioneers in the 1980s, the notion of human resource management is based on a philosophy which is fundamentally different from the personnel management practices of the time. In an article on strategic human resource management (one of the earliest uses of this term) Tichy et al (1982: 47) examined the role of human resource management in the implementation of the long-term plans of a company and commented that: 'The human resource department is a major player in driving organizational performance.' This point was made by Fombrun et al (1984: 37) in their classic statement that: 'The critical management task is to align the formal structure and human resource systems so that they drive the strategic objectives of the organization.' This approach became known as the 'matching model' of HRM.

The other major early contributors to the development of the philosophy of HRM were Beer et al (1984: 1), who, in their 'Harvard framework', proposed that: 'Human resource management involves all management decisions and actions that affect the nature of the relationship between the organization and employees – its human resources.' They expressed the belief that: 'Today... many pressures are demanding a broader, more comprehensive and more strategic perspective with regard to the organization's human resources' (ibid: 4). They also stressed that it was necessary to adopt 'a longer-term perspective in managing people and consideration of people as a potential asset rather than merely a variable cost' (ibid: 6). Beer and his colleagues emphasized that people should be treated as potential assets rather than variable costs. They suggested that HRM had two characteristic features: (1) line managers accept more responsibility for ensuring the alignment of competitive strategy and HR policies; and (2) HR has the mission of setting policies that govern how HR activities are developed and implemented in ways that make them more mutually reinforcing. Richard Walton followed this up with his seminal pieces advocating policies of enhancing commitment and mutuality: 'From control to commitment in the workplace' (1985a) and 'Towards a strategy of eliciting employee commitment based on principles of mutuality' (1985b).

As noted by Legge (2005: 101), following these American pioneers, the old term 'personnel management' increasingly gave way to 'human resource management' (HRM). She commented that 'quickly the term was taken up by both UK managers (for example, Armstrong, 1987; Fowler, 1987), and UK academics'. Hendry and Pettigrew (1990: 20) observed that: 'What HRM did at this point was to provide a label to wrap around some of the observable changes, while providing a focus for challenging deficiencies – in attitudes, scope, coherence, and direction – of existing personnel management.'

The development of the HRM concept

The original concept of HRM as conceived by its founding fathers was commented on and developed in a number of ways during the 1980s and 1990s. The observation made on this era by Guest (1990: 377) was: 'The 1980s was a good decade for advocates of human resource management (HRM) in the UK. To managers it seemed to offer an attractive alternative to the jaded image of personnel management and the dated rhetoric of traditional industrial relations.' However, he also noted that 'HRM is the repository of good intentions' (ibid: 392).

Explorations of the characteristics and goals of HRM were made by mainly British academics, many of whom produced strongly critical studies of it. During this period the concept of strategic human resource management (SHRM) was explored in depth. The importance of a considered approach to performance management and reward management emerged. So did competency-based HRM, which uses the notion of competency (an underlying characteristic of a person that results in effective or superior performance) and the results of competency analysis to inform and improve the processes of performance management, recruitment and selection, employee development and employee reward. In employee relations, the first partnership agreements were made in the 1990s. The notions of high-involvement management (Lawler, 1986), high-performance working (Osterman, 1994) and high-commitment management (Wood, 1996) also took root. Towards the end of the 1990s and into the 2000s a number of research projects tried to establish links between HRM and firm performance.

Characteristics of HRM as described during this development period

HRM was described by Storey (1989: 3) as a 'set of interrelated policies with an ideological and philosophical underpinning'. He listed four aspects that he believed constituted the meaningful version of HRM:

- a particular constellation of beliefs and assumptions;
- a strategic thrust informing decisions about people management;
- the central involvement of line managers;
- reliance upon a set of 'levers' to shape the employment relationship.

He made an influential distinction between the 'hard' and 'soft' versions of HRM, stating that: 'The hard one emphasizes the quantitative, calculative and business-strategic aspects of managing human resources in as "rational" a way as for any other economic factor. By contrast, the soft version traces its roots to the human relations school; it emphasizes communication, motivation and leadership' (ibid: 8). The soft approach to HRM stresses the need to gain the commitment – the 'hearts and minds' – of employees through involvement and other methods of developing a high-commitment, high-trust organization. Attention is also drawn to the key role of organizational culture.

The human relations school referred to by John Storey was founded by Elton Mayo (1933) but its leading exponent was Douglas McGregor (1960). His 'Theory Y' stressed the importance of recognizing the needs of both the organization and the individual and creating conditions which would reconcile these needs so that members of the organization could work together for its success and share in its rewards.

However, it was pointed out by Keenoy (1997: 838) that 'hard and soft HRM are complementary rather than mutually exclusive practices'. Based on research in eight UK organizations, Truss (1999) indicated that the distinction between hard and soft HRM was not as precise as some commentators had implied. Her conclusions were (ibid: 70):

> Even if the rhetoric of HRM is 'soft', the reality is almost always 'hard', with the interests of the organization prevailing over those of the individual. In all the organizations, we found a mixture of both hard and soft approaches. The precise ingredients of this mixture were unique to each organization, which implies that factors such as the external and internal environment of the organization, its strategy, culture and structure all have a vital role to play in the way in which HRM operates.

The goals of HRM

Views about the goals of HRM were expressed by a number of commentators in the 1980s and 1990s. Dyer and Holder (1988: 22–28) analysed management's HR goals under the headings of contribution (what kind of employee behaviour is expected?), composition (what headcount, staffing ratio and skill mix?), competence (what general level of ability is desired?) and commitment (what level of employee attachment and identification?). Ulrich and Lake (1990: 96) remarked that: 'HRM systems can be the source of organizational capabilities that allow firms to learn and capitalize on new opportunities.' Ulrich (1998: 125) suggested that HR departments should become an 'agent of continuous transformation'.

The following policy goals for HRM were proposed by Guest (1991: 154–59):

- commitment: behavioural commitment to pursue agreed goals and attitudinal commitment reflected in a strong identification with the enterprise;
- flexibility: functional flexibility and the existence of an adaptable organization structure with the capacity to manage innovation;
- quality: referring to all aspects of managerial behaviour which bear directly on the quality of goods and services provided, including the management of employees and investment in high-quality employees;
- strategic integration: the ability of the organization to integrate HRM issues into its strategic plans, ensure that the various aspects of HRM cohere, and provide for line managers to incorporate an HRM perspective into their decision making.

The emergence of the concept of strategic human resource management

Perhaps the most significant feature of HRM that emerged in the 1980s and 1990s was the importance attached to strategic integration. This involves vertical integration (fitting HR strategies with the business strategy) and horizontal integration. Legge (1989) argued that one of the common themes of the typical definitions of HRM is that human resource policies should be integrated with strategic business planning. Storey (1989: 6) noted that the concept 'locates HRM policy formulation firmly at the strategic level' and that 'a characteristic of HRM lies in its internally coherent approach'. Sisson (1990) stated that a feature increasingly associated with HRM is the emphasis on the integration of HR policies both with one another and with business planning more generally.

Earlier reservations about HRM

HRM was a controversial topic in academic circles during the 1990s. The main reservations were that HRM was unrealistic – it promises more than it delivers – and that its morality was suspect.

HRM is unrealistic

Noon (1992: 28) asserted that HRM has serious deficiencies as a theory: 'It is built with concepts and propositions, but the associated variables and hypotheses are not made explicit. It is too comprehensive.' He concluded that: 'If HRM is labelled a "theory" it raises expectations about its ability to describe and predict' (ibid: 29). Mabey et al (1998: 80) posed the questions: 'Is SHRM a promise that is not yet fulfilled or a disturbed dream? Is it a failed promise that could never work, or a dream that is most powerful in distorting the realities it advocates?' Their answer to both questions was yes. They also argued that the 'heralded outcomes (of SHRM) are almost without exception unrealistically high' and that 'The gap between SHRM theory and empirical reality is not an incidental feature of SHRM but is actually central to SHRM. SHRM is significant more as rhetoric or ideology than reality – as a large-scale attempt to manage meaning for managers and employees' (ibid: 525).

The immorality of HRM

HRM was accused by many academics in the 1990s of being manipulative, if not positively immoral. Keenoy (1990) claimed that it was a wolf in sheep's clothing. Keenoy and Anthony (1992: 239) argued that 'HRM has succeeded in placing itself at a new frontier of control, at that pinnacle of organizational influence that has always eluded personnel managers.' Willmott (1993) remarked that HRM operates as a form of insidious control by compliance when it emphasizes the need for employees to be committed to do what the organization wants them to do. It preaches mutuality but the reality is that behind the rhetoric it exploits workers. Referring to the HRM interest in cultural change he commented that: 'Under the guise of giving more autonomy to the individual than in organizations governed by bureau-cratic rules, corporate culture threatens to promote a new, hypermodern neo-authoritarianism which, potentially, is more insidious and sinister than its bureaucratic predecessor' (ibid: 541). Scott (1994) thought that HRM was a form of deceit which brainwashed workers to become willing slaves.

Comments on the reservations

The criticisms referred to above seem to be based on the assumption that the early HRM advocates, especially the Americans, were cynically advanc-ing views that they knew to be misleading. This is unlikely. Credit has to be given to people like Richard Walton that they believed what they said, even though their aspirations might have been unrealistic. The criticisms also imply that there is a single monolithic form of HRM. This is not the case. HRM comes in all sorts of shapes and sizes. Sometimes, as Armstrong (1987) observed, it is just personnel management under another name. Many organizations which rebranded their personnel departments as HR departments were not practising the sort of HRM attacked so vigorously, indeed frenetically, by the commentators quoted above.

The assertion that HRM wasn't happening was contradicted by research conducted by Guest and Conway (1997), covering a stratified random sam-ple of 1,000 workers, which established that a notably high level of HRM was in place. The HRM characteristics covered by the survey included the opportunity to express grievances and raise personal concerns on such mat-ters as scope for training and development, communications about business issues, single status, effective systems for dealing with bullying and harass-ment at work, making jobs interesting and varied, promotion from within, in-volvement programmes, no compulsory redundancies, performance-related pay, profit sharing and the use of attitude surveys.

The accusation that HRM treats employees as means to an end is often made. However, it could be argued that if organizations exist to achieve ends, which they obviously do, and if those ends can only be achieved through people, which is clearly the case, the concern of management for commitment and performance from those people is not unnatural and is not attributable to the concept of HRM – it existed in the good old days of personnel management before HRM was invented. What matters is, if man-agement does treat people as means to an end, how this is done and what management provides in return.

Much of the hostility to HRM expressed by a number of academics is based on the belief that it is against the interests of workers, ie that it is managerialist. However, the Guest and Conway (1997) research established that the reports of workers on outcomes showed that a higher number of HR practices were associated with higher ratings of fairness, trust and man-agement's delivery of their promises. Those experiencing more HR activities also felt a greater degree of security and satisfaction with their jobs. Motiva-tion was significantly higher for those working in organizations where more

HR practices were in place. In summary, as commented by Guest (1999), it appears that workers like their experience of HRM. These findings appear to contradict the 'radical critique' view proffered by some academics that HRM has been ineffectual, pernicious (ie managerialist) or both. Those who adopted this stance tended to dismiss favourable reports from workers about HRM on the grounds that they have been brainwashed by management. But there is no evidence to support this view. Moreover, as Armstrong (2000: 577) pointed out: 'HRM cannot be blamed or given credit for changes that were taking place anyway.'

There is something in what the academic critics of HRM in the 1990s had to say. Important contributors to the HRM concept such as Michael Beer and Richard Walton were undoubtedly idealistic (the 'American dream' referred to by Guest, 1990), but in effect to accuse them of a cynical attempt to misrepresent what HRM stood for is going too far. There is often a lot of rhetoric and not so much reality about HRM (Gratton et al, 1999). Karen Legge (1998: 28) pointed out that: 'In a world of scarce resources, as employees are used as means to an end, there will be some that lose out. For these people, the soft version of HRM may be an irrelevancy, while the hard version is likely to be an uncomfortable experience.' But it was left to a practitioner, Alan Fowler (1987: 3), to sum it all up:

> At the heart of the concept is the complete identification of employees with the aims and values of the business – employee involvement but on the company's terms. Power in the HRM system remains very firmly in the hands of the employer. Is it really possible to claim full mutuality when at the end of the day the employer can decide unilaterally to close the company or sell it to someone else?'

HRM today

Human resource management is now the most commonly accepted way of describing the process of managing people. In the words of John Storey (2001: 5), HRM has become 'a generic term simply denoting any approach to employment management'. However, some prefer 'people management' to avoid the use of 'human resources', with its implication that members of the workforce exist to be exploited as factors of production.

In the early 2000s, Storey (2001: 7) noted in line with earlier definitions that the beliefs of HRM included the assumptions that it is the human resource which gives competitive edge, that the aim should be to enhance employee commitment, that HR decisions are of strategic importance and that therefore HR policies should be integrated into the business strategy. Caldwell (2003: 997) added that 'One of the central assumptions of HRM is that greater employee involvement and commitment will improve business performance.' Kochan (2007: 600) directed attention to meeting employee as well as organizational needs when he wrote that: 'The central task is to achieve a better balance between employer and employee interests at work.'

Among the developments in HRM in the 2000s and into the 2010s were the following:

- the emergence of the concept of engagement (the situation in which people are committed to their work and the organization and motivated to achieve high levels of performance);
- the establishment of talent management (identifying, developing, recruiting, retaining and deploying talented people) as a major HR activity;
- the importance attached to human capital management (HCM) – the process of informing HRM decisions by obtaining, analysing and reporting on data relating to employees;
- a recognition of the importance of storing and sharing the wisdom, understanding and expertise accumulated in an organization about its processes, techniques and operations – knowledge management;
- the increased emphasis on learning rather than training and on developing learning cultures rather than creating a 'learning organization' (a concept which was increasingly criticized as being unrealistic);
- the realization that reward management, especially performance-related pay, was not the lever for change it was supposed to be, and the expansion of the notion of total rewards which stressed that non-financial rewards were just as important as, if not more important than, financial rewards;
- the emphasis on partnership and employee voice in employment relations;
- the focus on the need for HR people to be strategic, which was associated with the concept of HR specialists as strategic business partners (Ulrich, 1998).

But the application of these developments has not been universal or consistent. As Thompson and Harley (2007: 162) pointed out: 'The practice of HRM remains ambiguous and variable.' However, the overriding significance of the strategic role of HR is frequently expressed, for example by the CIPD in its 2009 HR profession map. Lawler and Mohrman (2003: 16) stated that: 'HR can make a logical case for being an important part of strategy development because of the importance of human capital in the ability of the firm to carry out its strategy.'

It can be argued that the relentless pressure to be strategic and 'add value' can be overdone. Referring to this 'strategy discourse', Alvesson (2009: 57) commented that: 'Sometimes one gets the impression that there is very little "non-strategic" HRM going on.' He thought that HR people were redefining themselves from being administrators and managers to becoming 'strategists' and that the role of the strategy discourse was to be a source of 'identification and boosting of status' for HR practitioners (ibid: 57). An HR practitioner interviewed by Raymond Caldwell summed up this dilemma bluntly: 'All this rubbish about strategy is simple self-delusion... personnel people are implementers' (Caldwell 2003: 1000).

The strategic focus has led to the popular use of the phrase 'adding value' to describe what HR professionals are there to do. Strictly speaking, adding value is the process of ensuring that the value of the contribution made by any activity to business performance exceeds its cost or generates an acceptable return on investment. But the term is often used more generally to signify the business-orientated approach HR professionals are expected to adopt and how they contribute to the creation of value by the firm. Francis and Keegan (2006: 239) report the following comment from a recruitment consultant, which illustrates how the term has become popular:

> Most HR professionals will now have 'value added' stamped on their foreheads, because they are always being asked to think in terms of the business objectives and how what they do supports the business objectives and the business plan.

To add value, HR focuses on improving performance and results by getting more out of HRM activities than were put into them. The imperative for HR people to 'add value' has become something of a mantra, but as Storey et al (2009: 9) pointed out: 'Adding value depends less on what HR does but on what HR delivers and to whom it delivers it. HR professionals have responsibility to help multiple stakeholders get value from the HR work they do. Employees should have a value proposition where those who deliver value get value back.' Kochan (2007: 604) warned that: 'In pursuing alignment with business goals HR professionals have lost any semblance of credibility as stewards of the social contract because most HR professionals have lost their ability to seriously challenge or offer an independent perspective on the policies and practices of the firm.'

As cited by Francis and Keegan (2006: 235), Grant and Shields (2002) argue that the emphasis typically placed on the business case for HRM suggests a one-sided focus on organizational outcomes at the expense of employees. This resonates with Winstanley and Woodall's (2000: 6) assertions that employee well-being and ethics within the unfolding field of HRM remain contentious, and that the ethical dimension of HR policy and practice has been almost ignored in recent texts on HRM, where the focus has shifted to 'strategic fit' and 'best practice' approaches. The CIPD (2010: 5) refers to HR as 'an applied business discipline first and a people discipline second'.

An alternative view was offered by Paauwe (2004: 3), who wrote that: 'Added value represents the harsh world of economic rationality, but HRM is also about moral values. It is about achieving fairness and legitimacy.' He also commented that 'The yardstick of human resource outcomes is not just economic rationality' and that a stakeholder perspective is required involving 'the development and maintenance of sustainable relationships with all the relevant stakeholders, not just customers and shareholders' (ibid: 67). It was contended by Kochan (2007: 601) that: 'The HR profession has always had a special professional responsibility to balance the needs of the firm with the needs, aspirations and interests of the workforce and the values and standards society expects to be upheld at work.' However, HRM in practice can tend to be business rather than people orientated, as the CIPD has made clear.

Conclusions

HRM has become something that organizations do rather than an aspiration or a philosophy. However, some of its more important messages such as the need for strategic integration, the desirability of gaining commitment, the virtues of partnership and participation and the key role of line managers are now generally accepted. HRM is the term most often used to describe the people-orientated activities of organizations, although 'people management' is sometimes adopted as an alternative. The hostile academics have largely subsided. Peter Boxall, John Purcell and Patrick Wright, representing the new generation of commentators, produced the following explanation of the meaning of HRM, which focuses on what HRM is in the later 2000s rather than on its philosophy (Boxall et al, 2007: 1):

> Human resource management (HRM), the management of work and people towards desired ends, is a fundamental activity in any organization in which human beings are employed. It is not something whose existence needs to be radically justified: HRM is an inevitable consequence of starting and growing an organization. While there are a myriad of variations in the ideologies, styles, and managerial resources engaged, HRM happens in some form or other. It is one thing to question the relative performance of particular models of HRM in particular contexts… It is quite another thing to question the necessity of the HRM process itself, as if organizations cannot survive or grow without making a reasonable attempt at organizing work and managing people.

KEY LEARNING POINTS

HRM defined

Human resource management (HRM) can be defined as a strategic, integrated and coherent approach to the employment, development and well-being of the people working in organizations.

Characteristics of HRM

Its characteristics are that it is diverse, strategic and commitment-orientated, adopts a unitary (the interests of management and employees coincide) rather than pluralist (the interests of management and employees differ) viewpoint and is founded on the belief that people should be treated as assets and is a management-driven activity.

Soft and hard HRM

A distinction was made by Storey (1989) between:

- Soft HRM: treating employees as valued assets, a source of competitive advantage through their commitment, adaptability and high quality;
- Hard HRM: people are important resources through which organizations achieve competitive advantage. The focus is on the quantitative, calculative and business-strategic aspects of managing human resources in as 'rational' a way as for any other economic factor.

HRM policy goals

The four policy goals for HRM proposed by Guest (1991) were commitment, flexibility, quality and strategic integration:

Strategic HRM defined

Strategic HRM (SHRM) is an approach to managing people which deals with how the organization's goals will be achieved through its human resources by means of integrated HR strategies, policies and practices.

Meanings of HRM

The four meanings of SHRM suggested by Hendry and Pettigrew (1986) were:

- the use of planning;
- a coherent approach to the design and management of HR;
- matching HRM activities and policies to some explicit business strategy;
- seeing the people of the organization as a 'strategic resource' for the achievement of 'competitive advantage'.

Reservations about HRM

HRM has been a controversial topic, especially in academic circles in the 1990s. The main reservations made then were that HRM is unrealistic – it promises more than it delivers – and that its morality is suspect.

Use of the term HRM

HRM is now the most commonly accepted way of describing the process of managing people.

Among the developments in HRM in the 2000s and into the 2010s were the following:

- the emergence of the concept of engagement;
- the establishment of talent management as a major HR activity;
- the importance attached to human capital management (HCM);
- the increased emphasis on learning rather than training;

- the realization that reward management, especially performance-related pay, was not the lever for change it was supposed to be;
- the focus on the need for HR people to be strategic.

References

Alvesson, M (2009) Critical perspectives on strategic HRM, in J Storey, P M Wright and D Ulrich (eds) *The Routledge Companion to Strategic Human Resource Management*, pp 3–13, Abingdon, Routledge, pp 53–68

Armstrong, M (1977) *A Handbook of Personnel Management Practice*, 1st edn, London, Kogan Page

Armstrong, M (1987) Human resource management: a case of the emperor's new clothes?, *Personnel Management*, August, pp 30–35

Armstrong, M (2000) The name has changed but has the game remained the same?, *Employee Relations*, **22** (6), pp 576–89

Beer, M, Spector, B, Lawrence, P, Quinn Mills, D and Walton, R E (1984) *Managing Human Assets*, New York, The Free Press

Boxall, P F (1996) The strategic HRM debate and the resource-based view of the firm, *Human Resource Management Journal*, **6** (3), pp 59–75

Boxall, P F, Purcell, J and Wright, P (2007), in (eds) P Boxall, J Purcell and P Wright, *The Oxford Handbook of Human Resource Management*, Oxford University Press, pp 1–18

Caldwell, R (2003) The changing roles of personnel managers: old ambiguities, new uncertainties, *Journal of Management Studies*, **40** (4), pp 983–1004

Caldwell, R (2004) Rhetoric, facts and self-fulfilling prophesies: exploring practitioners' perceptions of progress in implementing HRM, *Industrial Relations Journal*, **35** (3), pp 196–215

Chartered Institute of Personnel and Development (2010) *Next Generation HR*, London, CIPD

Dyer, L and Holder, G W (1988) Strategic human resource management and planning, in L Dyer (ed) *Human Resource Management: Evolving roles and responsibilities*, Washington DC Bureau of National Affairs, pp 1–46

Fombrun, C J, Tichy, N M and Devanna, M A (1984) *Strategic Human Resource Management*, New York, Wiley

Fowler, A (1987) When chief executives discover HRM, *Personnel Management*, January, p 3

Francis, H and Keegan A (2006) The changing face of HRM: in search of balance, *Human Resource Management Journal*, **16** (3), pp 231–49

Grant, D and Shields, J (2002) In search of the subject: researching employee reactions to human resource management, *Journal of Industrial Relations*, **44** (3), 178–93

Gratton, L A, Hailey, V H, Stiles, P and Truss, C (1999) *Strategic Human Resource Management*, Oxford, Oxford University Press

Guest, D E (1990) HRM and the American Dream, *Journal of Management Studies*, **27** (4), pp 377–97

Guest, D E (1991) Personnel management: the end of orthodoxy, *British Journal of Industrial Relations*, **29** (2), pp 149–76

Guest, D E (1999) Human resource management: the workers' verdict, *Human Resource Management Journal*, **9** (2), pp 5–25

Guest, D E and Conway, N (1997) *Employee Motivation and the Psychological Contract*, London, IPD

Hendry, C and Pettigrew, A (1986) The practice of strategic human resource management, *Personnel Review*, **15**, (5) pp 2–8

Hendry, C and Pettigrew, A (1990) Human resource management: an agenda for the 1990s, *International Journal of Human Resource Management*, **1** (1), pp 17–44

Keenoy, T (1990) HRM: a case of the wolf in sheep's clothing, *Personnel Review*, **19** (2), pp 3–9

Keenoy, T (1997) HRMism and the images of re-presentation, *Journal of Management Studies*, **34** (5), pp 825–41

Keenoy, T and Anthony, P (1992) HRM: metaphor, meaning and morality, in P Blyton and P Turnbull (eds) *Reassessing Human Resource Management*, London, Sage Publications, pp 233–55

Kochan, T A (2007) Social legitimacy of the HR profession, in P Boxall, J Purcell and P Wright (eds) *Oxford Handbook of Human Resource Management*, Oxford, Oxford University Press, pp 599–620

Lawler, E E (1986) *High-Involvement Management*, San Francisco, Jossey-Bass

Lawler E E and Mohrman S A (2003) What does it take to make it happen?, *Human Resource Planning*, **26** (3), pp 15–29

Legge, K (1989) Human resource management: a critical analysis, in J Storey (ed) *New Perspectives in Human Resource Management*, London, Routledge, pp 19–40

Legge, K (1998) *Human Resource Management: Rhetorics and Realities*, London, Macmillan

Legge, K (2005) *Human Resource Management: Rhetorics and Realities*, 2nd edn, Basingstoke, Palgrave Macmillan

Mabey, C, Salaman, G and Storey, J (1998) *Human Resource Management: A strategic introduction*, Oxford, Blackwell

Mayo, E (1933) Human Problems of an Industrial Civilisation, London, Macmillan

McGregor, D (1960) *The Human Side of Enterprise*, New York, McGraw-Hill

Noon, M (1992) HRM: a map, model or theory? in P Blyton and P Turnbull (eds) *Reassessing Human Resource Management*, London, Sage Publications, pp 16–32

Osterman, P (1994) How common is workplace transformation and who adopts it? *Industrial and Labor Relations Review*, **47** (2), pp 175–88

Paauwe, J (2004) *HRM and performance: Achieving long-term viability*, Oxford, Oxford University Press

Pigors, P J W (1951) *Personnel Administration: A point of view and a method*, New York, McGraw Hill

Schuler, R S (1992) Strategic human resource management: linking people with the strategic needs of the business, *Organizational Dynamics*, **21** (1), pp 18–32

Scott, A (1994) *Willing Slaves: British workers under human resource management*, Cambridge, Cambridge University Press

Sisson, K (1990) Introducing the Human Resource Management Journal, *Human Resource Management Journal*, **1** (1), pp 1–11

Storey, J (1989) From personnel management to human resource management, in J Storey (ed) *New Perspectives on Human Resource Management*, London, Routledge, pp 1–18

Storey, J (2001) Human resource management today: an assessment, in J Storey (ed) *Human Resource Management: A critical text*, London, Thompson Learning, pp 3–20

Storey, J, Ulrich, D and Wright, P M (2009) Introduction, in J Storey, P M Wright and D Ulrich (eds) *The Routledge Companion to Strategic Human Resource Management*, Abingdon, Routledge, pp 3–13

Thompson, P and Harley, B (2007) HRM and the worker: labour process perspectives, in P Boxall, J Purcell and P Wright (eds) *Oxford Handbook of Human Resource Management*, Oxford, Oxford University Press, pp 147–65

Tichy, N M, Fombrun, C J and Devanna, M A (1982) Strategic human resource management, *Sloan Management Review*, **23** (2), pp 47–61

Truss, C (1999) Soft and hard models of HRM, in L Gratton, V H Hailey, P Stiles and C Truss (eds) *Strategic Human Resource Management*, Oxford, Oxford Oxford University Press

Ulrich, D (1998) A new mandate for human resources, *Harvard Business Review*, January–February, pp 124–34

Ulrich, D and Lake, D (1990) *Organizational Capability: Competing from the inside out*, New York, Wiley

Walton, R E (1985a) From control to commitment in the workplace, *Harvard Business Review*, March–April, pp 77–84

Walton, R E (1985b) Towards a strategy of eliciting employee commitment based on principles of mutuality, in R E Walton and P R Lawrence (eds) *HRM Trends and Challenges*, Boston MA, Harvard Business School Press

Willmott, H (1993) Strength is ignorance, slavery is freedom: Managing culture in modern organizations, *Journal of Management Studies*, **30** (4), pp 515–52

Wilson, N A B (1973) *On the Quality of Working Life*, London, HMSO

Winstanley, D and Woodall, J (2000) The ethical dimension of human resource management, *Human Resource Management Journal*, **10** (2), pp 5–20

Wood, S (1996) High commitment management and organization in the UK, *International Journal of Human Resource Management*, **7** (1), pp 41–58

Wright, P M and McMahan, G C (1999) Theoretical perspectives for human resource management, in R S Schuler and S E Jackson (eds) *Strategic Human Resource Management*, Oxford, Blackwell, pp 49–72

Questions

1 What is human resource management (HRM)?

2 What are the fundamental characteristics of HRM?

3 What is the matching model of HRM?

4 What is the 'Harvard framework' of HRM?

5 What characteristics did John Storey attribute to HRM?

6 What is the difference between 'hard' and 'soft' HRM?

7 What are the goals of HRM as defined by Dyer and Holder?

8   What are the goals of HRM as defined by David Guest?

9   What is strategic integration?

10 What is strategic human resource management (SHRM)?

11 What are the four meanings attached to SHRM by Hendry and Pettigrew?

12 It has been said that strategic HRM is not just about formulating HR strategies. What is it, then?

13 Why do some commentators think that HRM is unrealistic?

14 Why do some commentators think that HRM is immoral?

15 What response might be made to someone who says that HRM is unrealistic, immoral or both?

16 What is the state of HRM today?

17 What are the key recent developments in HRM?

18 What is added value?

19 How can HRM add value?

20 What are the most important messages of HRM?

Delivering HRM

05

Key concepts and terms

- *Employee relations*
- *Employee value proposition*
- *Employer brand*
- *Employer of choice*
- *Employment relationship*
- *HR architecture*
- *HR delivery model*
- *HR philosophies, policies, practices, processes and programmes*
- *HR system*
- *Job design*
- *Learning and development*
- *Organization design*
- *Organization development*
- *Organizational learning*
- *Performance management*
- *Recruitment*
- *Resourcing*
- *Reward management*
- *Selection*
- *Talent management*
- *Workforce planning*

LEARNING OUTCOMES

On completing this chapter you should be able to define these key concepts. You should also understand:

- What the concept of HR architecture means
- What an HR system looks like
- The basic features of the key HR practices of organization design and development, employee resourcing, learning and development, performance and reward management, managing the employment relationship and employee relations
- The nature of an HR delivery model

Introduction

HRM is delivered through the HR architecture of an organization, which includes the HR system, HR practices and the HR delivery model adopted by the HR function.

HR architecture

HR architecture consists of the HR systems, processes and structure as well as employee behaviours. It is a comprehensive representation of all that is involved in HRM, not simply the structure of the HR function. As explained by Becker et al (2001: 12): 'We use the term HR architecture to broadly describe the continuum from the HR professionals within the HR function, to the system of HR-related policies and practices, through the competencies, motivation and associated behaviours of the firm's employees.' It was noted by Hird et al (2010: 25) that 'this architecture is seen as a unique combination of the HR function's structure and delivery model, the HR practices and system, and the strategic employee behaviours that these create'.

Purcell (1999: 38) suggested that the focus should be on 'appropriate HR architecture and the processes that contribute to organizational performance'. Becker and Huselid (2006: 899) stated that: 'It is the fit between the HR architecture and the strategic capabilities and business processes that implement strategy that is the basis of HR's contribution to competitive advantage.'

The HR system

The HR system contains the interrelated and jointly supportive HR activities and practices which together enable HRM goals to be achieved. Becker and

Huselid (1998: 95) observed that: 'The HRM system is first and foremost a vehicle to implement the firm's strategy.' Later (2006) they argued that it is the HR system which is the key HR asset. Boselie et al (2005: 73) pointed out that in its traditional form HRM can be viewed as 'a collection of multiple discrete practices with no explicit or discernible link between them. The more strategically minded system approach views HRM as an integrated and coherent bundle of mutually reinforcing practices.'

As illustrated in Figure 5.1, an HRM system brings together HR philosophies which describe the overarching values and guiding principles adopted in managing people. Taking account of the internal and external environments in which the organization operates, the system incorporates HR strategies which define the direction in which HRM intends to go in each of its main areas of activity, and HR policies which provide guidelines defining how these values, principles and strategies should be applied and implemented in specific aspects of HRM. The system also includes HR processes which comprise

FIGURE 5.1 The HRM system

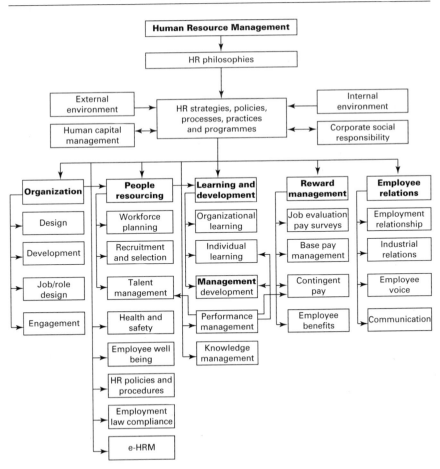

the formal procedures and methods used to put HR strategic plans and policies into effect, linked HR practices which consist of the approaches used in managing people, and HR programmes – the planned activities which enable HR strategies, policies and practices to be implemented according to plan.

HR practices

The key HR practices used by successful organizations as described below are organization design and development, job design, people resourcing (attracting and retaining employees and talent management), learning and development, performance and reward management, managing the employment relationship and employee relations.

Organization design

Organization design is the process of deciding how organizations should be structured and function. Organizations are not static things. Changes are constantly taking place in the business itself, in the environment in which the business operates, and in the people who work in the business. There is no such thing as an 'ideal' organization. The most that can be done is to optimize the processes involved, remembering that whatever structure evolves it will be contingent on the circumstances of the organization. It is important to remember that organizations consist of people working more or less cooperatively together. Inevitably, and especially at managerial levels, the organization may have to be adjusted to fit the particular strengths and attributes of the people available. The result may not conform to the ideal, but it is more likely to work than a structure which ignores the human element. It is always desirable to have an ideal structure in mind, but it is equally desirable to modify it to meet particular circumstances, as long as there is awareness of the potential problems that may arise.

In principle, organization design aims to:

- clarify the overall purposes of the organization – the strategic goals which govern what it does and how it functions;
- define how work should be organized to achieve that purpose, including the use of technology and other work processes;
- define as precisely as possible the key activities involved in carrying out the work;
- group these activities logically together to avoid unnecessary overlap or duplication;
- provide for the integration of activities and the achievement of cooperative effort and teamwork;
- build flexibility into the system so that organizational arrangements can adapt quickly to new situations and challenges;
- clarify individual roles, accountabilities and authorities.

In practice, however, organization design is seldom as considered an affair as this list of aims suggests. This is partly because organizations are run by people – the 'dominant coalition' – who do not necessarily react logically to new demands and are influenced by political pressures and power plays. It also arises from the dynamic nature of organizations as they adapt to ever-changing environmental conditions. This is why organizations often evolve rather than being designed. The aims as stated above will not always be achieved. However, many organizations seem to muddle though, primarily through the informal processes which have the greatest influence on how they function.

Organization development

Organization development (OD) is about taking systematic steps to improve organizational capability. It is concerned with process – how things get done. Organization development aims to help people work more effectively together, improve organizational processes such as the formulation and implementation of strategy, and facilitate the transformation of the organization and the management of change. As expressed by Beer (1980: 10), OD operates as 'a system-wide process of data collection, diagnosis, action planning, intervention and evaluation'.

OD programmes are concerned with system-wide change and have the following features:

- They are managed, or at least strongly supported, from the top but may make use of third parties or 'change agents' to diagnose problems and to manage change by various kinds of planned activity or intervention.
- The plans for organization development are based upon a systematic analysis and diagnosis of the strategies and circumstances of the organization and the changes and problems affecting it.
- They use behavioural science knowledge and aim to improve the way the organization copes in times of change through such processes as interaction, communications, participation, planning, and conflict management.
- They focus on ways of ensuring that business and HR strategies are implemented and change is managed effectively.

Job design

Job design specifies the contents, methods and relationships of jobs in order to satisfy work requirements for productivity, efficiency and quality, meet the personal needs of the job holder and thus increase levels of employee engagement. The process of job design starts with an analysis of the way in which work needs to be organized and what work therefore needs to be done – the tasks that have to be carried out if the purpose of the organization or an organizational unit is to be achieved. Account is taken of the need to satisfy the job characteristics specified by Hackman and Oldham (1974): variety, autonomy, required interaction, optional interaction, knowledge and skill required, and responsibility.

People resourcing

People resourcing is about the acquisition, retention, development and effective use of the people the organization needs. It is based on a resourcing strategy which is linked to the business strategy and is the basis for workforce planning activities. Workforce plans are implemented by means of the resourcing activities of attracting people, recruitment and selection, retention planning and talent management. In addition, learning and development programmes enhance the organization's skills base. The effectiveness with which human resources are used involves providing for flexibility and controlling absenteeism.

Workforce planning

Organizations need to know how many people and what sort of people they should have to meet present and future business requirements. This is the function of workforce planning, which consists of the following activities:

- Scenario planning – making broad assessments of future environmental developments and their likely impact on people requirements.
- Demand forecasting – estimating future needs for people and competences by reference to corporate and functional plans and forecasts of future activity levels.
- Supply forecasting – estimating the supply of people by reference to analyses of current resources and future availability, after allowing for wastage. The forecast will also take account of labour market trends relating to the availability of skills and to demographics.
- Forecasting requirements – analysing the demand and supply forecasts to identify future deficits or surpluses with the help of models, where appropriate.
- Action planning – preparing plans to deal with forecast deficits or surpluses of employees.

Attracting people to the organization

The aim is to become 'an employer of choice', a firm people want to work for and stay with. This means developing an employee value proposition which consists of what the organization has to offer for prospective or existing employees that they are likely to value and which would persuade them to join or remain with the business. It will include pay and benefits – which are important but can be overemphasized compared with other non-financial elements. The latter may be crucial in obtaining and retaining people and include the attractiveness of the organization, its reputation as a good employer, and the degree to which it acts responsibly, treats people with consideration and respect and provides for diversity and inclusion, work–life balance and personal and professional growth. The employee value proposition can be expressed as an employer brand – an image for prospective employees of the organization as a good employer.

Recruitment and selection

Recruitment is the process of finding and engaging the people the organization needs. Selection is an aspect of recruitment concerned with deciding which applicants or candidates should be appointed to jobs. The four stages of recruitment and selection are:

1 Defining requirements – preparing role profiles and person specifications; deciding terms and conditions of employment.

2 Planning recruitment campaigns.

3 Attracting candidates – reviewing and evaluating alternative sources of applicants, inside and outside the company: advertising, e-recruiting, agencies and consultants.

4 Selecting candidates – sifting applications, interviewing, testing, assessing candidates, assessment centres, offering employment, obtaining references; preparing contracts of employment.

Retention planning

It is not enough to attract good people to the organization. Steps have to be taken to encourage them to stay. This is the aim of retention planning which, on the basis of information about how many people leave and why they leave, establishes what needs to be done to retain those who are worth retaining. The possible actions are to:

- Ensure that selection and promotion procedures match the capacities of individuals to the demands of the work they have to do. Rapid turnover can be caused by poor selection or promotion decisions.
- Reduce losses of people who cannot adjust to their new job – the 'induction crisis' – by giving them proper training and support when they join the organization.
- Deal with uncompetitive, inequitable or unfair pay systems.
- Design jobs to maximize skill variety, task significance, autonomy, control over their work and feedback, and ensure that they provide opportunities for learning and growth. Some roles can be 'customized' to meet the needs of particular individuals.

- Increase job engagement through job design and by organizing work around projects with which people can identify..
- Encourage the development of social ties within the company.
- Take steps to improve work–life balance by developing family-friendly policies such as flexible working which recognize the needs of employees outside work.
- Eliminate as far as possible unpleasant working conditions or the imposition of too much stress on employees.
- Select, brief and train managers and team leaders so that they appreciate the positive contribution they can make to improving retention by the ways in which they lead their teams. Bear in mind that people often leave their managers rather than their organization.
- Ensure that policies for controlling stress, bullying and harassment exist and are applied.

Talent management

As defined by Duttagupta (2005: 2), 'Talent management is the strategic management of the flow of talent through an organization.' Talent management starts with the business strategy and what it signifies in terms of the talented people required by the organization. Ultimately, the aim is to create and maintain a pool of talented people through a talent management 'pipeline'.

Learning and development

Learning and development is the process of ensuring that the organization has the knowledgeable, skilled and engaged workforce it needs. It involves facilitating the acquisition by individuals and teams of knowledge and skills through experience, learning events and programmes provided by the organization, guidance and coaching provided by line managers and others and self-directed learning activities carried out by individuals. Learning and development activities comprise:

- Organizational learning: the development and acquisition in organizations of knowledge, understanding, insights, techniques and practices in order to improve organizational effectiveness.
- Individual and team learning: the processes and programmes used to ensure that individual employees and teams acquire and develop the new knowledge, skills, capabilities, behaviours and attitudes required to perform their roles effectively and to develop their potential.
- Management development: improving the performance of managers in their present roles and preparing them to take on greater responsibilities in the future.

- Learning needs analysis: a systematic process for determining what needs to be done and why it needs to be done, which provides the basis for designing learning and development programmes.
- Planning and delivering learning and development programmes or learning events: a learning and development programme is a sequence or group of learning activities which may include a mix of approaches (blended learning) which take place over a period of time. A learning event is a specific learning activity which might take the form of a course designed to meet established learning needs.
- Evaluation of learning and development: the assessment of the effectiveness of learning and development activities producing the outcomes specified (the criterion or terminal behaviour) when the activity was planned in order to indicate where improvements or changes are required.

Performance management

Performance management is a systematic process for improving organizational performance by developing the performance of individuals and teams. Individual performance is developed through performance management systems. They provide the framework for improving performance through the agreement of performance expectations and the formulation of performance development plans. As vehicles for feedback and recognition they have a major role in a performance and reward system. They inform contingent pay decisions.

The performance management cycle is shown in Figure 5.2.

FIGURE 5.2 The performance management cycle

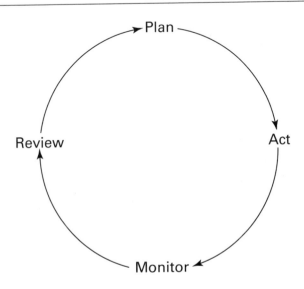

The performance management processes taking place in this cycle are:

- Plan: agree objectives and competency requirements as expressed in role profiles; identify the required behaviours; produce plans expressed in performance agreements for meeting objectives and improving performance; prepare personal development plans to enhance knowledge, skills and competence and reinforce the desired behaviours.
- Act: carry out the work required to achieve objectives by reference to the plans and in response to new demands.
- Monitor: check on progress in achieving objectives and responding to new demands; treat performance management as a continuous process – 'managing performance all the year round' – rather than an annual appraisal event.
- Review: hold a 'stock-taking' discussion of progress and achievements in a review meeting and identify where action is required to develop performance as a basis for completing the cycle and continuing into the planning stage.

Reward management

Reward management is concerned with the strategies, policies and processes required to ensure that the value of people and the contribution they make to achieving organizational, departmental and team goals are recognized and rewarded. It is about the design, implementation and maintenance of reward systems (interrelated reward processes, practices and procedures) which aim to satisfy the needs of both the organization and its stakeholders and to operate fairly, equitably and consistently. These systems will include arrangements for assessing the value of jobs through job evaluation and market pricing, base pay management (the design and management of grade and pay structures), performance management processes, schemes for rewarding and recognizing people according to their individual performance or contribution and/or team or organizational performance, and the provision of employee benefits.

But it should be emphasized that reward management is not just about pay and employee benefits. It is equally concerned with non-financial rewards such as recognition, learning and development opportunities and increased job responsibility (the concept of total rewards).

Managing the employment relationship

The employment relationship is one which is established whenever employers and employees work together. A positive employment relationship is required, one in which there is mutuality – the state that exists when management and employees are interdependent and both benefit from this interdependency – and trust. Such a relationship provides a foundation for employment and employee relations policies. It governs much of what organizations need to be aware of in developing and applying human resource management and employee relations processes, policies and procedures. These need to be considered in terms of what they will or will not contribute to furthering a productive and rewarding relationship between all the parties concerned.

The employment relationship is underpinned by the psychological contract. This is a set of unwritten expectations which exist between individual employees and their employers. As Guest (2007) noted, it is concerned with 'the perceptions of both parties to the employment relationship, organization and individual, of the reciprocal promises and obligations implied in that relationship'.

The nature of the employment relationship is strongly influenced by HR actions. These cover all aspects of HRM. The ways in which people are treated in such areas as recruitment, performance reviews, promotion, career development, reward, involvement and participation, grievance handling, disciplinary procedures and redundancy will be particularly important. How people are required to carry out their work (including flexibility and multi-skilling), how performance expectations are expressed and communicated, how work is organized and how people are managed will also have a significant impact on the employment relationship. HR specialists can contribute to the development of a positive and productive employment relationship in the following ways:

- during recruitment interviews – presenting the unfavourable as well as the favourable aspects of a job in a 'realistic job preview';
- in induction programmes – communicating to new starters the organization's HR policies and procedures and its core values, indicating to them the standards of performance expected in such areas as quality and customer service, and spelling out requirements for flexibility;
- by issuing and updating employee handbooks which reinforce the messages delivered in induction programmes;
- by encouraging the development of performance management processes which ensure that performance expectations are agreed and reviewed regularly;
- by encouraging the use of personal development plans which spell out how continuous improvement of performance can be achieved, mainly by self-managed learning;
- by using learning and development programmes to underpin core values and define performance expectations;
- by ensuring through manager and team leader training that managers and team leaders understand their roles in managing the employment

relationship through such processes as performance management and team leadership;

- by encouraging the maximum amount of contact between managers and team leaders and their team members to achieve mutual understanding of expectations and to provide a means of two-way communications;
- by adopting a general policy of transparency – ensuring that on all matters which affect them, employees know what is happening, why it is happening and the impact it will make on their employment, development and prospects;
- by developing HR procedures covering grievance handling, discipline, equal opportunities, promotion and redundancy and ensuring that they are implemented fairly and consistently;
- by developing and communicating HR policies covering the major areas of employment, development, reward and employee relations;
- by ensuring that the reward system is developed and managed to achieve equity, fairness, consistency and transparency in all aspects of pay and benefits;
- generally, by advising on employee relations procedures, processes and issues which further good collective relationships.

These approaches to managing the employment relationship cover all aspects of people management. It is important to remember, however, that this is a continuous process. The effective management of the relationship means ensuring that values are upheld and that a transparent, consistent and fair approach is adopted in dealing with all aspects of employment. It is also important to remember that perhaps the best way of improving the employment relationship is to develop a high-trust organization.

Employee relations

Employee relations consist of the approaches and methods adopted by employers to deal with employees either individually or collectively through their trade unions. They are concerned with managing and maintaining the employment relationship as described above. But they also involve handling the pay–work bargain (the agreement between employers and employees either individually or collectively of terms and conditions of employment), dealing with employment practices and issues arising from employment, providing employees with a voice and communicating with employees.

The term 'employee relations' encompasses that of 'industrial relations' which are about relationships between managements and trade unions involving collective agreements, collective bargaining, disputes resolution and dealing with issues concerning the employment relationship and the working environment.

The HR delivery model

In a sense HR is in the delivery business – providing the advice and services which enable organizations to get things done through people. The HR delivery model describes how those services are provided. These methods of delivery take place irrespective of the degree to which what is done corresponds with the conceptual HRM model described in Chapter 2.

The most celebrated delivery model was produced by Dave Ulrich. In his highly influential *Harvard Business Review* article he wrote that: 'HR should not be defined by what it does but by what it delivers – results that enrich the organization's value to customers, investors, and employees' (Ulrich, 1998: 124). More specifically, he suggested that HR can deliver in four ways: as a strategic partner, an administrative expert, an employee champion and a change agent. This first model was later modified by Ulrich and Brockbank (2005), who defined the four roles as employee advocate, human capital developer, functional expert, and strategic partner. The role of HR in delivering HRM is explored in more detail in the next chapter.

KEY LEARNING POINTS

HRM delivery

HRM is delivered through the HR architecture of an organization, which includes the HR system, HR practices, and the HR delivery model adopted by the HR function.

HR architecture

HR architecture includes the HR systems and processes and employee behaviours as well as the structure of the HR function.

The HR system

The HR system as part of the HR architecture consists of the interrelated and jointly supportive HR activities and practices which together enable HRM goals to be achieved.

HR practices

The key HR practices and activities are organization design and development, job design, resourcing (attracting and retaining employees and talent management), learning and development, performance and reward management, managing the employment relationship and employee relations:

- Organization design is the process of deciding how organizations should be structured and function.
- Organization development (OD) is about taking systematic steps to improve organizational capability.

- Job design specifies the contents, methods and relationships of jobs in order to satisfy work requirements for productivity, efficiency and quality, meet the personal needs of the job holder and thus increase levels of employee engagement.
- People resourcing is about the acquisition, retention, development and effective utilization of the people the organization needs.
- Recruitment is the process of finding and engaging the people the organization needs. Selection is an aspect of recruitment concerned with deciding which applicants or candidates should be appointed to jobs.
- Talent management is the process of identifying, developing, recruiting, retaining and deploying talented people.
- Learning and development is the process of ensuring that the organization has the knowledgeable, skilled and engaged workforce it needs.
- Performance management is a systematic process for improving organizational performance by developing the performance of individuals and teams.
- Reward management is concerned with the strategies, policies and processes required to ensure that the value of people and the contribution they make to achieving organizational, departmental and team goals are recognized and rewarded.
- The employment relationship is one which is established whenever employers and employees work together.
- Employee relations consist of the approaches and methods adopted by employers to deal with employees either individually or collectively through their trade unions. Providing the advice and services which enable organizations to get things done through people.

The HR delivery model

The HR delivery model describes how those services are delivered.

References

Becker, B E and Huselid, M A (1998) High-performance work systems and firm performance: a synthesis of research and managerial implications, *Research on Personnel and Human Resource Management*, **16**, Stamford, Connecticut, JAI Press, pp 53–101

Becker, B E and Huselid, M A (2006) Strategic human resource management: where do we go from here?, *Journal of Management*, **32** (6), pp 898–925

Becker, B E, Huselid, M A and Ulrich, D (2001) *The HR Scorecard: Linking people, strategy, and performance*, Boston MA, Harvard Business School Press

Beer, M (1980) *Organization Change and Development: A systems view*, Santa Monica CA, Goodyear Publishing

Boselie, P, Dietz, G and Boon, C (2005) Commonalities and contradictions in HRM and performance research, *Human Resource Management Journal*, **15** (3), pp 67–94

Duttagupta, R (2005) *Identifying and Managing Your Assets: Talent management*, London, PricewaterhouseCoopers

Guest, D (2007) HRM: Towards a new psychological contract, in P Boxall, J Purcell and P Wright (eds) *Oxford Handbook of Human Resource Management*, Oxford, Oxford University Press

Hackman, J R and Oldham, G R (1974) Motivation through the design of work: test of a theory, *Organizational Behaviour and Human Performance*, **16** (2), pp 250–79

Hird, M, Sparrow, P and Marsh, C (2010) HR structures: are they working? in P Sparrow, A Hesketh, M Hird and C Cooper (eds) *Leading HR*, Basingstoke, Palgrave Macmillan, pp 23–45

Purcell, J (1999) Best practice or best fit: chimera or cul-de-sac?, *Human Resource Management Journal*, **9** (3), pp 26–41

Ulrich, D (1998) A new mandate for human resources, *Harvard Business Review*, January–February, pp 124–34

Ulrich, D and Brockbank, W (2005) *The HR Value Proposition*, Cambridge MA, Harvard Press

Questions

1 How is HRM delivered?

2 What is HRM architecture?

3 What is the significance of the concept of HRM architecture?

4 What is an HR system?

5 What are the principal elements of an HR system?

6 What is an HR policy?

7 What is an HR strategy?

8 What are the key HR practices?

9 What is involved in organization design?

10 What is involved in organization development?

11 What is involved in job design?

12 What is involved in resourcing?

13 What is workforce planning?

14 What is involved in recruitment and selection?

15 What is involved in retention planning?

16 What is involved in talent management?

17 What is involved in learning and development?

18 What is involved in performance management?

19 What is the employment relationship?

20 What is the psychological contract?

21 What is involved in employee relations?

The role and organization of the HR and L&D functions

06

Key concepts and terms

- *Centre of expertise*
- *Human resource development*
- *Learning culture*
- *Shared service centre*
- *Social responsibility*
- *Strategic business partner*
- *Systematic training*
- *Three-legged stool model*
- *Transactional activities (HR)*
- *Transformational activities (HR)*

LEARNING OUTCOMES

On completing this chapter you should be able to define these key concepts. You should also understand:

- The role of HR
- The transformational and transactional activities carried out by the HR function
- The organization of the HR function
- Evaluating the HR function

- The HR role of line managers
- The role and organization of the L&D function
- The relationship between HRM and L&D

Introduction

This chapter describes the role and activities of the HR and L&D functions and how they are organized to deliver human resource management and learning and development. Reference is also made to the key role played by line managers in human resource management.

The role of HR

The HR function delivers HRM by providing insight, leadership, advice and services on matters affecting the management, employment, development, reward and well-being of people and the relationships between management and employees. Importantly, it makes a major contribution to the achievement of organizational effectiveness and success. The basic role of HR is to deliver HRM services. But it does much more than that. It plays a key part in the creation of an environment which enables people to make the best use of their capacities, to realize their potential to the benefit of both the organization and themselves, and to achieve satisfaction through their work.

Increasingly the role of HR is seen to be business orientated – contributing to the achievement of sustained competitive advantage. Becker and Huselid (1998: 97) argued that HR should be 'a resource that solves real business problems'. But one of the issues explored by Francis and Keegan (2006) is the tendency for a focus on business performance outcomes to obscure the importance of employee well-being in its own right. They quoted the view of Ulrich and Brockbank (2005: 201) that 'caring, listening to, and responding to employees remains a centrepiece of HR work'. The HR function and its members have to be aware of the ethical dimensions of their work.

HR activities

HR activities can be divided into two broad categories: (1) transformational (strategic) activities, which are concerned with developing organizational effectiveness and the alignment and implementation of HR and business strategies; and (2) transactional activities, which cover the main areas of

HR service delivery – resourcing, learning and development, reward and employee relations. A CEO's view on the HR agenda as quoted by Hesketh and Hird (2010: 105) was that it operates on three levels: 'There's the foundation level, which we used to call personnel, it's just pay and rations, recruitment, all that sort of stuff that makes the world go round, transactional work. Level two to me is tools, it could be engagement, reward, development, those sort of things. Level three is the strategic engagement.'

The organization of the HR function

The ways in which HR operates vary immensely. As Sisson (1990) commented, HR management is not a single homogeneous occupation – it involves a variety of roles and activities which differ from one organization to another and from one level to another in the same organization. Tyson (1987) claimed that the HR function is often 'Balkanized' – not only is there a variety of roles and activities but these tend to be relatively self-centred, with little passage between them. Hope-Hailey et al (1997: 17) believed that HR could be regarded as a 'chameleon function' in the sense that the diversity of practice established by their research suggests that 'contextual variables dictate different roles for the function and different practices of people management'.

The organization and staffing of the HR function clearly depend on the size of the business, the extent to which operations are decentralized, the type of work carried out, the kind of people employed and the role assigned to the HR function. A survey by Incomes Data Services (IDS, 2010) found that the overall median number of HR staff in the responding organizations was 14. In small and medium-sized companies (with 1 to 499 staff) the median number was 3.5, and in companies with 500 or more employees it was 20. While, as would be expected, large organizations employed more staff than small and medium enterprises (SMEs), they had on average, fewer HR staff per employee. For SMEs the median ratio of employees to HR staff was 62:1; in large employers it was 95:1. The overall ratio was 80:1.

A traditional organization might consist of an HR director responsible directly to the chief executive, with functional heads dealing, respectively, with recruitment and employment matters, learning and development, and reward management. Crail (2006: 15) used the responses from 179 organizations to an IRS survey of the HR function to produce a model of a HR department. He suggested that this 'might consist of a team of 12 people serving a workforce of around 1,200. The team would have a director, three managers, one supervisor, three HR officers and four assistants. Such a team would typically include a number of professionally qualified practitioners, particularly at senior level.' But there is no such thing as a typical HR function, although the 'three-legged stool' model as described below has attracted a lot of attention.

The three-legged stool model

The notion of delivering HR through three major areas – centres of expertise, business partners and HR service centres – emerged from the HR delivery model produced by Ulrich (1997, 1998), although, as reported by Hird et al (2010: 26): 'Ulrich himself has gone on record recently to state that the structures being implemented by HR based on his work are not actually his idea at all but an interpretation of his writing.' They noted that the first reference to the three-legged stool was in an article by Johnson (1999) two years after Ulrich published his delivery model. In this article Johnson quoted David Hilborn, an associate of William Mercer, management consultants, as follows (ibid: 44):

> The traditional design typically includes a vice president of HR, then a manager of compensation and benefits, a manager of HRIS and payroll, a manager of employment and so on. However, the emerging model is more like a three-legged stool. One leg of the stool includes an administrative service centre which processes payroll, benefits and the like and focuses on efficiency in transaction functions. The second leg is a centre of excellence (or expertise) in which managers and specialists work. These employees concentrate on design rather than transactions and will have line managers as their customers. HR business partners make up the third leg. They are generalists who usually report to line managers and indirectly to HR. These employees don't get involved in transactions, but instead act as consultants and planners, linking the business with appropriate HR programmes.

This exposition provided the blueprint for all subsequent versions of the model, which has evolved as follows:

- Centres of expertise – these specialize in the provision of high-level advice and services on key HR activities. The CIPD survey on the changing HR function (CIPD, 2007) found that they existed in 28 per cent of respondents' organizations. The most common expertise areas were training and development (79 per cent), recruitment (67 per cent), reward (60 per cent) and employee relations (55 per cent).

- Strategic business partners – these work with line managers to help them reach their goals through effective strategy formulation and execution. They are often 'embedded' in business units or departments.

- Shared service centres – these handle all the routine 'transactional' services across the business, which include such activities as recruitment, absence monitoring and advice on dealing with employee issues like discipline and absenteeism.

Although this model has attracted a great deal of attention, the Chartered Institute of Personnel and Development (CIPD) 2007 survey found that only 18 per cent of respondents had implemented all three 'legs', although

47 per cent had implemented one or two elements, with business partners being the most common (29 per cent). However, there are difficulties. Gratton (2003: 18) pointed out that: 'this fragmentation of the HR function is causing all sorts of unintended problems. Senior managers look at the fragments and are not clear how the function as a whole adds value.' And as Reilly (2007) commented, respondents to the CIPD survey mentioned other problems in introducing the new model. These included difficulties in defining roles and accountabilities, especially those of business partners, who risk being 'hung, drawn and quartered by all sides', according to one HR director. At the same time, the segmented nature of the structure gives rise to 'boundary management' difficulties, for example when it comes to separating out transactional tasks from the work of centres of expertise. The model can also hamper communication between those engaged in different HR activities. Other impediments were technological failure, inadequate resources in HR and skills gaps. Hird et al (2010: 31) drew attention to the following issues:

- an 'off-the-shelf' introduction of a new HR structure without careful thought as to how the model fits the organization's requirements;
- a lack of care in dealing with the boundary issues between elements of the HR structure which can easily be fragmented;
- a lack of attention to the new skill sets needed by business partners to ensure they can play at the strategic level;
- a lack of understanding on the part of managers as to the value of a new HR structure;
- a lack of skill on the part of line managers to make the required shift to greater responsibility for people issues implied by the new model;
- what is referred to as the 'polo' problem: a lack of provision of the execution of HR services as the business partner shifts to strategic work, and the centre of expertise to an advisory role.

However, some benefits were reported by respondents to the CIPD (2007) survey. Centres of expertise provide higher-quality advice. Business partners exercise better business focus, line managers are more engaged and the profile of HR is raised, while the introduction of shared services results in improved customer service and allows other parts of HR to spend more time on value-adding activities.

Evaluating the HR function

It is necessary to evaluate the contribution of the HR function in order to ensure that it is effective at both the strategic level and in terms of service delivery and support. The prime criteria for evaluating the work of the function are its ability to operate strategically and its capacity to deliver the levels of services required.

Research conducted by the Institute of Employment Studies (Hirsh, 2008) discovered that the factors that correlated most strongly with line managers' and employees' satisfaction with HR were:

- being well supported in times of change;
- HR giving good advice to employees;
- being well supported when dealing with difficult people or situations;
- HR getting the basics right.

However, the results showed that HR could do better in each of these areas. The conclusions reached were that HR must find out what its customers need and what their experiences of HR services are. HR has to be responsive – clear about what it is there for and what services it offers, and easy to contact.

The HR role of line managers

HR can initiate new policies and practices but it is the line that has the main responsibility for implementing them. In other words, 'HR proposes but the line disposes.' As Guest (1991: 159) commented: 'HRM is too important to be left to personnel managers.'

If line managers are not inclined favourably towards what HR wants them to do, they won't do it; or if compelled to, they will be half-hearted about it. On the basis of their research, Guest and King (2004: 421) noted that 'better HR depended not so much on better procedures but better implementation and ownership of implementation by line managers'.

As pointed out by Purcell et al (2003: 74) following their research, high levels of organizational performance are not achieved simply by having a range of well-conceived HR policies and practices in place. What makes the difference is how these policies and practices are implemented. That is where the role of line managers in people management is crucial: 'The way line managers implement and enact policies, show leadership in dealing with employees and in exercising control come through as a major issue.' Purcell and his colleagues noted that dealing with people is perhaps the aspect of their work in which line managers can exercise the greatest amount of discretion and they can use that discretion by not putting HR's ideas into practice. As they pointed out, it is line managers who bring HR policies to life.

A further factor affecting the role of line managers is their ability to do the HR tasks assigned to them. People-centred activities such as defining roles (job design), interviewing, reviewing performance, providing feedback, coaching, and identifying learning and development needs all require special skills. Some managers have them: many don't. Performance-related pay schemes sometimes fail because of untrained line managers.

Hutchinson and Purcell (2003) recommended that to improve the quality of the contribution line managers make to people management, it is necessary to give them time to carry out their people management activities, pay more attention to the behavioural competencies they need when selecting them, and support them with strong organizational values concerning leadership and people management. To which can be added that better implementation and better ownership by line managers of HR practices are more likely to be achieved if: (1) the practice demonstrably benefits them; (2) they are involved in the development and, importantly, the testing of the practices; (3) the practice is not too complicated, bureaucratic or time-consuming; (4) their responsibilities are defined and communicated clearly; and (5) they are provided with the guidance, support and training required to implement the practice.

The role of HR is to work in partnership with line managers to help them in whatever way possible to manage their people effectively and achieve their goals.

The role, purpose and organization of the L&D function

The learning and development (L&D) function is responsible for formulating and implementing learning and development strategies that are integrated with and support business strategies. The role of the function is to:

- develop and maintain a learning culture;
- Identify learning needs;
- promote workplace and self-directed learning;
- advise and guide line managers on their responsibilities for training and developing their staff;
- develop and deliver learning events and programmes to meet identified needs;
- evaluate the effectiveness of learning events.

Members of an L&D function or anyone responsible for L&D activities can be described as 'enablers of learning'.

The term 'learning and development' (L&D) is used rather than the alternative 'human resources development' (HRD) in accordance with the view expressed by Harrison (2009: 5) that: 'The term human resource development retains its popularity among academics but it has never been attractive to practitioners. They tend to dislike it because they see its reference to people as a "resource" to be demeaning. Putting people on a par with money, materials and equipment creates the impression of "development" as an unfeeling, manipulative activity.'

In practice, the two terms, HRD and L&D, are almost indistinguishable. They are indeed often used interchangeably by commentators and practitioners. However, the introduction of 'learning' has emphasized the belief that what matters for individuals is that they are given the opportunity to learn, often for themselves but with guidance and support, rather than just being on the receiving end of training administered by the organization.

The L&D function may exist as part of an all-embracing HR function (eg a centre of excellence), although in some smaller organizations there may not be a distinct function – L&D will be one of the responsibilities of HR generalists. L&D is sometimes but not often a separate function. However, the essential role of the function is unaffected by where it is placed in the organization in relation to HRM, although what is practised and how it is practised varies immensely according to the size and context of the organization; and the extent to which it can exert influence will be affected by the degree to which it has access to those ultimately responsible for managing the organization and its people.

Purpose and aims of the L&D function

The starting point in considering the role of the L&D (HRD) function is to answer the question 'What is its purpose?' As noted by McGoldrick et al (2001: 346), debates on the purpose of HRD 'centre on the learning versus performance perspectives. Should HRD practice focus on the well-being of the individual or should the interests of the shareholders predominate?' The answer is, of course, that L&D should be concerned with both. But Lee (2005: 105) commented that: 'HRD... finds itself in the forefront of the battleground between people-centred and for-profit motives and thus operating in an environment fraught with ethical quandaries.'

In meeting both purposes, the aims of the L&D function are to:

- ensure that L&D strategies support the achievement of business goals, satisfy the learning and development needs of employees and are integrated with complementary HR strategies;
- create and sustain a learning culture, ie an environment which promotes learning because it is recognized by all concerned as an essential organizational process to which they are committed and in which they engage continuously;
- identify organization, team and individual learning needs;
- develop organizational learning strategies to meet organizational needs;
- encourage and facilitate workplace learning for individuals and teams;
- plan and deliver learning events and programmes designed to satisfy identified needs;
- evaluate the effectiveness of organizational learning, workplace learning and learning programmes and events.

The approach to L&D

Mabey and Salaman (1995) identified six conditions which had to be met to demonstrate a rational and strategic approach to L&D:

- alignment with organization objectives;
- senior management support;
- involvement of line managers;
- quality of programme design and delivery;
- motivation of trainees;
- integration with HRM policy.

What L&D practitioners do

Potentially the most important activity of L&D specialists is to encourage, guide and help line managers deliver their training responsibilities. However, although the emphasis in current thinking is on enabling learning rather than just delivering training, the reality is that many L&D practitioners are still in the training business. As Poell (2005: 85) noted: 'Although it is common nowadays to assert that employees are self-responsible for their own learning and careers, in practice HRD professionals will spend most of their time coordinating, designing and delivering training to employees.' And on the basis of their trans-Europe research, Sambrook and Stewart (2005: 79) concluded that: 'Despite the wishes and, in some cases, the efforts of HRD professionals, learning and development practice still relies to a significant extent on traditional and formalized training interventions.'

It is not difficult to understand why this is happening. The systematic training approach, ie training specifically designed, planned, implemented and evaluated to meet defined needs, is traditionally what professional trainers are expected to do, so they do it. The promotion and facilitation of self-directed and workplace learning are not a recognized requirement and are more difficult, so they do not do these.

The delivery of formal learning events or programmes therefore continues to be a major activity and it is important to get it right. To ensure that a learning event or programme is effective, the L&D function has to do the following:

- Base the event or programme on a thorough evaluation of learning needs.
- Set clear objectives for the outcomes of the event or programme.
- Set standards for the delivery of the event or programme.
- Establish success criteria and methods of measuring success.
- Use a blend of learning and development methods – informal and formal – which are appropriate for the established needs of those taking part.

- Clarify the responsibilities for planning and delivering the event or programme. This will include careful briefing if the training is outsourced.
- Check that those responsible for the learning activity are well qualified in whatever role they are expected to play.
- Allocate adequate resources to the event or programme.
- Gain the support of top management.
- Check that the event or programme is implemented effectively as planned, within its budget and in accordance with the defined standards.
- Monitor the delivery of a programme regularly to check that it meets the defined objectives and standards.
- Evaluate the achievements of the event or programme against the success criteria and take swift corrective action to deal with any shortcomings.

The relationship between HRM and L&D

There has been considerable debate, mainly amongst academics, on the organizational relationship between HRM and L&D (HRD). Generally, however, the consensus has been that they are closely linked and in most organizations the L&D function is part of the HR function. The Cabinet Office, as quoted by Walton (1999: 146), summed this up in 1995 as follows:

> The usual definitions of HRM and HRD often seek to put boundaries between the two. But the theoretical and practical perimeters are extremely blurred. For example, most HRM systems (eg performance management) contain a strong HRD element. In practice it is not particularly useful to maintain artificial distinctions. Indeed it could be argued that the whole system of ideas embodied in an HR approach argues for a single, integrated set of policies covering all aspects of people management.

Sambrook and Stewart (1998) concluded that HRD has been born to accompany HRM. O'Donnell et al (2006: 9) claimed that: 'It is pragmatically impossible for HRD to escape from, or to function in splendid isolation from, its parental, twin or sibling (take your choice here – it makes not one whit of difference to practice) relationship with HRM.' O'Connell (2008: 42) quoted Barry Hopley, senior L&D manager at NCP Services, as saying: 'L&D is fundamentally a specialism but it still sits with HR in NCP Services. There isn't room for two directors (one for HR and one for L&D) on the board.'

But there are problems, as mentioned by Stewart and Harris (2003: 58), who stated that: 'The favoured choice is a single department to achieve integration, consistency and synergy in resources, policy and practice.' But they also remarked that their experience suggested that: 'the relationship between personnel and training will be troubled for a while yet, with training

continuing to be the Cinderella of the HR function, even by HR professionals. For now, it seems the relationship will continue to be "fractured" rather
than integrated.'

KEY LEARNING POINTS

Role of HR function

The role of the HR function is to provide insight, leadership, advice and services on
matters affecting the management, employment, development, reward and well-being of
people.

Aim and role of HR function

The aim of the HR function is to introduce and sustain HR strategies, policies and
practices which cater for everything concerning the employment, development and well-
being of people and the relationships that exist between management and the workforce.

Increasingly the role of HR is seen to be business orientated – contributing to the
achievement of sustained competitive advantage.

The HR function and its members have to be aware of the ethical dimensions of their
work.

HR activities

HR activities can be divided into two broad categories: (1) strategic (transformational),
which is concerned with the alignment and implementation of HR and business strategies
and developing organizational effectiveness; and (2) transactional, which covers the
main areas of HR service delivery – resourcing, learning and development, reward and
employee relations.

HR function organization

The organization and staffing of the HR function clearly depend on the size of the
business, the extent to which operations are decentralized, the type of work carried out,
the kind of people employed and the role assigned to the HR function.

HR management is not a single homogeneous occupation – it involves a variety of
roles and activities which differ from one organization to another and from one level to
another in the same organization.

The notion of delivering HR through three major areas – centres of expertise, business
partners and HR service centres – emerged from the HR delivery model produced by
Ulrich.

The learning and development function

The learning and development function is responsible for formulating learning and
development strategies that are integrated with and support business strategies,

developing and maintaining a learning culture, identifying learning needs, promoting workplace and self-directed learning, advising and guiding line managers on their responsibilities for training and developing their staff, developing and delivering learning events and programmes to meet identified needs, and evaluating their effectiveness.

Key aims of L&D

- Ensure that L&D strategies support the achievement of business goals, meet the learning and development needs of employees and are integrated with complementary HR strategies.
- Develop organizational learning strategies to meet organizational needs.
- Encourage and facilitate workplace learning for individuals and teams.
- Plan and deliver learning events and programmes designed to satisfy identified needs.

The role and organization of the L&D function

The L&D function may exist as part of an all-embracing HR function (eg a centre of excellence), although in some smaller organizations there may not be a distinct function – L&D will be one of the responsibilities of HR generalists. L&D is sometimes but not often a separate function.

References

Becker, B E and Huselid, M A (1998) High-performance work systems and firm performance: a synthesis of research and managerial implications, *Research on Personnel and Human Resource Management*, **16**, Stamford, Connecticut, JAI Press, pp 53–101

Cabinet Office, Office of Public Service and Science (1995) *A Strategic Approach to People Management*, London, Personnel Publications

Chartered Institute of Personnel and Development (2007) *The Changing HR Function*, London, CIPD

Crail, M (2006) HR roles and responsibilities 2006: benchmarking the HR function, *IRS Employment Review*, **839**, 20 January, pp 9–15

Francis, H and Keegan A (2006) The changing face of HRM: in search of balance, *Human Resource Management Journal*, **16** (3), pp 231–49

Gratton, L (2003) The Humpty Dumpty effect: A view of a fragmented HR function, *People Management*, 5 January, p 18

Guest, D E (1991) Personnel management: the end of orthodoxy, *British Journal of Industrial Relations*, **29** (2), pp 149–76

Guest, D E and King, Z (2004) Power, innovation and problem solving: the personnel managers' three steps to heaven?, *Journal of Management Studies*, **41** (3), pp 401–23

Harrison, R (2009) *Learning and Development*, 5th edn, London, CIPD

Hesketh, A and Hird, M (2010) Using relationships between leaders to leverage more value from people: building a golden triangle, in P Sparrow, A Hesketh,

M Hird and C Cooper (eds) *Leading HR*, Basingstoke, Palgrave Macmillan, pp 103–21

Hird, M, Sparrow, P and Marsh, C (2010), HR structures: are they working? in P Sparrow, A Hesketh, M Hird and C Cooper (eds) *Leading HR*, Basingstoke, Palgrave Macmillan, pp 23–45

Hirsh, W (2008) What do people want from you?, *People Management*, 18 September, pp 23–6

Hope-Hailey, V, Gratton, L, McGovern, P, Stiles, P and Truss, C (1997) A chameleon function? HRM in the 1990s, *Human Resource Management Journal*, 7 (3), pp 5–18

Hutchinson, S and Purcell, J (2003) *Bringing Policies to Life: The vital role of front-line managers in people management*, London, CIPD

IDS (2010) *HR Function Survey*, HR Study 928, October, London

Johnson, C (1999) Changing shapes: Trends in human resource reorganizations, *HR Magazine*, **44** (3), pp 40–48

Lee, M (2005) Critiquing codes of ethics, in C Elliott and S Turnbull (eds) *Critical Thinking in Human Resource Development*, Abingdon, Routledge, pp 105–15

Mabey, C and Salaman, G L (1995) *Strategic Human Resource Management*, Oxford, Blackwell

McGoldrick, J, Stewart, J and Watson, S (2001) Theorizing human resource development, *Human Resource Development International*, **4** (3), pp 343–56

O'Connell, G (2008) Crystal clear, *People Management*, 6 March, pp 40–42

O'Donnell, D, McGuire, D and Cross, C (2006) Critically challenging some assumptions in HRD, *International Journal of Training and Development*, **10** (1), pp 4–16

Poell, R F (2005) HRD beyond what HRD practitioners do, in C Elliott and S Turnbull (eds) *Critical Thinking in Human Resource Development*, Abingdon, Routledge, pp 85–95

Purcell, J, Kinnie, N, Hutchinson, S, Rayton, B and Swart, J (2003) *Understanding the People and Performance Link: Unlocking the black box*, London, CIPD

Reilly, P (2007) Facing up to the facts, *People Management*, 20 September, pp 43–45

Sambrook, S and Stewart, J (1998) No, I didn't want to be part of HR, *Human Resource Development International*, **1** (2), pp 171–87

Sambrook, S and Stewart, J (2005) A critical review of researching human resource development, in C Elliott and S Turnbull (eds) *Critical Thinking in Human Resource Development*, Abingdon, Routledge, pp 67–84

Sisson, K (1990) Introducing the Human Resource Management Journal, *Human Resource Management Journal*, **1** (1), pp 1–11

Stewart, J and Harris, L (2003) HRD and HRM: an uneasy relationship, *People Management*, 25 September, p 58

Tyson, S (1987) The management of the personnel function, *Journal of Management Studies*, **24** (5), pp 523–32

Ulrich, D (1997) *Human Resource Champions*, Boston MA, Harvard Business School Press

Ulrich, D (1998) A new mandate for human resources, *Harvard Business Review*, January–February, pp 124–34

Ulrich, D and Brockbank, W (2005) *The HR Value Proposition*, Boston MA, Harvard Business School Press

Walton, J (1999) *Strategic Human Resource Development*, Harlow, Financial Times/Prentice Hall

Questions

1 What is the fundamental role of the HR function?

2 How can HR further the achievement of sustained competitive advantage?

3 What do people mean when they say HR should be business orientated?

4 In what sense can HR be transformational?

5 What are the transactional activities of HR?

6 Are there any standardized ways in which the HR function can be organized?

7 What is the 'three-legged stool' model?

8 What is the function of a centre of expertise?

9 What is the function of a shared service centre?

10 What is the role of an HR strategic business partner?

11 What are the problems that might occur when a three-legged stool model is adopted? (Name at least three.)

12 What was the main finding of the research conducted by the CIPD in 2007 on the role and organization of the HR function?

13 What role do line managers play in HR?

14 What are the problems that might arise in enlarging the HR responsibilities of line managers?

15 How should those problems be overcome?

16 What is the overall role of the L&D function?

17 What is the purpose of the L&D function?

18 What are the key aims of the function?

19 What do L&D specialists need to do to plan and conduct effective learning events or programmes?

20 What is the relationship between L&D and HRM?

The contribution of HRM and L&D in different types of organization

07

Key concepts and terms

- *Big idea*
- *The black box*
- *Causal ambiguity*
- *Contingency variables*
- *Employee value proposition*
- *Employee champion*
- *Organizational effectiveness*
- *Reversed causality*

LEARNING OUTCOMES

On completing this chapter you should be able to define these key concepts. You should also understand:

- The overall contribution the HRM and L&G functions can make to organizational capability and effectiveness
- How HR makes an impact on organizational performance
- The contribution HR can make in the public and voluntary sectors, in small to medium-sized enterprises (SMEs) and international organizations

Introduction

This chapter starts with a study of the overall contribution of the human resources (HR) and learning and development (L&D) functions to organizational effectiveness and an analysis of how this contribution is made. The rest of the chapter is devoted to the contribution of HR in organizations in the public and voluntary sectors, in SMEs (small to medium-sized enterprises) and in international organizations.

The overall contribution of HR

In large private sector companies and in other sectors HR can:

- Provide insight – seek understanding of the issues affecting the organization and its employees, explore the implications of these issues for business and people management and convey these messages to management. The aim is to help organizations 'to find new ways of meeting current and future challenges' (CIPD, 2010a: 5).

- Participate in the formulation and implementation of business strategy – as Lawler and Mohrman (2003: 16) commented: 'HR can play an important role in the formulation of strategy by making explicit the human capital resources required to support various strategies and strategic initiatives, by playing a leadership role in helping the organization develop the necessary capabilities to enact the strategy, and by playing a strong role in implementation and change management.'

- Improve organizational effectiveness (the ability of an organization to achieve its goals by making effective use of the resources available) – plan and implement organization development programmes. As emphasized by the CIPD (2010a: 7): 'HR has a unique role to play in helping an organization succeed today in a way that lays the foundations for future, sustainable success.'

- Facilitate change – fulfil the role of change agent, leading and advising senior and line managers how best to manage organizational change. Ulrich (1998: 125) suggested that HR should become 'an agent of continuous transformation'.

- Deliver HR services – provide effective and efficient services in such fields as recruitment, learning and development, reward management and employee relations which meet the needs of the organization, its management and its employees.

- Provide expertise – in contributing to the achievement of the organization's strategy, developing HR strategies and delivering advice and services in accordance with good practice in each aspect of HRM.

- Provide advice – improve the quality of employment relationships by advising managers on the implementation of HR policies and procedures, on employment issues and on handling people problems.
- Develop the employee value proposition – take action to improve the value of what the organization offers to prospective or existing employees in order to persuade them to join or remain with the business.
- Promote the well-being of employees – help to improve the quality of the work environment, covering how people are treated at work in such areas as health and safety, reduction of stress and work–life balance issues.
- Promote social responsibility – formulate socially responsible HR policies on such issues as equal opportunity, the management of diversity, flexible working, harassment and bullying, and ensure they are implemented. Act as the guardian of the organization's values and ethical standards concerning people, pointing out when behaviour conflicts with those values or where proposed actions will be inconsistent with them. Ulrich (1998) called this the 'employee champion' role.
- Ensure compliance with employment law – develop and implement policies and procedures which ensure that the provisions of employment law are fully taken into account.

The contribution of learning and development

The CIPD research on the value of learning (Anderson, 2007) found that senior managers and L&D specialists believed generally that learning was expected to ensure the strategic readiness of employees; deliver performance improvement; deliver cost-effective labour, and enable effective career/talent management processes. In more detail, the contribution that L&D can make is to:

- provide insight – seek understanding of the issues affecting the organization and its employees, explore the implications of these issues for learning and development strategy and practice;
- improve organizational effectiveness – plan and implement learning and development policies designed to improve performance and help the organization achieve its goals;
- facilitate change – support change management programmes by developing the knowledge, skill and understanding required to implement change;
- help to ensure that the organization has the skilled, knowledgeable and engaged people it needs – contribute to talent management

programmes and organize learning and development events and programmes to meet identified needs;

- deliver L&D services – provide effective and efficient services in the provision of learning and development events and programmes which meet the needs of the organization, its management and its employees;

- promote individual development – encourage and support the development of individuals to their own benefit and that of the organization;

- provide expertise – to contribute to the achievement of the organization's strategy, develop L&D strategies and deliver advice and services in line with good practice in each aspect of L&D;

- provide advice – help managers to improve the quality of workplace learning.

The impact of HRM on Performance

As Guest (1997: 269) argued: 'The distinctive feature of HRM is its assumption that improved performance is achieved through the people in the organization.' If, therefore, appropriate HR policies and processes are introduced, it can also be assumed that HRM will impact on firm performance. Much research has been carried out showing that good HRM practice and firm performance are correlated; notable examples in the UK being Patterson et al (1997), Guest et al (2000a), Thompson (2002), West et al (2002) and Purcell et al (2003), as summarized in Table 7.1.

The problem of establishing how HRM makes an impact

Storey et al (2009: 4) observed that: 'The premise is that, in some shape or form, HR policies have an effect on HR practices and these in turn influence staff attitudes and behaviours which will, in turn again, impact on service offerings and customer perceptions of value.' However, Guest et al (2000b) commented that much of the research has demonstrated an association between HRM and performance but left uncertainties about cause and effect. Ulrich (1997: 304) pointed out that: 'HR practices seem to matter; logic says it is so; survey findings confirm it. Direct relationships between performance and attention to HR practices are often fuzzy, however, and vary according to the population sampled and the measures used.'

There are two issues which affect the determination of a link between HRM and firm performance: causal ambiguity and contingency factors. These contribute to what is known as 'the black box' phenomenon.

Causal ambiguity

The term 'causal ambiguity' refers to the numerous, subtle and often hidden interconnections between the factors influencing cause and effect. Boselie et al (2005: 75) referred to the causal distance between an HRM input and an output such as financial performance: 'Put simply, so many variables and events, both internal and external, affect organizations that this direct linkage strains credibility.'

A basic reason for ambiguity is multiple causation, which exists when there is more than one possible cause for an effect. HRM may have caused an improvement in performance but there may be many other economic or business factors that did so, and it could be difficult to unravel them. Another factor is the possibility of reversed causality (a situation where A might have caused B but B might well have caused A). As Purcell et al (2003: 2) expressed it: 'Although it is nice to believe that more HR practices lead to higher economic return, it is just as possible that it is successful firms that can afford more extensive (and expensive) HRM practices.'

Contingency factors

Causation will additionally be affected by the organization's context, the internal and external environmental factors which influence what happens within the organization.

The black box phenomenon

Causal ambiguity also stems from the black box phenomenon as illustrated in Figure 7.1. This is the situation in which while it may be possible to observe HRM inputs in the form of HR practices and measure firm performance outputs, it may be difficult or hard to be certain through research about what happened in between – what the HRM outcomes were which converted the input of HR practices into firm performance outputs. As Alvesson (2009: 56) commented: 'Research does not proceed beyond attempts to find an empirical association between HR practices and organizational performance. The phenomena are in a black box, only input and output are registered and what is happening remains clouded in the dark.'

FIGURE 7.1 The black box phenomenon

TABLE 7.1 Research on the link between HRM and firm performance

Researcher(s)	Methodology	Outcomes
Patterson et al (1997)	The research examined the link between business performance and organization culture and the use of a number of HR practices.	HR practices explained significant variations in profitability and productivity (19% and 18% respectively). Two HR practices were particularly significant: (1) the acquisition and development of employee skills and (2) job design, including flexibility, responsibility and variety.
Guest et al (2000a)	An analysis of the 1998 WERS survey which sampled some 2,000 workplaces and obtained the views of about 28,000 employees.	A strong association exists between HRM and both employee attitudes and workplace performance.
Thompson (2002)	A study of the impact of high-performance work practices such as team working, appraisal, job rotation, broad-banded grade structures and sharing of business information in UK aerospace establishments.	The number of HR practices and the proportion of the workforce covered appeared to be the key differentiating factor between more and less successful firms.

West et al (2002)	Research conducted in 61 UK hospitals obtaining information on HR strategy, policy and procedures, and mortality rates from chief executives and HR directors.	An association between certain HR practices and lower mortality rates was identified. As noted by Professor West: 'If you have HR practices that focus on effort and skill; develop people's skills; encourage cooperation, collaboration, innovation and synergy in teams for most if not all employees, the whole system functions and performs better.'
Purcell et al (2003)	A University of Bath longitudinal study of 12 companies to establish how people management impacts on organizational performance.	The most successful companies had 'the big idea'. They had a clear vision and a set of integrated values. They were concerned with sustaining performance and flexibility. Clear evidence existed between positive attitudes towards HR policies and practices, levels of satisfaction, motivation and commitment, and operational performance. Policy and practice implementation (not the number of HR practices adopted) is the vital ingredient in linking people management to business performance and this is primarily the task of line managers.

Explanations of how HRM makes an impact

David Guest (1997: 268) stated that: 'The assumption is that "appropriate" HRM practices tap the motivation and commitment of employees.' He explained how expectancy theory might help to explain the HR/performance link as follows. The expectancy theory of motivation provides one possible basis for developing a more coherent rationale about the link between HRM practices and performance. Although expectancy theory is concerned primarily with motivation, it is also a theory about the link between motivation and performance. Specifically, it proposes that high performance, at the individual level, depends on high motivation plus possession of the necessary skills and abilities and an appropriate role and understanding of that role. It is a short step to specify the HRM practices that encourage high skills and abilities, for example careful selection and high investment in training; high motivation, for example employee involvement and possibly performance-related pay; and an appropriate role structure and role perception, for example job design and extensive communication and feedback.

Following this contribution from David Guest, any explanation of the impact of HRM on organizational performance is likely to be based on three propositions: (1) that HR practices can make a direct impact on employee characteristics such as engagement, commitment, motivation and skill; (2) if employees have these characteristics it is probable that organizational performance in terms of productivity, quality and the delivery of high levels of customer service will improve; and (3) if such aspects of organizational performance improve, the financial results achieved by the organization will improve. These propositions highlight the existence of an intermediate factor between HRM and financial performance. This factor consists of the HRM outcomes in the shape of employee characteristics affected by HR practices. Therefore, HRM does not make a direct impact. A model of the impact of HRM taking the considerations of reverse causation and contingency effects mentioned earlier into account is shown in Figure 7.2.

But high performance is not just about HR practices. The case-based research by Purcell et al (2003) showed that the key to activating what they called the 'people–performance' link lies not only in well-crafted 'bundles' of HR practices, but in their conjunction with a powerful and cohering organizational vision (or 'big idea') and corporate leadership, together with front-line leadership's action and use of its discretionary power.

HRM in different contexts

The discussion so far in this chapter on the contribution and impact of HRM could be applied generally to any private sector firm and, in a number of respects to organizations in the public and voluntary sectors. The HR activities of organization design and development, resourcing, learning and development, reward and employee relations as described in Chapter 3 may

FIGURE 7.2 Impact of HRM on organizational performance (based on Paauwe, 2004)

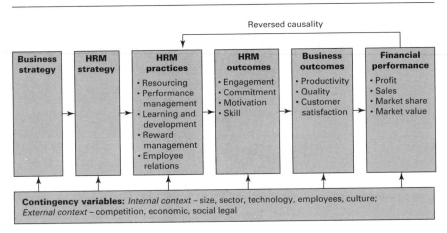

appear on the surface to be basically similar in any organization in which they take place. They are often presented as if this were the case. In practice, however, the way in which they are applied and to what extent will, in accordance with contingency theory, be dependent on the organization's environment and circumstances, ie the context in which HRM takes place. Two of the most important contextual factors are the organization's sector and its size.

The major distinction, as discussed in this chapter, is between private sector, public sector and voluntary organizations. Most of the discourse on HRM over the years has been focused on the private sector and to a large extent this applies to this book, so far. But there are significant differences in the HRM context between the private sector and the other two sectors and in the next two parts of this chapter these differences are analysed.

The other major contextual factor is the size of the organization. Again, descriptions of HRM often seem to assume that all organizations are alike, irrespective of sector and size. But SMEs are different in many ways and this affects how HRM takes place. These differences are therefore explored in this chapter after the public and voluntary sectors have been dealt with. Finally, there is the significant effect of international activities on HRM, which is considered in the last section of the chapter.

The contribution of HRM in the public sector

An analysis of the contribution of HRM in the public sector has to be made against the background of a definition of the public sector and by descriptions of the considerations affecting the sector and its main characteristics. These are dealt with in the first three parts of this section. The role and the contribution of HRM in the sector are examined in the next two parts of the section.

Definition of the public sector

The public sector was first defined by Adam Smith (1776: 1220) as:

> ...those public institutions and those public works, which though they may be in the highest degree advantageous to a great society, are, however, of such a nature that the profit could never repay the expense to any individual, or small number of individuals, and, therefore, it cannot be expected that any individual, or small number of individuals, should erect or maintain.

Today, the public sector can be defined as containing those organizations and activities that exist to provide services for the state, the community and individual citizens. Public sector organizations at national or local level execute political policy decisions but senior or specialized members of such institutions will provide advice to politicians on the factors affecting political policies and on their implementation. Public sector organizations are concerned with revenues and expenditures but do not exist to create profits. They are, in effect, owned by the public and not, as is the case in private sector businesses, by shareholders.

Considerations affecting the public sector

The considerations affecting public sector organizations as noted by Vere (2005: 5–6) are:

- smaller government;
- better delivery;
- improved efficiency;
- cost reduction;
- release resources to the front line.

Characteristics of the public sector

The main characteristics of the public sector are summarized below.

- Public scrutiny. As Bach and Kessler (2007: 470–71) noted: 'The degree of public scrutiny and the amount of direct and indirect intervention has no direct equivalent in the private sector.'
- Range of stakeholders. Truss (2008: 1073) commented that: 'public organizations have a much broader range of stakeholders than their private sector counterparts. Compared with the more

limited number of stable goals that exist for private sector firms, these bring a multiplicity of objectives and priorities. This creates a complex and qualitatively different working environment for public managers.'

- Governance. Top managers in the public sector are very much subject to the will and sometimes the foibles of their masters – the politicians. As Parry et al (2005: 590) noted: 'Management of human resources in the public sector is subject to direct and indirect political intervention brought about by the tripartite nature of the relationship among employer, employee and government. Historically, public sector employment has been influenced by the desire of the government to be a "model employer".'

- Funding uncertainties. Funding uncertainties and funding constraints are endemic to public services, as exemplified by the cuts imposed by the UK coalition government in 2011.

The HR function in the public sector

Vere and Butler (2007: viii) stated that: 'Public sector organizations are under continual pressure to provide better services with fewer resources at a time of increasing expectations from stakeholders, customers and taxpayers.' Truss (2008: 1071–72) observed that there has been 'increasing pressure from government on organizations to emulate private sector managerial practices, including performance management, customer orientation, and a heightened strategic focus'. She pointed out that: 'Since, in the public sector, salaries can amount to up to 80 per cent of organizational costs, the domain of human resource management (HRM) has received renewed attention under these reforms.' She also argued that: 'Historically, compared with other more powerful groups vying for resources, the HR function in the public sector has lacked credibility and been regarded as peripheral and relatively powerless' (ibid: 1072–73).

Challenges to the HR function in the public sector

HR in the public sector is involved in the same transactional activities such as recruitment, training and pay administration as in other sectors. But it is much more concerned with industrial relations than in the majority of private sector firms and it is particularly involved in ensuring that the organization sets an example in people management in such areas as equal opportunity, diversity and employee well-being. The CIPD (2010b: 7) highlighted particular areas of performance management in the public sector that need to improve to support more effective service delivery, namely: managing absence, managing stress, managing conflict.

What HR can contribute in the public sector

Apart from providing efficient and effective transactional HR services, HR in the public sector can make the following key contributions:

- Enable an integrated strategic approach to HRM to be adopted which responds to the challenges presented by multiple stake holders, governance issues and funding uncertainties and ensures that the organization has the skilled and engaged workforce it needs and that a cooperative climate of employee relations is maintained.
- Meet the exacting demands of good practice in the fields of equal opportunity, equal pay, diversity management and employee well-being.
- Contribute to the management of constant and often unpredictable change.

The contribution of HRM in the voluntary sector

The voluntary sector, sometimes called the third sector, consists of organizations such as charities, whose purpose is to help people, provide services or promote causes. The larger charities, especially international ones, are often referred to as 'non-governmental organizations' (NGOs). Voluntary organizations function on a 'not-for-profit' basis and their income is obtained from voluntary contributions, gifts, earnings from the services they provide to the public or to government and local government organizations on a contractual basis, and funding from the state or local government. They are typically governed by unelected boards of trustees.

The sector is large, complex and fragmented. According to Sargeant (2005: 7): 'One of the oldest surviving charities in England is Weeks' charity, an organization originally set up in the fifteenth century to provide faggots (bundles of sticks) for burning heretics.' Cunningham (2010: 344) recorded that 608,000 people are employed in the voluntary sector and 21.4 million people in the UK volunteer at least once a year. The voluntary sector contributes £21 billion to the economy.

Voluntary sector issues

On the basis of their research, Birdi et al (2007) noted that the performance of voluntary organizations is closely related to the knowledge and skills of their employees. The human factor is indeed an important issue as discussed below.

Managing people with particular values and beliefs

In many charities a large proportion of employees are professionally qualified and 'knowledge workers' – individuals who may be averse to bureaucratic HR policies. The writer observed on the basis of his extensive experience in the voluntary sector that employees, especially those concerned with service delivery, were often highly committed but that this high commitment has its downside. Individuals are reluctant to change or recognize any priorities other than their own. The organization is perceived as an unnecessary distraction, and this can make the life of a personnel director who is trying to establish a consistent approach to personnel management practices very difficult (Armstrong, 1992: 30).

Hudson (1999: 16) observed that:

> Managing third-sector organizations is subtly different from managing in the private or public sectors. Managers who have transferred from either the public or the private sector quickly discover that there is something intrinsically different in making things happen in a not-for-profit context. It is difficult to spot the relevant differences and distinguish them from the superficial ones. The symbols of informal dress, cramped offices and seemingly endless meetings hide more deep-seated differences in people's values and beliefs. Yet it is these values and beliefs that are at the root of the differences.

Kendall (2003: 215) wrote of voluntary sector organizations: 'These organizations are awkward customers. They cannot be steered by fiat or finance to the extent that state entities or for-profit organizations can.'

Governance issues

As noted by Brewster and Lee (2006a: 135) 'Governance problems in the NGOs vary considerably and depend on the type of organization that is being considered. However, a crucial distinctive element in the nature of governance in NGOs is that it remains the ultimate responsibility of part-time volunteers, usually meeting no more than four or six times a year in the form of a trustee board or committee of management.'

Funding and regulatory pressures

Cunningham (2008: 1034–35) pointed out that: 'HR practitioners will operate across a spectrum of "high" and "low" road employment strategies in an effort to coordinate organizational responses to divers and contradictory external funding and regulatory constraints while at the same time attempting to exercise degrees of strategic freedom from the funding bodies.'

The role of HR in the voluntary sector

Parry et al (2005: 591) commented that in the voluntary sector, 'people management had traditionally taken a back seat to the management of fundraising activities and service delivery'. Sargeant (2005) observed that HRM specialist skills at board level in non-profit organizations are often under-represented or non-existent, dwarfed by the more urgent priorities associated strategically with the demands of resource attraction (fundraising and marketing) and resource allocation (service provision, campaigning and education).

Research conducted by Brewster and Lee (2006a) in NGOs found that HR issues were frequently overlooked in favour of campaigning programmes, with HR specialists – where they existed – rarely represented at senior levels. As Brewster and Lee (2006b: 44) commented: 'The success of NGOs hinges on their people – but HR is neglected in the sector.' They also found that HR usually had no place on trustee boards and pointed out that the HRM function is often characterized as:

- a supporting rather than a leading function when viewed in terms of its contribution towards mission achievement;
- an administrative function that is predominately reactive to the decisions of others, not proactive in its own right;
- being emasculated by comparison with staff and budget resource allocated to other functions (ie service delivery, income generation etc);
- lacking in participation in the identification and selection process associated with the appointment of the most senior staff and trustees;
- uninvolved in corporate strategy.

However, research by Birdi et al (2007) established that non-profit organizations did appear to be better than private or public sector organizations in the range of individual learning opportunities offered to, and taken up by, their employees.

What HR can contribute in the voluntary sector

The four core needs for charities which can be addressed by HR and L&D are effective management, enhancing performance, staff development, and governance – with board-level leadership development being an urgent priority. As in the public sector, the function can provide efficient and effective transactional HR services but beyond this, the role of HR in the voluntary sector is not easy. Ideally, it should be there to ensure that a strategic approach to managing and developing people is adopted which will meet the needs of both the charity and those it employs. But this can be difficult if the function is not represented at the highest level (which is often the case) and if in practice HR strategies for a large part of the workforce and for volunteers are evolved elsewhere, if they exist at all.

The contribution of HRM in SMEs

Small and medium-sized enterprises are defined in terms of the number of employees – up to 250. SMEs play an important part in the economy – they account for 59 per cent of private sector employment in the UK (Storey et al, 2010: 306). In the private sector they are usually founded by entrepreneurs and often remain family owned as they grow. They may be more proactive and innovative than larger firms and more prepared to take risks.

SMEs are generally regarded as providing a friendlier and less formal working environment than larger firms. As Stavrou-Costea and Manson (2006: 111) pointed out: 'The major strength of SMEs is flexibility in the way they manage human resources.' Storey et al (2010: 306) commented that: 'The process of managing a small firm differs from that of the large firm, for small firms face distinct forms of risk and they organize their human resources differently and often informally.'

HR issues in SMEs

One of the major challenges facing SMEs is that of finding and utilizing human resources effectively and efficiently. But they may lack the resources in the shape of a full-time HR professional to deal with this challenge. As a result, HR activities such as recruitment and deciding on terms and conditions of employment (typically done on an individual basis) are often carried out by the general manager or other senior line manager who may not have the skills or the time to do them properly.

In a research study of human resource development practices in SMEs, Matlay (2002) found that the needs of family members were seen in terms of firm-specific HRD issues while those of non-family members focused on individual learning needs. Most owner-managers did not view training as being crucial to their business strategy. Small firms lacking professional HR advice may fail to comply with the requirements of employment law. However, because they tend not to be unionized, this does not necessarily mean that they have to cope with a multitude of legal challenges.

The HR contribution in SMEs

The work of an HR specialist in an SME will, of course, vary according to the context. There will, for example, be differences in the HR role between a software firm, a small manufacturer employing skilled workers and a distribution firm employing drivers and warehouse staff. The fundamental contribution that an HR specialist can make in an SME is to 'professionalize' the transactional elements of HR practice such as recruitment, training, managing reward and the employment relationship. They can also provide for legal compliance. More importantly, they can make a strategic contribution by working closely with senior management (easier in a smaller establishment) and getting to know how the business works and what it needs to do about its organization and human resources to succeed. They can help to develop a more persuasive employee value proposition and to create a good working environment.

International HRM

International human resource management is the process of managing people across international boundaries by multinational companies. It involves the world-wide management of people, not just the management of expatriates.

Michael Dickman of the Cranfield School of Management, as reported by Welfare (2006), believes that the main contrast between national and global HR practice is the need to see the bigger picture. Sensitivity is necessary in dealing with different cultures and there are complex challenges involved when operating in different business environments. Understanding the local context is key and an international HR person needs to be asking questions such as 'What is the business environment here? What is the role of the trade unions? What is the local labour law? Are these people different? Are their motivation patterns different?'

Issues in international HRM

There are a number of issues which specifically affect the practice of international as distinct from domestic HRM. These issues comprise the impact of globalization, the influence of environmental and cultural differences, the extent to which HRM policy and practice should vary in different countries (convergence or divergence), and the approaches used to employ and manage expatriates.

Globalization

Globalization is the process of international economic integration in world-wide markets. It involves the development of single international markets for goods or services accompanied by an accelerated growth in world trade. As Ulrich (1998: 126) put it, globalization requires organizations 'to move people, ideas, products, and information around the world to meet local needs. They must add new and important ingredients to the mix when making strategy: volatile political situations, contentious global trade issues, fluctuating exchange rates, and unfamiliar cultures. They must be more literate in the ways of international customers, commerce, and competition than ever before. In short, globalization requires that organizations increase their ability to learn and collaborate and to manage diversity, complexity, and ambiguity.'

Research conducted over a number of years by Brewster and Sparrow (2007: 48) demonstrated the growth of what they called globalized HRM. They noted that 'whereas international human resource management has tended to operate in the same way as local HRM but on a wider scale, globalized HRM exploits the new technologies available in order to manage all the company's staff around the world in the same way that it has traditionally managed staff in the home country.'

Cultural differences

Cultural differences must also be taken into account. Hiltrop (1995) noted the following HR areas which may be affected by national culture:

- decisions of what makes an effective manager;
- giving face-to-face feedback;
- readiness to accept international assignments;
- pay systems and different concepts of social justice;
- approaches to organizational structuring and strategic dynamics.

Convergence and divergence

According to Brewster et al (2002), the dilemma facing all multinational corporations is that of achieving a balance between international consistency and local autonomy. They have to decide on the extent to which their HR policies should either 'converge' worldwide to be basically the same in each location, or 'diverge' to be differentiated in response to local requirements.

Global HR policies and practices

The research conducted by Brewster et al (2005) identified three processes that constitute global HRM: talent management/employee branding, international assignments management, and managing an international workforce. It was established by the Global HR Research Alliance research (Stiles, 2007) that global HR policies and practices were widespread in the areas of maintaining global performance standards, the use of common evaluation processes, common approaches to rewards, the development of senior managers, the application of competency frameworks and the use of common performance management criteria.

Generally the research has indicated that while global HR policies in such areas as talent management, performance management and reward may be developed, communicated and supported by centres of excellence, often through global networking, a fair degree of freedom has frequently been allowed to local management to adopt their own practices in accordance with the local context as long as in principle these are consistent with global policies.

Managing expatriates

Expatriates are people working overseas on long- or short-term contracts who can be nationals of the parent company or 'third country nationals' (TCNs) – nationals of countries other than the parent company who work abroad in subsidiaries of that company.

The management of expatriates is a major factor determining success or failure in an international business. Expatriates are expensive; they can cost three or four times as much as the employment of the same individual at home. They can be difficult to manage because of the problems associated with adapting to and working in unfamiliar environments, concerns about their development and careers, difficulties encountered when they re-enter their parent company after an overseas assignment, and how they should be remunerated. Policies to address all these issues are required.

Contribution of HR to international management

The contribution HR can make to international management is to:

- formulate strategies for the development and deployment of talented people to meet worldwide needs;
- advise on the cultural factors involved in managing overseas businesses;
- create HR systems based on successful policies and practices in the parent company which can be adapted to fit local contexts and conditions;
- facilitate the transfer of good practice from wherever it may be found in the international organization;
- ensure that expatriates are managed effectively with regard to assignments, terms and conditions, career development and return to the parent company.

KEY LEARNING POINTS

HR contribution

The contribution that HR can make is to:

- provide insight;
- contribute to the formulation and implementation of business strategy;
- improve organizational effectiveness;
- facilitate change;

- provide expertise;
- promote social responsibility;
- deliver HR services;
- provide advice;
- develop an employee value proposition;
- promote the well-being of employees.

The contribution of L&D

- provide insight;
- improve organizational effectiveness;
- help to ensure that the organization has the skilled, knowledgeable and engaged people it needs;
- promote individual development;
- provide expertise;
- deliver L&D services;
- provide advice;
- facilitate change.

Issues in the public sector

- public scrutiny;
- range of stakeholders;
- governance;
- funding uncertainties and constraints;
- the bureaucratic role.

What HR can contribute in the public sector

- Enable an integrated strategic approach to HRM.
- Meet the exacting demands of good practice in the fields of equal opportunity, equal pay, diversity management and employee well-being.
- Contribute to the management of constant and often unpredictable change.

HR in the voluntary sector

The HRM function in charities is often characterized as:

- a supporting rather than a leading function when viewed in terms of its contribution towards mission achievement;
- an administrative function that is predominately reactive to the decisions of others, not proactive in its own right;

- being emasculated by comparison with staff and budget resource allocated to other functions (ie service delivery, income generation, etc);
- lacking in participation in the identification and selection process associated with the appointment of the most senior staff and trustees;
- uninvolved in corporate strategy.

The four core needs for charities which could be addressed by HR and L&D are effective management, enhancing performance, staff development, and governance – with board-level leadership development as an urgent priority.

HR issues in SMEs

One of the major challenges facing SMEs is that of finding and utilizing human resources effectively and efficiently but they may lack the resources in the shape of a full-time HR professional to deal with this challenge. This is because they have limited funds or they do not see the necessity.

The fundamental contribution that an HR specialist can make in an SME is to 'professionalize' the transactional elements of HR practice such as recruitment, training, managing reward and the employment relationship. They can also provide for legal compliance.

HR international issues

International human resource management is the process of managing people across international boundaries by multinational companies. It involves the worldwide management of people, not just the management of expatriates.

There are a number of issues which specifically affect the practice of international as distinct from domestic HRM. These issues comprise the impact of globalization, the influence of environmental and cultural differences, the extent to which HRM policy and practice should vary in different countries (convergence or divergence), and the approaches used to employ and manage expatriates.

The contribution HR can make to international management is to:

- develop strategies for the development and deployment of talented people to meet worldwide needs;
- advise on the cultural factors involved in managing overseas businesses;
- create HR systems based on successful policies and practices in the parent company which can be adapted to fit local contexts and conditions;
- facilitate the transfer of good practice from wherever it may be found in the international organization;
- ensure that expatriates are managed effectively with regard to assignments, terms and conditions, career development and return to the parent company.

References

Alvesson, M (2009) Critical perspectives on strategic HRM, in J Storey, P M Wright and D Ulrich (eds) *The Routledge Companion to Strategic Human Resource Management*, Abingdon, Routledge, pp 53–68

Anderson, V (2007) *The Value of Learning: From return on investment to return on expectation*, London, CIPD

Armstrong, M (1992) A charitable approach to personnel, *Personnel Management*, December, pp 28–32

Bach, S and Kessler, I (2007) HRM and the new public management, in P Boxall, J Purcell and P Wright (eds) *Oxford Handbook of Human Resource Management*, Oxford, Oxford University Press, pp 469–88

Birdi, K S, Patterson, M G and Wood, S J (2007) Learning to perform? A comparison of learning practices and organizational performance in profit- and non-profit-making sectors in the UK, *International Journal of Training and Development*, 11 (4), pp 265–81

Boselie, P, Dietz, G and Boon, C (2005) Commonalities and contradictions in HRM and performance research, *Human Resource Management Journal*, 15 (3), pp 67–94

Brewster, C and Lee, S (2006a) HRM in not-for-profit international organizations: different but also alike, in H H Larsen and W Mayrhofer (eds) *Managing Human Resources in Europe*, London, Routledge, pp 131–48

Brewster, C and Lee, S (2006b) The success of NGOs hinges on their people – but HR is neglected in the sector, *People Management*, 23 March, p 44

Brewster, C and Sparrow, P (2007) Advances in technology inspire a fresh approach to international HRM, *People Management*, 8 February, p 48

Brewster, C, Harris, H and Sparrow, P (2002) *Globalizing HR*, CIPD, London

Brewster, C, Sparrow, P and Harris, H (2005) Towards a new model of globalizing HRM, *The International Journal of Human Resource Management*, 16 (6), pp 949–70

Chartered Institute of Personnel and Development (2007) *The Value of Learning*, London, CIPD

Chartered Institute of Personnel and Development (2010a) *Next Generation HR*, London, CIPD

Chartered Institute of Personnel and Development (2010b) *Building productive public sector workplaces*, London, CIPD

Cunningham, I (2008) A race to the bottom? Exploring variations in employment conditions in the voluntary sector, *Public Administration*, 86 (4), pp 1033–53

Cunningham, I (2010) HRM in the not-for profit sector, in I Roper, R Prouska and U Ayudhya (eds) *Critical Issues in Human Resource Management*, London, CIPD, pp 341–55

Guest, D E (1997) Human resource management and performance; a review of the research agenda, *The International Journal of Human Resource Management*, 8 (3), 263–76

Guest, D E, Michie, J, Sheehan, M and Conway, N (2000a) *Employee Relations, HRM and Business Performance: An Analysis of the 1998 Workplace Employee Relations Survey*, London, CIPD

Guest, D E, Michie, J, Sheehan, M, Conway, N and Metochi, M (2000b) *Effective People Management: Initial findings of future of work survey*, London, CIPD

Hiltrop, J M (1995) The changing psychological contract: the human resource challenge of the 1990s, *European Management Journal*, **13** (3), pp 286–94

Hudson, M (1999) *Managing Without Profit*, Harmondsworth, Penguin Books

Kendall, J (2003) *The Voluntary Sector: Comparative prospects in the UK*, London, Routledge

Lawler E E and Mohrman S A (2003) What does it take to make it happen?, *Human Resource Planning*, **26** (3), pp 15–29

Matlay, H (2002) Training and HRD strategies in family and non-family owned small businesses: a comparative approach, *Education & Training*, **44** (8/9), pp 357–70

Paauwe, J (2004) *HRM and Performance: Achieving long-term viability*, Oxford, Oxford University Press

Paauwe, J and Richardson, R (1997) Introduction, *International Journal of Human Resource Management*, **8** (3), pp 257–62

Parry, E, Kelliher, C, Mills, T and Tyson, S (2005) Comparing HRM in the voluntary and public sectors, *Personnel Review*, **34** (5), pp 599–602

Patterson, M G, West, M A, Lawthom, R and Nickell, S (1997) *Impact of People Management Practices on Performance*, London, IPD

Purcell, J, Kinnie, N, Hutchinson, S, Rayton, B and Swart, J (2003) *Understanding the People and Performance Link: Unlocking the black box*, London, CIPD

Richards, J (2006) Working where money isn't everything, *The Times* Public Agenda, 10 October, p 8

Sargeant, A (2005) *Marketing Management for Non-profit Organizations*, 2nd edn, Oxford, Oxford University Press

Smith, Adam (1776) *The Wealth of Nations*, Letchworth, Dent

Stavrou-Costea, E and Manson, B (2006) HRM in small and medium enterprises: typical but typically ignored, in H H Larsen and W Mayrhofer (eds) *Managing Human Resources in Europe*, London, Routledge, pp 107–30

Stiles, P (2007) A world of difference?, *People Management*, 15 November, pp 36–41

Storey, D J, Saridakis, G, Sen-Gupta, S, Edwards, P K and Blackburn, R A (2010) Linking HR formality with employee job quality: The role of firm and workplace size, *Human Resource Management*, **49** (2), pp 305–29

Storey, J, Wright P M and Ulrich D (2009) Introduction, in J Storey, P M Wright and D Ulrich (eds) *The Routledge Companion to Strategic Human Resource Management*, Abingdon, Routledge, pp 3–13

Thompson, M (2002) *High-performance Work Organization in UK Aerospace*, London, The Society of British Aerospace Companies

Truss, C (2008) Continuity and change: the role of the HR function in the modern public sector, *Public Administration*, **86** (4), pp 1071–88

Ulrich, D (1997) *Human Resource Champions*, Boston MA, Harvard Business School Press

Ulrich, D (1998) A new mandate for human resources, *Harvard Business Review*, January–February, pp 124–34

Vere, D (2005) *Fit for Business: Building a Strategic HR Function in the Public Sector*, London, CIPD

Vere, D and Butler, L (2007) *Fit for Business: Transforming HR in the Public Service*, London, CIPD

Welfare, S (2006) A whole world out there: managing global HR, *IRS Employment Review*, **862**, 29 December, pp 8–12

West, M A, Borrill, C S, Dawson, C, Scully, J, Carter, M, Anclay, S, Patterson, M and Waring, J (2002) The link between the management of employees and patient mortality in acute hospitals, *International Journal of Human Resource Management*, **13** (8), pp 1299–310

Questions

1 What is the overall contribution the HRM function can make to organizational effectiveness?

2 Research by the CIPD published in *Next Generation HR* (2010a) stressed that HR practitioners need 'insight' to ensure that their function maximizes its contribution. What does the CIPD mean by this and how is insight developed?

3 What is the overall contribution the L&D function can make to organizational effectiveness?

4 How does HR make an impact on organizational effectiveness?

5 What are the most significant outcomes of research into the impact of HRM conducted within the last 10 years in the UK? Refer to at least two projects.

6 What is the 'black box'?

7 What is meant when reference is made to 'contingency variables' in research on the link between HR and performance?

8 What is meant by reverse causality?

9 What are the characteristics of the public sector that might affect HRM?

10 What are the challenges to HRM in the public sector?

11 What contribution can HRM make in the public sector?

12 What are the issues in the voluntary sector that are likely to affect HRM?

13 What is the role of HRM in the voluntary sector?

14 What contribution can HRM make in the voluntary sector?

15 What are the characteristics of SMEs (small to medium-sized enterprises)?

16 What are the HR issues in SMEs?

17 What contribution can HRM make in an SME?

18 What is international human resource management?

19 What are the key issues in international organizations that affect HRM?

20 What contribution can HR make to international management?

The professional and ethical approach to HRM and L&D

08

Key concepts and terms

- *Bounded rationality*
- *Core values*
- *Deontological ethics theory*
- *Discourse ethics theory*
- *Distributive justice*
- *Ethics*
- *Fair dealing*
- *Morality*
- *Morals*
- *Natural justice*
- *Procedural justice*
- *Social justice*
- *Stakeholder theory*
- *Utilitarianism*

LEARNING OUTCOMES

On completing this chapter you should be able to define these key concepts. You should also understand:

- The nature of professionalism
- What constitutes a professional ethos

- The role of professional codes of conduct
- The nature of professional ethical standards
- The role and nature of organizational codes of conduct
- The meaning of ethics
- The nature of ethical decisions and judgements
- The ethical concepts of deontology, utilitarianism, stakeholder theory and discourse theory
- The significance of the concepts of equity, justice and fair dealing
- The ethical dimension of HRM
- HRM ethical guidelines
- Ethical dilemmas and how to deal with them
- What is involved in managing within the expectations of the law

Introduction

The theme of this chapter is that there is an ethical dimension to human resource management which requires HR specialists to act professionally. To do this they need initially to appreciate what professionalism means in terms of ethical standards, and the role of professional and organizational codes of conduct. To grasp the ethical dimension in their work they need to understand the nature and principles of ethics, the ethical role of HR and the ethical guidelines they can use. They should also know about approaches to resolving ethical dilemmas and the issues relating to managing within the law.

Professionalism

A profession is defined in the *Compact Oxford Dictionary* (1971: 2316) as: 'A vocation in which professional knowledge of some department of learning is used in its application to the affairs of others or in the practice of an art founded upon it.' Professionalism is defined as: 'Professional quality, character, method or conduct; the stamp of a particular profession' (ibid: 2316).

More loosely, professionalism can be defined as the conduct exhibited by people who are providing advice and services which require expertise and which meet defined or generally accepted standards of behaviour. Work done by a professional is usually distinguished by its reference to a framework of fundamental concepts which reflect the skilful application of specialized education, training and experience. It is accompanied by a sense of responsibility and an acceptance of recognized standards. Even more loosely, people can be described as acting 'professionally' when they do their work well and act responsibly.

Fletcher (2004) stated that a professional ethos is characterized by the following ingredients:

- the possession of specialized knowledge and skills;
- power and status based on expertise;
- self-discipline and adherence to some aspirational performance standards;
- the opportunity to display high levels of autonomy;
- the ability to apply some independence of judgement;
- operating, and being guided by, a code of ethics;
- allegiance to a professional body.

Like those in other fields, HR professionals are required to uphold the standards laid down by their professional body but they must also adhere to their own ethical values. Additionally, they are bound by organizational codes of conduct expressed formally or accepted and understood as core values (the basic values adopted by an organization which set out what is believed to be important about how people and the organizations should behave).

Codes of professional conduct

Codes of professional conduct define the ethical standards that members of a profession should adhere to. The CIPD Code of Professional Conduct (2008) states, inter alia, that:

> CIPD members are expected to exercise relevant competence in accordance with the Institute's professional standards and qualifications. In the public interest and in the pursuit of its objects, the Chartered Institute of Personnel and Development is committed to the highest possible standards of professional conduct and competency. To this end members are required to exercise integrity, honesty, diligence and appropriate behaviour in all their business, professional and related personal activities.

The standards set out in the Recruitment and Employment Confederation code of practice are:

- respect for work relationships;
- respect for honesty and transparency;
- respect for confidentiality and privacy;
- respect for laws;
- respect for diversity;
- commitment to professional development.

The National School of Government (2010) has produced a code of ethics and practice for learning and development specialists which includes the following 'issues of responsibility':

- You should demonstrate a commitment to professional and ethical practice.

- You should ensure that your relationships with learners are not exploitative or a misuse of your role or power.
- You should behave with sensitivity and professionalism, being an ambassador for your organization and your profession.
- You should at all times make every effort to avoid bringing the profession into disrepute.
- You should demonstrate a respect for individuals and their needs.
- You should deal with trainees fairly, consistently and with impartiality.
- You should avoid language that could be regarded as offensive, suggestive or discriminatory.
- You should avoid behaviour that could be regarded as harassment, bullying, exploitation or intimidation.

Professional ethical standards

Professional ethics are the moral principles and values governing professional behaviour which may or may not be enshrined in codes of practice. The ethical principles of the HR profession require HR professionals to take account of the dignity and rights of employees when making employment decisions.

The ethical frameworks for judging HR practices are the basic rights of people, the principles of social, natural, procedural and distributive justice (these are defined later), the need to achieve fairness, equity and consistency in managing people, and the obligation to treat them with respect and consideration.

These principles can conflict with organizational objectives to maximize performance, increase shareholder value and achieve more with less. They are also affected by issues such as pressure for more flexibility, work intensification, the use of HR techniques such as performance-related pay and performance management, and management practices such as expecting people to meet demanding performance targets and closely monitoring employee performance.

HR specialists are part of management. But there will be occasions when in their professional capacity they should speak out against plans or actions which are not in accord with the ethical standards or values professed by the organization in its code of conduct, if it has one. If not, HR professionals should speak out in accordance with the standards and values they believe in. And they should do their best to develop more exacting ethical standards and influence changes in core values where they feel they are necessary. They must not tolerate injustice or inequality of opportunity. But speaking out is probably the most demanding task that HR people have to do. It is never easy to challenge a course of action proposed or taken by management which may well be supported by a compelling business case. It takes courage and determination and it is, of course, advisable to be sure that there are good grounds for doing so.

HR professionals may often find themselves in a hardnosed, entrepreneurial environment. But this does not mean that they can remain unconcerned about developing and helping to uphold organizational core values in line with their own values on the ethical principles which govern how people should be managed. These may not always be reconcilable, and if this is strongly the case, the HR professional may have to make a choice on whether he or she can remain with the organization.

Professionalism in human resource management means acting in accordance with ethical standards. It means recognizing that there is an important ethical dimension to the work of HR professionals. All the more reason to be surprised that the current CIPD professional standards map issued in 2009 did not indicate that ethical considerations apply to HR at all apart from one passing reference to the need to adopt an ethical approach when managing conflict situations.

Organizational codes of practice (ethics policies)

Organizational codes of practice provide rules, policies and guidelines on what is considered to be appropriate ethical behaviour. The Institute of Business Ethics (2011) has stated that the proportion of larger UK companies with explicit ethics policies has risen over the last 10 years from a third to more than a half. Having an ethics policy is now considered a hallmark of a well managed company. The ethics policy is normally expressed in a code of business ethics, sometimes called a code of business conduct or principles. As described by the Institute of Business Ethics, an ethics policy:

- details an organization's ethical values, standards and commitments to stakeholders that will underpin the way that it does business;
- confirms leadership commitment to the above;
- describes how this will be achieved and monitored through an ethics programme; GARY
- identifies the main ethical issues faced by the organization/sector;
- identifies other policies and documents that support and detail aspects of the ethics policy – such as a code of ethics, a speak-up policy, a bullying and harassment policy, a gifts and hospitality policy, an environment policy, etc.

Aims

The main aims of an ethics policy, code and programme can be set out under the following headings:

- Values – to embed a set of ethical values into the organization's goals and strategies and the way it seeks to do what it does.

- Ethical behaviour – to provide guidance and support to staff for making decisions and carrying out their work in a way that is compatible with the organization's ethical values and standards.
- Corporate culture – to consolidate and strengthen a culture of integrity and openness so as to facilitate a sustainable business.
- Risk – to minimize operational and integrity risks.
- Reputation – to enhance trust among stakeholders so as to facilitate business success.
- Sustainability – to minimize the organization's negative impacts on and maximize its positive contribution to the social, economic and environmental well-being of wider society.

Examples

Here are some extracts from company codes to provide a flavour of what they can contain.

Santander – respect for people

- Harassment, abuse, intimidation, lack of respect and consideration are unacceptable and will not be permitted or tolerated in the workplace.

- Those employees with personnel reporting to them in the group's organizational units should ensure, with the resources available to them, that such situations do not occur.

- All employees, especially those with managerial responsibilities, shall uphold, at all times and at all professional levels, relations based on respect for the dignity of others, participation, equality and reciprocal cooperation, fostering a respectful and positive working environment.

Shell code of conduct

- You should base hiring, evaluation, promotion, training, development, discipline, compensation and termination decisions on qualifications, merit, performance and business considerations only.

- Do not discriminate according to race, colour, religion, age, gender, sexual orientation, marital status, disability, ethnic origin or nationality.

- Be aware of local legislation and cultural factors that may impact decisions.

Unilever code of business principles – employees

Unilever is committed to diversity in a working environment where there are mutual trust and respect and where everyone feels responsible for the performance and reputation of our company. We will recruit, employ and promote employees on the sole basis of the qualifications and abilities needed for the work to be performed. We are committed to safe and healthy working conditions for all employees. We will not use any form of forced, compulsory or child labour. We are committed to working with employees to develop and enhance each individual's skills and capabilities. We respect the dignity of the individual and the right of employees to freedom of association. We will maintain good communications with employees through company-based information and consultation procedures.

Reservations about codes of ethics

Codes of ethics are desirable but they are not the whole answer. As Bagley (2003: 19) commented:

> It would be naive to think that devising a corporate ethics policy is easy or that simply having a policy will solve the ethical dilemmas companies face. Directors, managers, and employees need to exercise their own fundamental sense of right and wrong when making decisions on behalf of the corporation and its shareholders. There is a lesson in the story of the pension fund manager who was asked whether she would invest in a company doing business in a country that permits slavery. 'Do you mean me, personally, or as a fund manager?' she responded. When people feel entitled or compelled to compromise their own ethics to advance the interests of a business or its shareholders, it is an invitation to mischief.

Reservations have also been expressed by Webley and Werner (2008: 405–06). They observed that: 'Though necessary, having an ethics policy based solely on a code of ethics is not sufficient to affect employee attitudes and behaviour.' This conclusion was similar to that reached by Schwartz (2004), whose research established that the mere existence of a code is unlikely to influence employee behaviour and that companies simply possessing a code could be subject to allegations of window dressing.

Webley and Werner (2008: 406) also commented that many of the businesses being singled out by the media as less than ethical have had an explicit ethics policy: 'Enron is but one dramatic example... This is what Kenneth Lay wrote in 2000: "We want to be proud of Enron and know that it enjoys a reputation for fairness and honesty and that it is respected."' They also reported on research by the UK Institute of Business Ethics which was conducted in 2005, covering 759 full-time employees. In the survey, one in two respondents said that they had noticed unethical behaviour but had failed to report it. Further analysis revealed that two out of three of the employees who had noticed unethical behaviour worked for organizations that had a code of ethics. Webley and Werner argued that formal ethics programmes can be deficient for any or all of the following reasons:

- They only encompass a narrow set of issues without addressing wider obligations.
- They might be compliance based, simply consisting of a set of rules that the employees are expected to follow ('Do it or else').
- The code is not company specific, reflecting real issues and involving employees in their identification.
- Management commitment is absent.
- The code is not sufficiently communicated and embedded in the organization.
- The code is inconsistent with embedded corporate culture, for example pressure on managers to meet targets.

The point about embedding is especially pertinent. As Collier and Estaban (2007: 30) concluded:

> It is not enough to have mission statements and codes of ethics. It is necessary for ethics to be embedded in the cultural fabric of the business as well as in the hearts and minds of its members.

This is where HR professionals come in, as explained later in this chapter. But to play a part in embedding ethics and resolving ethical dilemmas it is necessary to understand the nature of ethics and the ethics dimension as described below.

The meaning and nature of ethics

Ethics, as a system, is concerned with making judgements and decisions about what is the right course of action to take. It is defined by the *Compact Oxford Dictionary* (1971: 900) as being 'related to morals, treating of moral questions', and 'ethical' is defined as 'relating to morality'. Morals define what is right rather than wrong. Morality is behaving in a moral or ethical way: possessing moral qualities.

Petrick and Quinn (1997: 42) wrote that ethics is 'the study of individual and collective moral awareness, judgement, character and conduct'. Hamlin et al (2001: 98) noted that ethics is concerned with rules or principles that help us to distinguish right and wrong.

Ethics and morality are sometimes treated as being synonymous although Beauchamp and Bowie (1983: 1–2) suggested that they are different: 'Whereas morality is a social institution with a history and code of learnable rules, ethical theory refers to the philosophical study of the nature of ethical principles, decisions and problems.' Clearly, ethics is concerned with matters of right and wrong and therefore involves moral judgements. Even if they are not the same, the two are closely linked. Clegg et al (2007: 111) wrote: 'We understand ethics as the social organizing of morality.'

The nature of ethical decisions and judgements

As defined by Jones (1991: 367), an ethical decision is one that is morally acceptable to the larger community. He also noted that: 'A moral issue is present where a person's actions, when freely performed, may harm or benefit others. In other words, the action or decision must have consequences for others and must involve choice, or volition, on the part of the actor or decision maker' (ibid: 367).

Winstanley and Woodall (2000a: 8–9) pointed out that:

> Ethics is not about taking statements of morality at face value; it is a critical and challenging tool. There are no universally agreed ethical frameworks... Different situations require ethical insight and flexibility to enable us to encapsulate the grounds upon which competing claims can be made. Decisions are judgements usually involving choices between alternatives, but rarely is the choice between right and wrong... Moral disagreement and judgements are concerned with attitudes and feelings, not facts.

Clegg et al (2007: 112) emphasized that: 'Ethical decisions emerge out of dilemmas that cannot be managed in advance through rules.' People have to make choices. Foucault (1997: 284) asked: 'What is ethics, if not the practice of freedom?'

Ethics can be described in terms of a framework which is based on ethical theory and makes use of particular concepts such as equity, justice and fair dealing which guide ethical behaviour. Such frameworks can be used to develop, apply and evaluate HRM policies and practices.

Ethical theories

There are a number of theories explaining the nature of ethics. The main ones are deontology, utilitarianism, stakeholder theory and discourse theory, as described below.

Deontological theory

Deontological (from the Greek for 'what is right') theory maintains that some actions are right or wrong irrespective of their consequences. It is associated with Kant's notion of the categorical imperative, which contains two main propositions: (1) that one should follow the principle that what is right for one person is right for everyone, and thus you must do to others as you would be done by; and (2) that you should respect all people and treat them as ends in themselves, not as the means to an end.

Utilitarianism

Utilitarianism is the belief that actions are justified when they result in the greatest good to the greatest number. Actions should be judged in terms of their consequences. This is sometimes interpreted as supporting the dubious principle that the end justifies the means.

Stakeholder theory

In accordance with the ideas of Freeman (1984), stakeholder theory states that the organization should be managed on behalf of its stakeholders: its owners, employees, customers, suppliers and local communities. As Karen Legge (1998: 22) described it, management must act in the interests of the stakeholders as their agent, and also act in the interests of the organization to ensure the survival of the firm, safeguarding the long-term stakes of each group.

Discourse ethics

Foucault (1972) defined discourse as the taken-for-granted ways that people are collectively able to make sense of experience. Discourse ethics as explained by Winstanley and Woodall (2000a: 14) suggests that 'the role of ethicists is not to provide solutions to ethical problems, but rather to provide a practical process and procedure which is both rational and consensus enhancing, through which issues can be debated and discourse can take place.'

Ethical concepts

The ethical concepts of equity, justice and fair dealing complement the theories described above by providing more specific guidance on ethical behaviour.

Equity

Equity theory, as formulated by Adams (1965), is concerned with the perceptions people have about how they are being treated as compared with others. To be dealt with equitably is to be treated fairly in comparison with another group of people (a reference group) or a relevant other person. Equity involves feelings and perceptions and it is always a comparative process. It is not synonymous with equality, which means treating everyone the same, since this would be inequitable if they deserve to be treated differently.

Justice

Justice is the process of treating people in a way that is inherently fair, right and proper. An egalitarian theory of justice was proposed by Rawls (2005), and contained two principles:

- Every person has the right to basic liberty compatible with similar liberty for others.
- Inequalities should be arranged so that they are expected to be to everyone's advantage and attached to positions open to all.

There are four types of justice: social justice, natural justice, procedural justice and distributive justice.

Social justice

Social justice means treating people in accordance with the principles of human rights, human dignity and equality. In society, as argued by Rawls (2005: 3):

> Each person possesses an inviolability founded on justice that even the welfare of society as a whole cannot override. For this reason justice denies that the loss of freedom for some is made right by a greater good shared by others.

Rawls thus rejected the principle of utilitarianism and the pernicious belief that the end justifies the means.

In organizations, social justice means relating to employees generally in ways which recognize their natural rights to be treated justly, equitably and with respect.

Natural justice

According to the principles of natural justice, employees should know the standards they are expected to achieve and the rules to which they are expected to conform; they should be given a clear indication of where they are failing or what rules have been broken and, except in cases of gross misconduct, they should be given a chance to improve before disciplinary action is taken.

Procedural justice

Procedural justice (Adams, 1965 and Leventhal, 1980) involves treating people in ways which are fair, consistent, transparent and properly consider their views and needs. It is concerned with fair process and the perceptions employees have about the fairness with which company procedures in such areas as performance appraisal, promotion and discipline are being operated. The five factors that affect perceptions of procedural justice as identified by Tyler and Bies (1990) are:

- adequate consideration of an employee's viewpoint;
- suppression of personal bias towards an employee;
- applying criteria consistently across employees;

- providing early feedback to employees about the outcome of decisions;
- providing employees with an adequate explanation of decisions made.

Distributive justice

Distributive justice (Adams, 1965 and Leventhal, 1980) means ensuring that people are rewarded equitably in comparison with others in the organization and in accordance with their contribution, and that they receive what was promised to them.

Fair dealing

Fair dealing occurs when people are treated according to the principles of social, natural, procedural and distributive justice, and when the decisions or policies that affect them are transparent in the sense that they are known, understood, clear and applied consistently.

The ethical dimension of HRM

Karen Legge (1998: 20–21) commented that: 'In very general terms I would suggest that the experience of HRM is more likely (but not necessarily) to be viewed positively if its underlying principles are ethical.' HR professionals have a special responsibility for guarding and promoting core values in the organization on how people should be managed and treated generally. They are particularly concerned with values relating to just and fair treatment. They need to take a deontological stance which emphasizes that some actions are right or wrong irrespective of their consequences and that all people should be respected and treated as ends in themselves, not as the means to an end. This is not easy. Ethical decisions may not be clear cut. Interests conflict. But it is a necessary part of professionalism in HRM.

An important role for HR professionals is to do whatever they can to embed the consistent application of ethical values in the organization so that they can become values in use rather than simply professed values in a code of practice or values statement. As Winstanley and Woodall (2000b: 7) observed: 'HR professionals have to raise awareness of ethical issues, promote ethical behaviour, disseminate ethical practices widely among line managers, communicate codes of ethical conduct, ensure people learn about what constitutes ethical behaviours, manage compliance and monitor arrangements.'

To do all this, HR professionals may sometimes have to nag away without appearing to nag. But as necessary they need the courage to stand up and be counted. They need determination, persuasive skills and the ability to deal with the ethical dilemmas that they and line managers face in as rational a manner as possible. In the field of organizational ethics, HR people can lead by example. They can handle ethical issues in ways which become part of the organization's culture – 'the way we do things around here'.

The difficulties that HR professionals face in doing all this have been well-described by Guest and King (2004: 421) as follows:

> Much management activity is typically messy and ambiguous. This appears to apply more strongly to people management than to most other activities. By implication, the challenge lies not in removing or resolving the ambiguities in the role but in learning to live with them. To succeed in this requires skills in influencing, negotiating and learning when to compromise. For those with a high tolerance of ambiguity, the role of HR specialist, with its distinctive opportunity to contribute to the management of people in organizations, offers unique challenges; for those only comfortable if they can resolve the ambiguities, the role may become a form of purgatory.

HRM ethical guidelines

The guidelines set out below relate to how employees are treated in general and to the major HRM activities of organization development, recruitment and selection, learning and development, performance management, reward management, employee relations, and employment practices concerning the work environment, employee well-being, equal opportunities, managing diversity, handling disciplinary matters and grievances, job security and redundancy.

General guidelines

- Recognize that the strategic goals of the organization should embrace the rights and needs of employees as well as those of the business. This is in line with the comment made by Boxall et al (2007: 5) that: 'While HRM does need to support commercial outcomes (often called "the business case"), it also exists to serve organizational needs for social legitimacy.'
- Recognize that employees are entitled to be treated as full human beings with personal needs, hopes and anxieties.
- Do not treat employees simply as means to an end or mere factors of production. This accords with the comment made by Osterby and Coster (1992: 31) that: 'The term "human resources" reduces people to the same category of value as materials, money and technology – all resources, and resources are only valuable to the extent they can be exploited or leveraged into economic value.'
- Relate to employees generally in ways which recognize their natural rights to be treated justly, equitably and with respect.

Organization development

- Agree in advance with clients and individuals the goals, content and risks of an OD programme.
- Make explicit any values or assumptions used in the programme.
- Obtain the maximum involvement of all concerned in the programme so that they understand the processes involved and how they can benefit from them.
- Work with clients to plan and implement change to the benefit of all stakeholders.
- Enable individuals to continue with their development on completing the programme.
- Protect confidentiality.

Recruitment and selection

- Treat candidates with consideration – applications should be acknowledged, candidates should be kept informed without undue delay of decisions made about their application and they should not be kept waiting for the interview.
- Avoid intrusive questioning in interviews.
- Do not put candidates under undue stress in interviews.
- Do not criticize any aspect of the candidate's personality or experience.
- Use relevant selection criteria based on a proper analysis of job requirements.
- Give candidates reasonable opportunity to present their case and to ask questions.
- Avoid jumping to conclusions about candidates on inadequate evidence or as a result of prejudice.
- Give accurate and complete information to candidates about the job, prospects, security and terms and conditions of employment.
- Only use properly validated tests administered by trained testers.
- Do not use discriminating or biased tests.
- Monitor tests for impact and unintended bias.
- Ensure that candidates are not unfairly disadvantaged by testing processes.
- Give candidates feedback on test results unless there are compelling reasons why feedback should not be given.
- Ensure that selection decisions are free of discrimination or bias on the grounds of sex, sexual orientation, race, age or disability.
- Give unsuccessful candidates the reason for the decision if they request it.

Learning and development

- Respect individual rights for dignity, self-esteem, privacy and autonomy.
- Recognize that it is necessary and legitimate to provide individuals with learning opportunities which enable them to gain the knowledge and skills required to perform well in their jobs and develop their potential. But note that individuals should still be allowed autonomy to choose the extent to which they pursue learning and development programmes beyond this basic requirement.
- Accept that while the organization has the right to conduct learning and development activities which enhance performance, individuals also have the right to be provided with opportunities to develop their own knowledge, skills and employability.
- Ensure that people taking part in learning events feel 'psychologically safe' in accordance with the view expressed by Schein (1993: 91) that: 'To make people feel safe in learning, they must have a motive, a sense of direction, and the opportunity to try out new things without the fear of punishment.'
- Avoid manipulating people to accept imposed organizational values.

Performance management

Performance management ethical principles have been defined by Winstanley and Stuart-Smith (1996) as follows:

- Respect for the individual – people should be treated as 'ends in themselves' and not merely as 'means to other ends'.
- Mutual respect – the parties involved in performance management should respect each other's needs and preoccupations.
- Procedural fairness – the procedures incorporated in performance management should be operated fairly in accordance with the principles of procedural justice.
- Transparency – people affected by decisions emerging from performance management processes should be given the opportunity to scrutinize the basis upon which decisions were made.

Reward management

- Generally apply the principles of procedural and distributive justice.
- Ensure that reward policies and practices are fair, equitable and transparent and that they are applied consistently.
- Reward people according to their contribution.

- Ensure that people know in general the basis upon which rewards are provided and in particular how their own reward package is determined.
- Maintain reasonable and defensible pay differentials.
- Ensure that equal pay is provided for work of equal value.
- Base decisions on performance pay or bonuses on fair and equitable criteria.
- Avoid bonus schemes which encourage undesirable behaviour.

Employee relations

- Deliver the deal.
- Be open to employees' input and responsive to justifiable questions and concerns about employment policies and practices.
- Provide genuine opportunities and channels for employees to express their views and influence decisions on matters that affect them.
- Negotiate in good faith.
- Recognize that the interests of management and employees do not necessarily coincide, and develop and implement employee relations policies accordingly.

Employment practices

- Create a healthy, safe and fulfilling work environment.
- Promote the well-being of employees by improving the quality of working life provided for them, exercising concern for work/life balance and developing family-friendly policies.
- Provide equal opportunities for all with regard to recruitment and selection, learning and development, talent management, career progression and promotion.
- Manage diversity by recognizing the differences between people and ensuring that everyone feels valued and that the talents of all employees will be properly utilized.
- Handle disciplinary matters according to the principles of natural justice.
- Recognize that people may have legitimate grievances and respond to them promptly, fully and sympathetically.
- Preserve job security as far as possible and take alternative action to avoid compulsory redundancies.
- If compulsory redundancy is unavoidable, do whatever is possible to alleviate the distress by, for example, helping people to find work.

Ethical dilemmas

'Ethics will be enacted in situations of ambiguity where dilemmas and problems will be dealt with without the comfort of consensus or certitude' (Clegg et al, 2007: 109). As Baumann, quoted in Bauman and Tester (2001: 44), remarked: 'Morality concerns choice first of all – it is the predicament human beings encounter when they must make a selection amongst various possibilities.' And Derrida (1992) commented that ethical responsibility can exceed rational calculation.

Typical ethical dilemmas, with examples and approaches to dealing with them are examined below.

Ethical dilemma situations

The following is a sample of the sort of HRM situations which might create ethical dilemmas:

- There is tension between the needs of the organization and the needs of individuals, for example when an organization changes working arrangements and prejudices the work–life balance of some but not all employees.
- There is conflicting evidence in a disciplinary case and it is difficult to decide who to believe.
- The pressure to achieve targets creates corner-cutting in achieving results involving contraventions of company rules.
- There are apparently mitigating circumstances in a disciplinary case and the question is whether these justify not taking action.
- An accusation of bullying has been made but it is difficult to ascertain whether this is a clear case of bullying or overreaction on the part of the complainant to the normal pressures of day-to-day work.

Resolving ethical dilemmas

As Adam Smith (1759) wrote in *The Theory of Moral Sentiments* (quoted by Harrison, 2009: 246):

> When ethically perplexed, the question we should always ask is: would a disinterested observer, in full possession of the relevant facts, approve or disapprove of our actions?

This guidance is just as compelling and relevant today.

Woodall and Winstanley (2000: 285) pointed out that 'being ethical is not so much about finding one universal principle to govern all action, but more about knowing how to recognize and mediate between often unacknowledged differences of view'. By definition, an ethical dilemma is one that will be difficult to resolve. There may be all sorts of issues surrounding the situation, some of which will be unclear or contentious. The extent to which people react or behave rationally may be limited by their capacity to understand the complexities of the situation they are in and affected by their emotional reactions to it (the concept of bounded rationality). Faced with factors such as these, the process of ethical dilemma resolution can be hard going.

There is no 'one right way' to deal with an ethical dilemma, but an approach based on systematic questioning, analysis and diagnosis to get at the facts and establish the issues involved is more likely to produce a reasonably satisfactory outcome than one relying purely on 'gut feeling'. The following checklist – used judiciously and selectively according to the circumstances – can provide a basis for such questioning and analysis:

- What are the known facts about the situation and is it possible that there are facts or circumstances that have not come to light; and if so, what can be done to uncover them?
- In disciplinary or conduct cases, to what extent does the conduct contravene the organization's code of ethical conduct (if one exists) or any other relevant organizational policy guidelines and rules?
- Have different versions or interpretations of the facts and circumstances been offered and if so, what steps can be taken to obtain the true and full picture?
- Is the proposed action in line with both the letter and the spirit of the law?
- Are the proposed action and any investigations leading to it consistent with the principles of natural, procedural or distributive justice?
- Will the proposed action benefit the organization and if so, how?
- Is there any risk of the proposed action doing harm to the organization's reputation for fair dealing?
- Will the proposed action be harmful to the individual affected or to employees generally in any way and if so, how?
- Do the facts as established and confirmed justify the proposed action?
- Are there any mitigating circumstances (in disciplinary cases)?

Managing within the expectations of the law

HR professionals must clearly comply with the requirements of employment law but they also have the important responsibility of ensuring the compliance of managers and individual employees to it.

Providing for compliance means that HR should educate and inform managers and team leaders of their legal obligations and how they can best fulfil them. This can be done formally through guidance notes and training but there is a continuing need to provide advice and guidance on specific issues and to help deal with problems that require a deeper knowledge of employment law than it would be reasonable to expect managers to possess. This is an area of management where HR is expected to take the lead. The HR function will be judged on the extent to which it minimizes references to employment tribunals, but HR professionals should go beyond simple compliance and also be concerned with seeing that the spirit of the law in such areas as discrimination and equal pay is upheld.

KEY LEARNING POINTS

Professionalism

Professionalism can be defined as the conduct exhibited by people who are providing advice and services which require expertise and which meet defined or at least generally accepted standards of behaviour.

HR professionals

HR professionals are required to uphold the standards laid down by their professional body but they must also adhere to their own ethical values.

Codes of professional conduct

Codes of professional conduct define the ethical standards that members of the profession should adhere to. Professional ethics are the moral principles and values governing professional behaviour which may or may not be enshrined in codes of practice.

Organizational codes of practice

Organizational codes of practice provide rules and guidelines on what is considered to be appropriate ethical behaviour. Professionalism in human resource management means acting in accordance with ethical standards. It means recognizing that there is an important ethical dimension to the work of HR professionals. Codes of ethics are desirable but they are not the whole answer.

Ethics and morality defined

Ethics as a system is defined by the *Compact Oxford Dictionary* (1971: 900) as being 'related to morals, treating of moral questions', and 'ethical' is defined as 'relating to morality'. 'Morality' is defined as 'having moral qualities or endowments' and 'moral' is defined as 'of or pertaining to the distinction between right and wrong'. Simplistically, ethics could be described as being about behaviour while morality is about beliefs.

Ethics is concerned with making ethical decisions and judgements. It can be described in terms of an ethical framework which sets out different approaches and can be extended to embrace particular concepts which affect and guide ethical behaviour, namely: equity, justice, and fair dealing. An ethical decision is one that is morally acceptable to the larger community.

Ethical concepts

The ethical concepts of deontology, utilitarianism, stakeholder theory and discourse theory provide frameworks which can be used to evaluate HRM policies and practices.

Fair dealing

Fair dealing occurs when people are treated according to the principles of natural, procedural and distributive justice, and when the decisions or policies that affect them are transparent in the sense that they are known, understood, clear and applied consistently.

The role of HR

HR professionals have a special responsibility for guarding and promoting core values in the organization on how people should be managed and treated generally. They are particularly concerned with values relating to just and fair treatment.

An important role for HR professionals is to do whatever they can to embed the consistent application of ethical values in the organization so that they can become values in use rather than simply professed values in a code of practice or values statement.

Ethical guidelines

Ethical guidelines exist which set out how employees are treated in general and relate to the major HRM activities of organization development, recruitment and selection, learning and development, performance management, reward management, employee relations, and employment practices concerning the work environment, employee well-being, equal opportunities, managing diversity, handling disciplinary matters and grievances, job security and redundancy.

Handling ethical dilemmas

There is no 'one right way' to deal with an ethical dilemma but an approach based on systematic questioning, analysis and diagnosis to get at the facts and establish the issues involved is more likely to produce a reasonably satisfactory outcome than one relying purely on 'gut feeling'. An ethical dilemma is one that will be difficult to resolve. There may be all sorts of issues surrounding the situation, some of which will be unclear or contentious.

Managing within the expectations of the law

HR professionals must clearly comply with the requirements of employment law but they also have the important responsibility of ensuring the compliance of managers and individual employees to it.

References

Adams, J S (1965) Injustice in social exchange, in L Berkowitz (ed) *Advances in Experimental Psychology*, New York, Academic Press

Bagley, C E (2003) The ethical leader's decision tree, *Harvard Business Review*, February, pp 18–19

Bauman, Z and Tester, K (2001) *Conversations with Zygmunt Bauman*, Cambridge, Polity Press

Beauchamp, T L and Bowie, N E (1983) *Ethical Theory and Business*, 2nd edn, New Jersey, Prentice Hall

Boxall, P F, Purcell, J and Wright, P (2007) Human resource management; scope, analysis and significance, in P Boxall, J Purcell and P Wright (eds) *The Oxford Handbook of Human Resource Management*, Oxford, Oxford University Press, pp 1–18

Chartered Institute of Personnel and Development (2008) *Code of Professional Conduct*, at http://www.cipd.co.uk/about/profco.htm (accessed 30 January 2011)

Clegg, S, Kornberger, M and Rhodes, C (2007) Business ethics as practice, *British Journal of Management*, **18** (2), pp 107–22

Collier, J and Esteban, R (2007) Corporate social responsibility and employee commitment, *Business Ethics: A European Review*, **16** (1), pp 28–52

Compact Oxford Dictionary (1971) Oxford, Oxford University Press

Derrida, J (1992) Forces of law: the mystical foundation of authority, in D Cornell, M Rosenfeld and D G Carlson (eds) *Deconstruction and the Possibility of Justice*, London, Routledge, pp 3–68

Fletcher, C (2004) *Appraisal and Feedback: Making performance review work*, 3rd edn, London, CIPD

Foucault, M (1972) *The Archaeology of Knowledge and the Discourse on Language*, New York, Pantheon Books

Foucault, M (1997) *Ethics, Subjectivity and Truth. Essential Works of Foucault, 1954–1984*, ed P Rabinow, New York, The New Press

Freeman, R E (1984) *Strategic Management: A stakeholder perspective*, Englewood Cliffs NJ, Prentice Hall

Guest, D E and King, Z (2004) Power, innovation and problem solving: the personnel manager's three steps to heaven?, *Journal of Management Studies*, [b] (3), pp 401–23

Hamlin, B, Keep, J and Ash, K (2001) *Organizational Change and Development: A reflective guide for managers*, London, Financial Times/Pitman

Harrison, R (2009) *Learning and Development*, 5th edn, London, CIPD

Institute of Business Ethics http://www.ibe.org.uk/index.asp?upid=57&msid=11 (accessed 29 January 2011)

Jones, T M (1991) Ethical decision making by individuals in organizations: an issue-contingent model, *Academy of Management Review*, **16** (2), pp 366–95

Legge, K (1998) The morality of HRM, in C Mabey, D Skinner and T Clark (eds) *Experiencing Human Resource Management*, London, Sage, pp 14–32

Leventhal, G S (1980) What should be done with equity theory?, in G K Gergen, M S Greenberg and R H Willis (eds) *Social Exchange: Advances in Theory and Research*, New York, Plenum

National School of Government (2010) *Code of Ethics for Learning and Development Specialists* NationalSchool.gov.uk/about_us/jobs/associate_working/CodeOEthics.pdf (accessed February 2011)

Osterby, B and Coster, C (1992) Human resource development – a sticky label, *Training and Development*, April, pp 31–32

Petrick, J A and Quinn, J F (1997) *Management Ethics: Integrity at work*, London, Sage

Rawls, J (2005) *A Theory of Justice*, Cambridge MA, Harvard University Press

Schein, E (1993) How can organizations learn faster? The challenge of entering the green room, *Sloan Management Review*, 34 (2), pp 85–92

Schwartz, M (2004) Effective corporate codes of practice: perception of code users, *Journal of Business Ethics*, 55 (4), pp 323–43

Smith, A (1759) *The Theory of Moral Sentiments*, London, A Millar

Tyler, T R and Bies, R J (1990) Beyond formal procedures: the interpersonal context of procedural justice, in J S Carrol (ed) *Applied Social Psychology and Organizational Settings*, Hillsdale NJ, Lawrence Earlbaum

Webley, S and Werner, A (2008) Corporate codes of ethics: necessary but not sufficient, *Business Ethics: A European Review*, 17 (4), pp 405–15

Winstanley, D and Stuart-Smith, K (1996) Policing performance: the ethics of performance management, *Personnel Review*, 25 (6), pp 66–84

Winstanley, D and Woodall, J (2000a) Introduction, in D Winstanley and J Woodall (eds) *Ethical Issues in Contemporary Human Resource Management*, Basingstoke, Macmillan, pp 3–22

Winstanley, D and Woodall, J (2000b) The ethical dimension of human resource management, *Human Resource Management Journal*, 10 (2), pp 5–20

Woodall, J and Winstanley, D (2000) Concluding comments: ethical frameworks for action, in D Winstanley and J Woodall (eds) *Ethical Issues in Contemporary Human Resource Management*, Basingstoke, Macmillan, pp 3–22

Questions

1   What is a profession?

2   What is professionalism?

3   What are the main elements of a professional ethos? (Name at least three.)

4   What is a code of professional conduct?

5   What are the key points made in the CIPD code of professional conduct?

6   What are professional ethics?

7   What is the ethical framework for judging HR practices?

8   What is the purpose of organizational codes of ethics?

9   What reservations can be made about the effectiveness of organizational codes of ethics?

10 What are ethics?

11 What is the nature of ethical judgements?

12 What is the deontological theory of ethics?

13   What is the utilitarian theory of ethics?

14   What did Rawls have to say about social justice?

15   What is stakeholder theory?

16   What is procedural justice?

17   What is distributive justice?

18   What is the ethical dimension of HRM?

19   What are commonly accepted general guidelines on HR ethical behaviour? (Name at least three.)

20   How should ethical dilemmas be dealt with? (List at least three approaches.)

PART THREE
People management processes

Employee engagement

LEARNING OUTCOMES

On completing this chapter you should be able to define these key concepts. You should also know about:

- The meaning of employee engagement
- Job engagement
- Organizational engagement
- The theory of engagement
- The drivers of engagement
- Outcomes of engagement
- Enhancing overall engagement
- The drivers of engagement
- Methods of enhancing engagement

Introduction

The concept of employee engagement, crudely defined as 'going the extra mile', has attracted a lot of attention recently. It has become a new management mantra. Reilly and Brown (2008) noted that the terms job satisfaction, motivation and commitment are generally being replaced now in business by 'engagement' because it appears to have more descriptive force and face validity.

Everyone believes that engagement is a good thing but many, although they think they know it when they see it, are vague about what it really is. Perhaps this is because the concept of engagement is defined in so many different ways. It is often used loosely as a notion which embraces pretty well everything the organization is seeking to do with regard to the contribution and behaviour of its employees in terms of job performance, discretionary effort, organizational citizenship and commitment. Furthermore, it is not clear where the concept of motivation fits in. Is it just an aspect of engagement or is it something that needs to be treated separately?

The vagueness of the term is illustrated by the difficulty of answering the question 'Engagement to what?' Are employees engaged with their job, their career or their organization – or all three or any two of them?

Some definitions avoid this dilemma by referring to engagement as a condition which is solely related to the jobs people do. Others define it as, in effect, identification with the purposes and values of the organization. Only Saks (2006) and, following him, Balain and Sparrow (2009) make a clear distinction between the two. This distinction is important because without it the development of programmes for enhancing engagement which deal with the job aspects of engagement as distinct from the organizational aspects will be difficult. Faced with this confusion, David Guest (2009) suggested that the concept of employee engagement needs to be more clearly defined or it should be abandoned.

But the notion of employee engagement seems to excite managers, HR practitioners and academics. It is here to stay. This chapter therefore begins with an attempt to clarify its meaning and define its significance. This leads to an assessment of the drivers of engagement and a discussion of one of the key notions associated with it – that of discretionary effort. The chapter ends with a review of approaches to engaging employees.

The meaning of employee engagement

Kahn (1990), one of the earliest writers to consider engagement, regarded it as a psychological state experienced by employees in relation to their work, together with associated behaviours. A definition based on research by Maslach et al (2001: 74) referred to engagement as: 'A positive, fulfilling, work-related state of mind that is characterized by vigour, dedication, and absorption.' Macey et al (2009: 7) produced the following working definition:

> Engagement is an individual's purpose and focused energy, evident to others in the display of personal initiative, adaptability, effort and persistence directed towards organizational goals.

On the basis of their research, MacLeod and Clarke (2009) concluded that: 'The way employee engagement operates can take many forms.' So can descriptions of what it means. There are three approaches to definition as described below.

Job engagement

The term 'engagement' can be used in a specific job-related way to describe what takes place when people are interested in and positive, even excited, about their jobs, exercise discretionary behaviour and are motivated to achieve high levels of performance. Erickson (2005) described the job as the key antecedent of the state of engagement. Truss et al (2006: ix) stated that: 'Put simply, engagement means feeling positive about your job.' They went on to explain that: 'The engaged employee is the passionate employee, the employee who is totally immersed in his or her work, energetic, committed and completely dedicated' (ibid: 1). Gallup, as quoted by Balain and Sparrow (2009: 8), defined engagement as: 'The individual's involvement and satisfaction with as well as enthusiasm for work.'

Other sources have defined engagement on similar lines, often emphasizing the importance of discretionary behaviour as the key outcome or distinguishing feature of an engaged employee. Watkin (2001: 4) defined 'engaged performance' as: 'A result that is achieved by stimulating employees' enthusiasm for their work and directing it towards organizational success. This result can only be achieved when employers offer an implied contract to their employees that elicits specific positive behaviours aligned with the organization's goals.'

Organizational engagement

Organizational engagement focuses on attachment to or identification with the organization as a whole. The Conference Board (2006) defined employee engagement as the heightened connection that employees feel for their organization. Robinson et al (2004: 9) emphasized the organizational aspect of engagement when they referred to it as 'a positive attitude held by the employee towards the organization and its values'. This definition of engagement strongly resembles the traditional notion of commitment as discussed in Chapter 10.

TABLE 9.1 Antecedents, types and consequences of engagement (Balain and Sparrow, 2009)

Antecedents of engagement	Types of employee engagement	Consequences
• Enriched and challenging jobs (job characteristics) • Quality of the employee–organization relationship (perceived organizational support) • Quality of the employee–supervisor relationship (perceived supervisor support) • Rewards and recognition • Fairness in the processes that allocate resources or resolve disputes (procedural justice) • What is considered just or right in the allocation of goods in a society (distributive justice)	• Job engagement • Organizational engagement	• Job satisfaction • Organizational commitment • Level of intention to quit • Organizational citizenship behaviour

Analytical definitions

Perhaps the most illuminating and helpful approach to definition is to analyse the concept specifically in terms of both job and organizational engagement. A good example of this is the explanation of the antecedents, types and consequences of engagement shown in Table 9.1 produced by Balain and Sparrow (2009: 17) and based on the work of Saks (2006).

Engagement defined

On the basis of the Balain and Sparrow analysis, engagement can be defined as follows. Engagement happens when people are committed to their work and the organization and motivated to achieve high levels of performance. It has two interrelated aspects: (1) job engagement, which takes place when employees exercise discretionary effort because they find their jobs interesting, challenging and rewarding; and (2) organizational engagement when they identify with the values and purpose of their organization and believe that it is a great place in which to work and to continue to work.

The theory of engagement

The variety of definitions quoted above illustrates the elusiveness of the concept of engagement. As Alfes et al (2010: 4) commented: 'In theoretical, conceptual and empirical terms, we in fact know relatively little about the concept of employee engagement.' They also noted that most consultancies and survey firms regard engagement as something that is done to employees. In contrast, some academics such as May et al (2004) suggest that engagement is experienced by individuals, a state of being that may be affected by management strategies and approaches, but is not in itself such a strategy. The latter view was the one adopted by Alfes et al as the basis for their research.

As discussed below, the concept of engagement has been further explored in terms of its components, its facets, its underpinning theory and the notion of discretionary behaviour.

Components of engagement

The Institute for Employment Studies has modelled the components of engagement as shown in Figure 9.1:

- Commitment is the relative strength of the individual's identification with, and involvement in, an organization.
- Organizational citizenship behaviour as defined by Organ (1988) is employee behaviour that goes above and beyond the call of duty, that is discretionary and not explicitly recognized by the employing organization's formal reward system, and that contributes to organizational effectiveness.

FIGURE 9.1 IES model of employee engagement
(source: Armstrong et al, 2010)

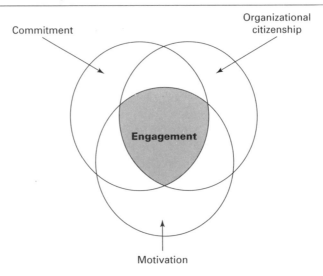

- Motivation is the force that energizes, directs and sustains behaviour. It can be intrinsic, ie behaviour is affected by factors which may arise from the work itself and are self-generated, or extrinsic, which occurs when things are done to or for people to motivate them. The motivation element in engagement is intrinsic. As Macey et al (2009: 67) observed: 'When the work itself is meaningful it is also said to have intrinsic motivation. This means that it is not the pay or recognition that yields positive feelings of engagement but the work itself.' They also commented that engaged employees 'feel that their jobs are an important part of what they are' (ibid: 127).

Facets of engagement

Alfes et al (2010: 5) see engagement as having three core facets:

- intellectual engagement – thinking hard about the job and how to do it better;
- affective engagement – feeling positively about doing a good job;
- social engagement – actively taking opportunities to discuss work-related improvements with others at work.

Ultimately, engagement will have behavioural outcomes leading to what can be described as an 'engaged employee'.

A theory of engagement

Balain and Sparrow (2010: 183) considered that engagement should be seen as a 'belief' and not an attitude, ie it is largely a cognitive construct (intellectual engagement) rather than an affective or behavioural one. They suggested that engagement will have affective and behavioural outcomes but it is necessary to separate the cause from the effect.

Saks (2006) suggested that a strong theoretical rationale for engagement is provided by social exchange theory. As he described it: 'Social exchange theory argues that obligations are generated through a series of interactions between parties who are in a state of reciprocal interdependence. A basic tenet of social exchange theory is that relationships evolve over time into trusting, loyal and mutual commitments as long as the parties abide by certain "rules" of exchange... usually involve reciprocity or repayment rules such that the actions of one party lead to a response or actions by the other party' (ibid: 603). This is consistent with the description of engagement by Robinson et al (2004) as a two-way relationship between the employer and the employee. Balain and Sparrow (2009: 16) concluded that: 'To understand what really causes engagement, and what it causes in turn, we need to embed the idea in a well-founded theory. The one that is considered most appropriate is social exchange theory, which sees feelings of loyalty, commitment, discretionary effort as all being forms of social reciprocation by employees to a good employer.'

Discretionary behaviour

Employee engagement is associated with the notion of discretionary behaviour or effort. As described by Purcell et al (2003), discretionary behaviour refers to the choices that people at work often have in the way they do the job and the amount of effort, care, innovation and productive behaviour they display. It can be positive when people 'go the extra mile' to achieve high levels of performance. It can be negative when they exercise their discretion to slack at their work. Discretionary behaviour is hard for the employer to define, monitor and control. But positive discretionary behaviour can happen when people are engaged with their work.

Drivers of employee engagement

The following drivers of engagement were listed by MacLeod and Clarke (2009):

- leadership which ensures a strong, transparent and explicit organizational culture which gives employees a line of sight between their job and the vision and aims of the organization;
- engaging managers who offer clarity, appreciation of employees' effort and contribution, who treat their people as individuals and who ensure that work is organized efficiently and effectively so that employees feel they are valued, and equipped and supported to do their job;
- employees who feel that they are able to voice their ideas and be listened to, both about how they do their job and in decision

making in their own department, with joint sharing of problems and challenges and a commitment to arrive at joint solutions;

- a belief among employees that the organization lives its values, and that espoused behavioural norms are adhered to, resulting in trust and a sense of integrity.

Macey et al (2009) placed greater emphasis on the work environment and the jobs people do. They noted that: 'Engagement requires a work environment that does not just demand more but promotes information sharing, provides learning opportunities and fosters a balance in people's lives, thereby creating the bases for sustained energy and personal initiative' (ibid: 11). They also commented that 'When people have the opportunity to do work in a way that: (a) effectively uses their skills; (b) fits their values; and (c) provides them the freedom to exercise choice, they will be fully motivated to engage in their work' (ibid: 126). They observed that 'Engaged employees feel that their jobs are an important part of who they are' (ibid: 127).

Research conducted by Alfes et al (2010: 2) established that the main drivers of engagement are meaningful work (the most important), senior management vision and communication, positive perceptions of one's line manager and employee voice – having a say in matters that concern them. 'HR practices do not impact directly on engagement; the relationship is mediated by person–job fit and line management style.'

Outcomes of engagement

Research conducted by the Institute for Employment Studies (Robinson et al, 2004) led to the conclusion that an engaged employee:

- is willing to 'go the extra mile';
- believes in and identifies with the organization;
- wants to work to make things better;
- understands the business context and the 'bigger picture';
- respects and help colleagues.

David Guest (2009) explained that the benefits of engagement were as follows. Employee engagement will be manifested in positive attitudes (for example, job satisfaction, organizational commitment and identification with the organization) and behaviour (low labour turnover and absence and high citizenship behaviour) on the part of employees; and evidence of perceptions of trust, fairness and a positive exchange within a psychological contract where two-way promises and commitments are fulfilled.

Alfes et al (2010: 2) concluded that engaged employees perform better, are more innovative than others, are more likely to want to stay with their employers, enjoy greater levels of personal well-being and perceive their workload to be more sustainable than others.

Enhancing overall employee engagement

Promoting the engagement of their employees is what every employer wants to do. But how can they do it? There are no universal prescriptions and any actions taken should be based on evidence, including measurements of levels of engagement, trends in those levels and benchmarking. This data needs to be analysed and assessed to provide information on what might be done (approaches to measurement are examined in the last section of this chapter).

MacLeod and Clarke (2009: 6) pointed out that: 'Engagement is about establishing mutual respect in the workplace for what people can do and be.' They also observed that: 'Engagement is two way: organizations must work to engage the employee, who in turn has a choice about the level of engagement to offer the employer. Each reinforces the other' (ibid: 9).

Following their research, Alfes et al (2010: 2) concluded that engagement requires a work environment that does not just demand more but promotes information sharing, provides learning opportunities and fosters a balance in people's lives, thereby creating the bases for sustained energy and personal initiative.

To enhance engagement, employers have to address issues concerning both aspects of engagement – job and organizational engagement. These are interrelated and any actions taken to enhance either aspect will be mutually supporting. However, it is useful to consider what can be done specifically in each area bearing in mind the particular circumstances and needs of the organization.

To summarize, job engagement will be affected by work and job design, the quality of leadership exercised by line managers and the reward system. Organizational engagement will be affected by the quality of life provided by the working environment and by having an employee value proposition which ensures that the organization is an employer of choice.

Enhancing job engagement

Job engagement can be enhanced through good job design, learning and development programmes, performance management, and improving the quality of leadership provided by line managers. In addition, rewards in the broadest sense, ie non-financial as well as financial, can play a part.

Job design

Job design has a key role to play in enhancing engagement. As Herzberg (1968: 96) remarked: 'If you want someone to do a good job, give them a good job to do.' And Macey et al (2009: 69) commented that: 'People come to work for pay but get engaged at work because the work they do is meaningful.' Intrinsic motivation and therefore increased engagement can be generated by the work itself if it provides interest and opportunities for achievement and self-fulfilment.

An early but influential perspective on the factors affecting job design and motivation was provided by Hackman and Oldham (1974), whose job characteristics model indicated that the features of jobs that need to be taken into account in job design were variety, autonomy, required interaction, optional interaction, knowledge and skill required and responsibility.

A later suggestion on the approaches to job design was made by Robertson and Smith (1985), who suggested that the aim should be to influence (1) skill variety by providing opportunities for people to do several tasks and combining tasks; (2) task identity by combining tasks and forming natural work units; (3) task significance by informing people of the importance of their work; (4) autonomy by giving people responsibility for determining their own working systems; and (5) feedback on how well they are doing.

These approaches may be used when setting up new work systems, and jobs and guidance and advice along these lines should be provided to those responsible for such developments. But the greatest impact on the design of work systems or jobs is made by line managers on a day-to-day basis. An engagement strategy should therefore include arrangements for educating them as part of a leadership development programme in the importance of good work and job design and what they can do to improve intrinsic motivation.

The work environment

A strategy for increasing job engagement through the work environment will be generally concerned with developing a culture which encourages positive attitudes to work, promoting interest and excitement in the jobs people do, reducing stress and recognizing the importance of social interaction. Land's End believes that staff who are enjoying themselves, who are being supported and developed and who feel fulfilled and respected at work will provide the best service to customers.

Learning and development programmes

Learning and development programmes can ensure that people have the opportunity and are given the encouragement to learn and grow in their roles. This includes the use of policies which focus on role flexibility – giving people the chance to develop their roles by making better and extended use of their talents. It also means going beyond talent management for the favoured few and developing the abilities of the core people on whom the organization depends. The philosophy should be that everyone has the ability to succeed and the aim should be to 'achieve extraordinary results with ordinary people'. It includes using performance management primarily as a developmental process with an emphasis on personal development planning.

The strategy should also cover career development opportunities and how individuals can be given the guidance, support and encouragement they need if they are to fulfil their potential and achieve a successful career with the organization in tune with their talents and aspirations. The actions required to provide men and women of promise with a sequence of learning activities and experiences that will equip them for whatever level of responsibility they have the ability to reach should be included in the strategy.

Line managers

As Harter et al (2002) observed, engagement at work is best enhanced when employees feel they are supported, recognized and developed by their managers. Line managers play a vital and immediate part in increasing levels of job engagement. They do this by exercising leadership and ensuring that their team members are clear about what they have to do, acquire the skills required and appreciate the significance of their contribution. They have considerable influence over job and work design and are there to provide support, encouragement and coaching with the help of the performance management system. They need guidance on what they are expected to do and help in developing the skills they need.

Developing engagement through reward

Reilly and Brown (2008) contended that appropriate reward practices and processes, both financial and non-financial and managed in combination (ie a total rewards approach) can help to build and improve employee engagement, and that badly designed or executed rewards can hinder it. Their model based on research of how reward policies influence performance through engagement is shown in Figure 9.2.

FIGURE 9.2 How reward policies influence performance through engagement (source: Reilly and Brown, 2008)

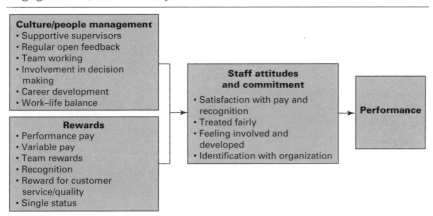

Enhancing organizational engagement

It was suggested by David Guest (2009) that engagement can be achieved 'through effective leadership of a strong, positive culture that ensures the enactment of organizational values; through strong management that supports employees' work and well-being; through careful design of systems and jobs to enable employees to contribute through full use of their knowledge and skills; through effective employee voice; and through provision of appropriate resources, tools and information to perform effectively'.

A basis for enhancing organizational engagement was established by the longitudinal research in 12 companies conducted by Professor John Purcell and his colleagues (Purcell et al, 2003) They found that the most successful companies had 'the big idea'. This meant that: 'They had a clear vision and a set of integrated values. They were concerned with sustaining performance and flexibility. Clear evidence existed between positive attitudes towards HR policies and practices, levels of satisfaction, motivation and commitment, and operational performance. Policy and practice implementation (not the number of HR practices adopted) is the vital ingredient in linking people management to business performance and this is primarily the task of line managers.'

At Land's End the thinking behind how the company inspires its staff is straightforward – employees' willingness to do that little bit extra arises from their sense of pride in what the organization stands for, ie quality, service and value. It makes the difference between a good experience for customers and a poor one.

High-involvement management

Organizational engagement can be developed through high-involvement management. This term was first used by Lawler (1986) to describe management systems based on commitment and involvement, as opposed to the old bureaucratic model based on control. The underlying hypothesis is that each employee will increase their involvement with the company if they are given the opportunity to manage and understand their work. Lawler claimed that high-involvement practices worked well because they acted as a synergy and had a multiplicative effect.

High-involvement management involves treating employees as partners in the enterprise whose interests are respected and who have a voice on matters that concern them. It is concerned with communication and participation. The aim is to create a climate in which a continuing dialogue between managers and the members of their teams takes place in order to define expectations and share information on the organization's mission, values and objectives. This establishes mutual understanding of what is to be achieved and a framework for managing and developing people to ensure that it will be achieved.

TABLE 9.2 Example of an engagement survey

Engagement survey				
Please circle the number which most closely matches your opinion.				
		Strongly agree	**Agree**	**Disagree**	**Strongly disagree**
1	I am very satisfied with the work I do	1	2	3	4
2	My job is interesting	1	2	3	4
3	I know exactly what I am expected to do	1	2	3	4
4	I am prepared to put myself out to do my work	1	2	3	4
5	I have plenty of freedom to decide how to do my work	1	2	3	4
6	I get lots of opportunities to use and develop my skills in this job	1	2	3	4
7	The facilities/equipment/ tools provided are excellent	1	2	3	4
8	I get good support from my boss	1	2	3	4
9	My boss gives me helpful feedback on how well I am doing	1	2	3	4
10	I am rewarded well for my contribution	1	2	3	4
11	I think this organization is a great place in which to work	1	2	3	4

TABLE 9.2 Example of an engagement survey (continued.)

	Engagement survey Please circle the number which most closely matches your opinion.	Strongly agree	Agree	Disagree	Strongly disagree
12	I would recommend this organization to people as a good employer	1	2	3	4
13	I believe I have a good future in this organization	1	2	3	4
14	I intend to go on working for this organization	1	2	3	4
15	I am happy about the values of this organization – the ways in which it conducts its business	1	2	3	4
16	I believe that the products/ services provided by this organization are excellent	1	2	3	4
17	The management of this organization is really concerned about the well-being of employees	1	2	3	4
18	I have no problems in achieving a balance between my work and my private life	1	2	3	4
19	I like working for my boss	1	2	3	4
20	I get on well with my work colleagues	1	2	3	4

Measuring engagement

Interest in engagement has been stimulated by the scope for measuring levels and trends through engagement surveys. These provide the basis for the development and implementation of engagement strategies through the 'triple-A' approach: Analysis, Assessment and Action. An example of a survey is given in Table 9.2. The first 10 questions focus on job engagement and the next 10 are more concerned with organizational engagement.

KEY LEARNING POINTS

The meaning of employee engagement

Engagement happens when people are committed to their work and the organization and motivated to achieve high levels of performance. It has two interrelated aspects: (1) job engagement, which takes place when employees exercise discretionary effort because they find their jobs interesting, challenging and rewarding; and (2) organizational engagement when they identify with the values and purpose of their organization and believe that it is a great place in which to work and to continue to work.

Elements of engagement

Commitment, organizational citizenship behaviour and motivation.

Facets of engagement

- intellectual engagement – thinking hard about the job and how to do it better;
- affective engagement – feeling positively about doing a good job;
- social engagement – actively taking opportunities to discuss work-related improvements with others at work;
- behavioural outcomes.

Theories of engagement

Engagement will have behavioural outcomes leading to what can be described as an 'engaged employee'.

Saks (2006) suggested that a strong theoretical rationale for engagement is provided by social exchange theory.

Discretionary behaviour

Discretionary behaviour refers to the choices that people at work often have on the way they do the job and the amount of effort, care, innovation and productive behaviour they display.

Drivers of engagement

Macey et al (2009) emphasize the importance of the work environment and the jobs people do.

Alfes et al (2010) established that the main drivers of engagement are meaningful work (the most important), senior management vision and communication, positive perceptions of one's line manager and employee voice – having a say in matters that concern them.

Enhancing engagement

Job engagement can be enhanced through good job design, learning and development programmes, and improving the quality of leadership provided by line managers. In addition, rewards in the broadest sense, ie non-financial as well as financial, can play a part.

It was suggested by David Guest (2009) that organizational engagement can be enhanced 'through effective leadership of a strong, positive culture that ensures the enactment of organizational values; through strong management that supports employees' work and well-being; through careful design of systems and jobs to enable employees to contribute through full use of their knowledge and skills; through effective employee voice; and through provision of appropriate resources, tools and information to perform effectively.'

References

Alfes, K, Truss, C, Soane, E C, Rees, C and Gatenby, M (2010) *Creating an Engaged Workforce*, London, CIPD

Armstrong, M, Brown, D and Reilly, P (2010) *Evidence-Based Reward Management*, London, Kogan Page

Balain, S and Sparrow, P (2009) *Engaged to Perform: A new perspective on employee engagement*, Lancaster, Lancaster University Management School

Balain, S and Sparrow, P (2010) Understanding the value of engagement, in P Sparrow, A Hesketh, M Hird and C Cooper (eds) *Leading HR*, Basingstoke, Palgrave Macmillan, pp 162–88

Conference Board (2006) *Employee Engagement: A review of current research and its implications*, New York, Conference Board

Erickson, T J (2005) Testimony submitted before the US Senate Committee on Health, Education, Labor and Pensions, May 26

Guest, D (2009) *Review of Employee Engagement: Notes for a discussion* (unpublished), prepared specifically for the MacLeod and Clarke 2009 review of employee engagement

Hackman, J R and Oldham, G R (1974) Motivation through the design of work: test of a theory, *Organizational Behaviour and Human Performance*, **16** (2), pp 250–79

Harter, J K, Schmidt, F L and Hayes, T L (2002) Business-unit-level relationship between employee satisfaction, employee engagement, and business outcomes: A meta-analysis, *Journal of Applied Psychology*, **87**, pp 268–79

Herzberg, F (1968) One more time: how do you motivate employees?, *Harvard Business Review*, January–February, pp 109–20

Kahn, W A (1990) Psychological conditions of personal engagement and disengagement at work, *Academy of Management Journal*, 33 (4), pp 692–724

Lawler, E E (1986) *High-Involvement Management*, San Francisco, Jossey-Bass

Macey, W H, Schneider, B, Barbera, K M and Young, S A (2009) *Employee Engagement*, Malden MA, Wiley-Blackwell

MacLeod, D and Clarke, N (2009) *Engaging for Success: Enhancing performance through employee engagement*, London, Department for Business Innovation and Skills

Maslach, C, Schaufeli, W B and Leiter, M P (2001) Job Burnout, *Annual Review of Psychology*, 52, pp 397–422

May, D R, Gilson, R L and Harter, L M (2004) The psychological conditions of meaningfulness, safety and availability and the engagement of the human spirit at work, *Journal of Occupational & Organizational Psychology*, 77 (1), pp 11–37

Organ, D W (1988) *Organizational Citizenship Behaviour: The good soldier syndrome*, Lexington MA, Lexington Books

Purcell, J, Kinnie, N, Hutchinson, S, Rayton, B and Swart, J (2003) *People and Performance: How People Management Impacts on Organizational Performance*, London, CIPD

Reilly, P and Brown, D (2008) Employee engagement: future focus or fashionable fad for reward management?, *World at Work Journal*, 17 (4), pp 37–49

Robertson, I T and Smith, M (1985) *Motivation and Job Design*, London, IPM

Robinson, D (2008) *Employee engagement: an IES perspective*, presentation to the IES HR Network, unpublished

Robinson, D, Perryman, S and Hayday, S (2004) *The Drivers of Employee Engagement*, Brighton, Institute for Employment Studies

Saks, A M (2006) Antecedents and consequences of employee engagement, *Journal of Managerial Psychology*, 21 (6), pp 600–19

Truss, C, Soane, E, Edwards, C, Wisdom, K, Croll, A and Burnett, J (2006) *Working Life: Employee attitudes and engagement*, London, CIPD

Watkin, C (2001) Engage employees to boost performance, *Selection & Development Review*, 18 (2), pp 3–6

Questions

1 What is employee engagement

2 What is job engagement?

3 What is organizational engagement?

4 What are the components of engagement?

5 What is organizational citizenship behaviour?

6 What is the relationship between engagement and commitment?

7 What is the relationship between engagement and motivation?

8 What are the facets of engagement?

9 What are the main outcomes of engagement? (Name at least four.)

10 What are the main conclusions about engagement reached by the research conducted by Saks (2006)?

11 What are the main conclusions about engagement reached by the research conducted by Balain and Sparrow (2009)?

12 What are the main conclusions about engagement reached by the research conducted by MacLeod and Clarke (2009)?

13 What are the main conclusions about engagement reached by the research conducted by Alfes et al (2010)?

14 What is social exchange theory?

15 What is discretionary behaviour?

16 What are the main drivers of engagement as listed by MacLeod and Clarke? (Name at least three.)

17 How can job engagement be enhanced?

18 What is the role of job design in job engagement?

19 How can organizational engagement be enhanced?

20 What is high-involvement management?

Motivation

Key concepts and terms

- *Content (needs) motivation theory*
- *Equity theory*
- *Expectancy theory*
- *Extrinsic motivation*
- *Goal theory*
- *Herzberg's two-factor model of motivation*
- *Intrinsic motivation*
- *Instrumentality*
- *Line of sight*
- *Management by objectives*
- *Motivation*
- *Process theory*
- *Reinforcement*
- *Self-efficacy*

LEARNING OUTCOMES

On completing this chapter you should be able to define these key concepts. You should also understand:

- The meaning of motivation
- Types of motivation
- The process of motivation
- The different motivation theories
- The points that have been made in critically evaluating those theories
- Approaches to developing a motivation strategy

Introduction

Motivation is the force that energizes, directs and sustains behaviour. High performance is achieved by well-motivated people who are prepared to exercise discretionary effort. Even in fairly basic roles, Hunter et al (1990) found through their research that the difference in value-added discretionary performance between 'superior' and 'standard' performers was 19 per cent. For highly complex jobs it was 48 per cent.

The meaning of motivation

A motive is a reason for doing something. Motivation is concerned with the strength and direction of behaviour and the factors that influence people to behave in certain ways. The term 'motivation' can refer variously to the goals individuals have, the ways in which individuals choose their goals and the ways in which others try to change their behaviour.

Types of motivation

A distinction is made between extrinsic and intrinsic motivation. Extrinsic motivation occurs when things are done to or for people to motivate them, which include rewards, such as incentives, increased pay, praise, or promotion, and punishments, such as disciplinary action, withholding pay, or criticism. Intrinsic motivation is provided by the work itself and is associated with the concept of engagement as explained in Chapter 9.

The process of motivation

The process of motivation can be modelled in a number of ways. Two of the best-known models are provided by content or needs theory and expectancy theory.

Content (needs) theory

This theory focuses on the content of motivation in the shape of needs. Its basis is the belief that an unsatisfied need creates tension and a state of disequilibrium. To restore the balance, a goal is identified which will satisfy the need, and a behaviour pathway is selected which will lead to the achievement of the goal and the satisfaction of the need. Behaviour is therefore motivated by unsatisfied needs. A content theory model is shown in Figure 10.1. Content theory, as the term implies, indicates the components of motivation but it does not explain how motivation affects performance – a necessary requirement if the concept is to provide guidance on HR policy and practice. This was the role of expectancy theory as described below.

FIGURE 10.1 The process of motivation according to content theory

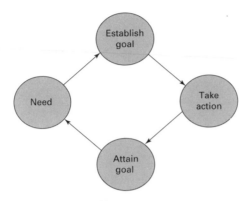

Expectancy theory

Expectancy theory states that motivation to perform will be high when people know what they have to do to get a reward, expect that they will be able to get the reward and expect that the reward will be worthwhile. Motivation is only likely when a clearly perceived and usable relationship exists between performance and outcome, and the outcome is seen as a means of satisfying needs. Porter and Lawler (1968) spelt out that the level of effort was affected by the value of rewards and the probability that reward followed effort. But they pointed out that effort was not enough to achieve high performance. Two additional factors affecting performance had to be taken into account: (1) ability – individual characteristics such as intelligence, knowledge, skills; and (2) role perceptions – what individuals want to do or think they are required to do. A model of their theory is shown in Figure 10.2.

Motivation theories

The main motivation theories including content and expectancy theory are summarized in Table 10.1.

FIGURE 10.2 Motivation model (Porter and Lawler, 1968)

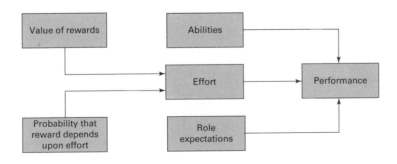

TABLE 10.1 Summary of motivation theories

Category	Type	Theorist(s)	Summary of theory	Implications
Instrumentality	Taylorism	Taylor (1911)	If we do one thing it leads to another. People will be motivated to work if rewards and punishments are directly related to their performance.	Basis of crude attempts to motivate people by incentives. Often used as the implied rationale for performance-related pay, although this is seldom an effective motivator.
Reinforcement	The motivation process	Hull (1951)	As experience is gained in satisfying needs, people perceive that certain actions help to achieve goals while others are unsuccessful. The successful actions are repeated when a similar need arises.	Provide feedback which positively reinforces effective behaviour.
Content (needs) theory	Hierarchy of needs	Maslow (1954) Alderfer (1972)	People are motivated by their needs, which are translated into goals for them to attain. The content of motivation is therefore those needs and the goals they generate to which people aspire. In Maslow's theory a hierarchy of needs exists: physiological, safety, social, esteem, self-fulfilment. Needs at a higher level only emerge when a lower need is satisfied. Alderfer (1972) produced a simpler three-factor non-hierarchical theory identifying three basic needs.	Focuses attention on the various needs that motivate people and the notion that a satisfied need is no longer a motivator. The concept of a hierarchy has no practical significance.

Theory	Reference	Summary	Implications
Two-factor model	Herzberg et al (1957)	Two groups of factors affect job satisfaction: (1) those intrinsic to the work itself; (2) those extrinsic to the job (extrinsic motivators or hygiene factors) such as pay and working conditions.	Identifies a number of fundamental needs within the two-factor model, ie achievement, recognition, advancement, autonomy and the work itself. It also indicates that satisfaction from a pay increase (extrinsic motivation) does not last long. The research methodology has been strongly criticized and the underpinning assumption that everyone has the same needs is invalid. But it has influenced approaches to job design (job enrichment) and it supports the proposition that reward systems should provide for both financial and non-financial rewards.
Process/ cognitive theory Expectancy theory	Vroom (1964) Porter and Lawler (1968)	Effort (motivation) depends on the likelihood that rewards will follow effort and that the reward is worthwhile.	The key theory informing approaches to rewards, ie that there must be a link between effort and reward (line of sight), the reward should be achievable and should be worthwhile.
Goal theory	Latham and Locke (1979)	Motivation will improve if people have demanding but agreed goals and receive feedback.	Influences performance management and learning and development practices.
Equity theory	Adams (1965)	People are better motivated if treated equitably, ie treated fairly in comparison with another group of people (a reference group) or a relevant other person.	Need to have equitable reward and employment practices.

Critical evaluation of motivation theories

Instrumentality

This theory emerged in the second half of the 19th century with its emphasis on the need to rationalize work and on economic outcomes. It assumes that people will be motivated to work if rewards and penalties are tied directly to their performance; thus the awards are contingent upon effective performance. Instrumentality theory has its roots in the scientific management methods of Taylor (1911).

The theory provides a rationale for incentive pay, albeit a dubious one. Motivation using this approach has been and still is widely adopted and can be successful in some circumstances, eg piece work. But it relies exclusively on a system of external controls and does not recognize a number of other human needs. It also fails to appreciate the fact that the formal control system can be seriously affected by the informal relationship existing between workers.

Reinforcement

It has been suggested that behavioural theories based on the principle of reinforcement pay insufficient attention to the influence of expectations, and no indication is given of any means of distinguishing in advance the class of outcomes which would strengthen responses and those which would weaken them. They are limited because they imply, in Allport's (1954) vivid phrase, a 'hedonism of the past'. They assume that the explanation of the present choices of individuals is to be found in an examination of the consequences of their past choices.

Content/needs theory

Content or needs theory has a considerable amount of face validity; it seems almost self-evident that people are motivated by unsatisfied needs. In particular, Maslow's needs hierarchy has an intuitive appeal and has been very popular. But his theory has not been verified by empirical research such as that conducted by Wahba and Bridwell (1979). It has been criticized first for its apparent rigidity – different people may have different priorities; second, because it is difficult to accept that needs progress steadily up the hierarchy; and third for the misleading simplicity of Maslow's conceptual language. In fact, Maslow himself expressed doubts about the validity of a strictly ordered hierarchy.

Alderfer (1972) produced a more convincing and simpler theory identifying three primary categories:

- Existence needs, such as hunger and thirst. Pay, fringe benefits and working conditions are other types of existence needs.

- Relatedness needs, which acknowledge that people are not self-contained units but must engage in transactions with their human environment. Acceptance, understanding, confirmation and influence are elements of the relatedness process.

- Growth needs, which involve people in finding the opportunities 'to be what they are most fully and to become what they can'.

Together, the content model of motivation shown in Figure 10.1 and the Alderfer concept usefully emphasize the significance of needs and goals as factors affecting motivation and how they function. But content or need theory ignores the important factor of expectations, which is covered by expectancy theory. This means that it does not really explain how people make choices about their goals and behaviour.

Herzberg's two-factor model

Herzberg's two-factor theory in effect identifies needs but it has been attacked by, for example, Opsahl and Dunnette (1966). The research method has been criticized because no attempt was made to measure the relationship between satisfaction and performance. It has been claimed that the two-factor nature of the theory is an inevitable result of the questioning method used by the interviewers. It has also been suggested that wide and unwarranted inferences have been drawn from small and specialized samples and that there is no evidence to suggest that the satisfiers do improve productivity. The underpinning assumption that everyone has the same needs is invalid. Rousseau (2006: 263) summed up the views of academics about Herzberg as follows: 'Herzberg's long discredited two-factor theory is typically included in the motivation section of management textbooks, despite the fact that it was discredited over thirty years ago.'

In spite of these criticisms the Herzberg two-factor theory continues to thrive; partly because it is easy to understand and seems to be based on 'real life' rather than academic abstractions, and partly because it convincingly emphasizes the positive value of the intrinsic motivating factors. It is also in accord with a fundamental belief in the dignity of labour and the Protestant ethic – that work is good in itself. As a result, Herzberg had immense influence on the job enrichment movement, which sought to design jobs in a way which would maximize the opportunities to obtain intrinsic satisfaction from work and thus improve the quality of working life.

Expectancy theory

Expectancy theory focuses on how motivation affects performance and describes how people make choices about desired goals. It is generally accepted as the leading theory of motivation and has become an important basis for explaining what motivates people to work. It used to inform decisions on the design and management of contingent pay schemes and to measure the effectiveness of such schemes.

The theory was developed by Vroom (1964) but has its origins in the ancient Greek principle of hedonism, which assumes that behaviour is directed toward pleasure and away from pain. Individuals will choose from alternative courses of action that behaviour which they think will maximize their pleasure or minimize their pain.

But research has not provided unequivocal backing for the theory. Connolly (1976) noted that: 'The expectancy model appears to have enjoyed substantial if uneven support.' House et al (1974) commented that: 'Evidence for the validity of the theory is very mixed.' They also established that there were a number of variables affecting expectations which make it difficult to predict how they function. These are:

- leadership behaviour – the function of the leader in clarifying expectations, guiding, supporting and rewarding subordinates;
- individual characteristics – the subjects' perception of their ability to perform the required task;
- nature of the task – whether accomplishing the task provides the necessary reinforcements and rewards;
- the practices of the organization – its reward and control systems and how it functions.

Research conducted by Behling and Starke (1973) established that individuals:

- make crucial personal decisions without clearly understanding the consequences;
- do not in practice consistently evaluate their order of preference for alternative actions;
- have to assign two values when making a decision – its desirability and its achievability – but they tend to be influenced mainly by desirability: they let their tastes influence their beliefs;
- may be able to evaluate the extrinsic rewards they expect but may find it difficult to evaluate the possibility of achieving intrinsic rewards;
- may find it difficult to distinguish the benefits of one possible outcome from another.

Behling and Starke concluded that: 'Expectancy theory can account for some of the variations in work effort but far less than normally attributed to it.'

The findings of research by Reinharth and Wahba (1975), based on a survey of the salesforces of four industrial companies, showed no support for either the Vroom expectancy model or its components. Reinharth and Wahba concluded:

> The findings of the study point to the theory's ability to explain at best a very limited portion of human behavior. It may be that the theory, founded on considerations of rationality, can serve as a useful predictor in situations where contingencies between acts and outcomes and between first-level

and second-level outcomes are clearly perceived by the individual, whereas ambiguous situations force the individual to develop a choice mechanism not based on the expectancy variables. In short, the earlier optimism for the universality of the theory appears to have been dashed.

Overall, the outcomes of research suggest that while expectancy theory offers what appears to be a convincing explanation of the factors affecting the motivation to work, it does not provide a universal explanation because of individual differences in the approach to decision making, the circumstances in which the scheme operates and the impact of social forces on individuals.

However, when designing an incentive scheme and assessing its effectiveness, expectancy theory has considerable face validity as a common-sense explanation of the factors affecting motivation and what makes incentive schemes work, ie the incentive has to be worthwhile and attainable. It provides the theoretical basis for the concept of 'line of sight' developed by Lawler (1988), which states that for a scheme to be effective there has to be a clear and easily perceived link between effort and reward.

Goal theory

Goal theory provides the rationale for performance management, goal setting and feedback. But its universality has been questioned. For example, Harackiewicz et al (2002) warned that goals are only effective when they are 'consistent with and match the general context in which they are pursued'. And Pintrich (2000) noted that people have different goals in different circumstances and that it is hard to justify the assumption that goals are always accessible and conscious. But support for goal theory was provided by Bandura and Cervone (1983), who emphasized the importance of self-evaluation and self-efficacy (a belief in one's ability to accomplish goals).

Goal theory is in line with the 1960s concept of management by objectives or MBO (a process of managing, motivating and appraising people by setting objectives or goals and measuring performance against those objectives). But management by objectives fell into disrepute because it was tackled bureaucratically without gaining the real support of those involved and, importantly, without ensuring that managers were aware of the significance of the processes of agreement, reinforcement and feedback, and were also skilled in practising them. Goal theory, however, plays a key part in performance management

Equity theory

Equity theory has been criticized because it is oversimplified and is based on laboratory rather than real-life research (Huseman et al, 1982). It has also been suggested by Carrell and Dittrich (1978) that equity can be perceived not only on a person-to-person basis, as the theory posits, but also by reference

TABLE 10.2 Factors affecting motivation strategies and the HR contribution

Factors affecting motivation strategies	The HR contribution
The complexity of the process of motivation means that simplistic approaches based on instrumentality or needs theory are unlikely to be successful.	Avoid the trap of developing or supporting strategies that offer prescriptions for motivation based on a simplistic view of the process or fail to recognize individual differences.
People are more likely to be motivated if they work in an environment in which they are valued for what they are and what they do. This means paying attention to the basic need for recognition.	Encourage the development of performance management processes which provide opportunities to agree expectations and to recognize accomplishments.
Extrinsic motivators such as incentive pay can have an immediate and powerful effect, but will not necessarily last long. The intrinsic motivators, which are concerned with the 'quality of working life' (a phrase and movement which emerged from this concept), are likely to have a deeper and longer-term effect because they are inherent in individuals and the work they do and not imposed from outside in such forms as performance-related pay.	• Develop total reward systems which provide opportunities for both financial and non-financial rewards to recognize achievements. Bear in mind, however, that financial rewards systems are not necessarily appropriate and the lessons of expectancy, goal and equity theory need to be taken into account in designing and operating them. • Pay particular attention to recognition as a means of motivation and developing intrinsic motivation through job design.
Some people will be much more motivated by money than others. It cannot be assumed that money motivates everyone in the same way and to the same extent.	It is naive to think that the introduction of a performance-related pay scheme will miraculously transform everyone overnight into well-motivated, high-performing individuals.

The need for work which provides people with the means to achieve their goals, a reasonable degree of autonomy and scope for the use of skills and competences should be recognized.	Advise on processes for the design of jobs which take account of the factors affecting the motivation to work, providing for job enrichment in the shape of variety, decision-making responsibility and as much control as possible in carrying out the work.
The need for the opportunity to grow by developing abilities and careers.	• Provide facilities and opportunities for learning through such means as personal development planning processes as well as more formal training. • Develop career planning processes.
The cultural environment of the organization in the shape of its values and norms will influence the impact of any attempts to motivate people by direct or indirect means.	Advise on the development of a culture which supports processes of valuing and rewarding employees.
Motivation will be enhanced by leadership which sets the direction, encourages and stimulates achievement and provides support to employees in their efforts to reach goals and improve their performance generally.	• Devise competency frameworks which focus on leadership qualities and the behaviours expected of managers and team leaders. • Ensure that leadership potential is identified through performance management and assessment centres. • Conduct leadership development programmes.

to the fairness of processes in the organization as a whole. But the need to have equitable reward and employment practices which are supported by equity theory cannot be questioned. The problem is how to achieve equity.

Conclusions

In a sense, all the theories referred to above make a contribution to an understanding of the processes that affect motivation. But some, such as reinforcement and instrumentality, have considerable limitations, as do the needs hierarchy and two-factor theories of Maslow and Herzberg. Gerhart and Rynes (2003) pointed out that: 'Although Maslow's and Herzberg's theories were intuitively appealing to many people, research has not supported either theory to any great extent.' In fact, people are far more varied and complex than these theories suggest. To state that there are strong similarities between people leads to the conclusion that there is 'one best way' to motivate and reward them, which is simply not true.

Process theories concerned with expectancy, goal setting and equity are based on more realistic ideas and are much more relevant than the theories of Maslow and Herzberg. Expectancy theory is particularly appropriate when dealing with contingent pay (incentive schemes) but it is still dangerous to generalize that everyone is motivated in the same way by the same pattern of expectations.

Motivation strategies based on the lessons learnt from motivation theory are considered below.

Motivation strategies

Motivation strategies aim to create a working environment and to develop policies and practices which will provide for higher levels of performance from employees. The factors affecting them and the HR contribution are summarized in Table 10.2.

KEY LEARNING POINTS

The process of motivation

Motivation is goal-directed behaviour. People are motivated when they expect that a course of action is likely to lead to the attainment of a goal and a valued reward – one that satisfies their needs and wants.

Types of motivation

The two basic types are intrinsic and extrinsic motivation.

Motivation theories

There are a number of motivation theories which, in the main, are complementary to one another. The most significant theories are those concerned with expectancy, goal setting and equity, which are classified as process or cognitive theories.

Motivation strategies

Motivation strategies aim to create a working environment and to develop policies and practices that will provide for higher levels of performance from employees. They include the development of total reward systems and performance management processes, the design of intrinsically motivating jobs and leadership development programmes.

References

Adams, J S (1965) Injustice in social exchange, in L Berkowitz (ed) *Advances in Experimental Psychology*, New York, Academic Press

Alderfer, C (1972) *Existence, Relatedness and Growth*, New York, The Free Press

Allport, G (1954) The historical background of modern social psychology, in G Lindzey (ed) *Theoretical Models and Personality*, Cambridge MA, Addison-Wesley

Bandura, A and Cervone, D (1983) Self-evaluation and self-efficacy mechanisms governing the motivational effects of goal systems, *Journal of Personality and Social Psychology*, 45 (5), pp 1017–28

Behling, O and Starke, F A (1973) The postulates of expectancy theory, *Academy of Management Journal*, 16 (3), pp 375–88

Carrell, M R and Dittrich, J E (1978) Equity theory: the recent literature, methodological considerations and new directions, *Academy of Management Review*, 3 (2), pp 202–10

Connolly, T (1976) Some contested and methodological issues in expectancy models of work performance motivation, *Academy of Management Review*, 1 (4), pp 32–47

Gerhart, B and Rynes, S L (2003) *Compensation: Theory, evidence and strategic implications*, Thousand Oaks CA, Sage

Harackiewicz, J M, Barron, P R, Pintrich, P R, Elliot, A J and Thrash, T M (2002) Revision of goal theory: necessary and illuminating, *Journal of Educational Psychology*, 94 (3), pp 638–45

Herzberg, F W, Mausner, B and Snyderman, B (1957) *The Motivation to Work*, New York, Wiley

Herzberg, F (1968) One more time: how do you motivate employees?, *Harvard Business Review*, January–February, pp 109–20

House, R J, Shapiro, H J and Wahba, M A (1974) Expectancy theory as a predictor of work behaviour and attitude: a re-evaluation of empirical evidence, *Decision Science*, 5 (3), pp 481–506

Hull, C (1951) *Essentials of Behavior*, New Haven CT, Yale University Press

Hunter, J E, Schmidt, F L and Judiesch, M K (1990) Individual differences in output variability as a function of job complexity, *Journal of Applied Psychology*, 75 (1), pp 28–42

Huseman, R C, Hatfield, J D and Milis, E W (1982) A new perception on equity theory: the equity sensitivity constant, *Academy of Management Review*, **12** (2), pp 222–34

Latham, G and Locke, R (1979) Goal setting – a motivational technique that works, *Organizational Dynamics*, Autumn, pp 68–80

Lawler, E E (1988) Pay for performance: making it work, *Personnel*, October, pp 25–29

Maslow, A (1954) *Motivation and Personality*, New York, Harper & Row

Opsahl, R C and Dunnette, M D (1966) The role of financial compensation in individual motivation, *Psychological Bulletin*, **56**, pp 94–118

Pintrich, P R (2000) An achievement goal perspective on issues in motivation technology, theory and research, *Contemporary Educational Psychology*, **25**, pp 92–104

Porter, L W and Lawler, E E (1968) *Managerial Attitudes and Performance*, Homewood IL, Irwin-Dorsey

Reinharth, L and Wahba, M A (1975) Expectancy theory as a predictor of work motivation, effort expenditure and job performance, *Academy of Management Journal*, **18** (3), pp 520–37

Rousseau, D M (2006) Is there such a thing as evidence-based management?, *Academy of Management Review*, **31** (2), pp 256–69

Taylor, F W (1911) *Principles of Scientific Management*, New York, Harper

Vroom, V (1964) *Work and Motivation*, New York, Wiley

Wahba, M A and Bridwell, L G (1979) Maslow reconsidered: a review of research on the need hierarchy theory, in R M Sters and L W Porter (eds) *Motivation and Work Behavior*, New York, McGraw Hill

Questions

1 What is motivation?
2 What is the difference between extrinsic and intrinsic motivation?
3 What is instrumentality?
4 What is reinforcement?
5 What is content or needs theory?
6 How valid is Maslow's concept of the hierarchy of human needs?
7 How valid is Herzberg's two-factor theory of motivation?
8 What is expectancy theory?
9 What is goal theory?
10 What is equity theory?
11 Which motivation theory provides the best guide on the principles of performance-related pay and why?
12 What message for HR policy is provided by the belief that motivation is a highly complex process?
13 Why is recognition so important as a means of motivation?
14 Why are there limitations in the power of money to motivate?
15 Why is intrinsic motivation through the work itself likely to be more effective in the longer term than extrinsic motivation?

Commitment

LEARNING OUTCOMES

On completing this chapter you should be able to define these key concepts. You should also understand:

- The meaning of organizational commitment
- The importance of commitment
- Commitment and engagement
- Problems with the concept of commitment
- The impact of high commitment
- Factors affecting commitment
- Developing a commitment strategy

Introduction

Commitment represents the strength of an individual's identification with, and involvement in, a particular organization. It is a concept which has played an important part in HRM philosophy. As Guest (1987: 503) suggested, HRM policies are designed to 'maximize organizational integration, employee commitment, flexibility and quality of work'. Beer et al (1984: 20) identified commitment in their concept of human resource management as a key dimension because it 'can result not only in more loyalty and better performance for the organization, but also in self-worth, dignity, psychological involvement, and identity for the individual'.

The meaning of organizational commitment

Commitment refers to attachment and loyalty. It is associated with the feelings of individuals about their organization. The three characteristics of commitment identified by Mowday et al (1982) are:

- a strong desire to remain a member of the organization;
- a strong belief in and acceptance of the values and goals of the organization;
- a readiness to exert considerable effort on behalf of the organization.

Appelbaum et al (2000: 183) rephrased this definition as: 'Organizational commitment is a multidimensional construct that reflects a worker's identification with the organization (loyalty), attachment to the organization (intention to stay), and willingness to expand effort on the organization's behalf (discretionary effort).'

An alternative, although closely related, definition of commitment emphasizes the importance of behaviour in creating commitment. Three features of behaviour are important in binding individuals to their acts: the visibility of the acts, the extent to which the outcomes are irrevocable, and the degree to which the person undertakes the action voluntarily. Commitment, according to Salancik (1977) can be increased and harnessed to obtain support for organizational ends and interests through such ploys as participation in decisions about actions.

The importance of commitment

The importance of commitment was highlighted by Walton (1985b). His theme was that improved performance would result if the organization moved away from the traditional control-orientated approach to workforce management, which relies upon establishing order, exercising control and achieving efficiency. He proposed that this approach should be replaced by a commitment strategy which would enable workers to respond best – and most creatively – not when they are tightly controlled by management, placed in narrowly defined jobs, and treated like an unwelcome necessity, but, instead, when they are given broader responsibilities, encouraged to contribute and helped to achieve satisfaction in their work. He described the commitment-based approach as follows (ibid: 79):

> Jobs are designed to be broader than before, to combine planning and implementation, and to include efforts to upgrade operations, not just to maintain them. Individual responsibilities are expected to change as conditions

change, and teams, not individuals, often are the organizational units accountable for performance. With management hierarchies relatively flat and differences in status minimized, control and lateral coordination depend on shared goals. And expertise rather than formal position determines influence.

Expressed like this, a commitment strategy sounds idealistic ('the American dream' as Guest, 1990, put it) but does not appear to be a crude attempt to manipulate people to accept management's values and goals, as some have suggested. In fact, Walton did not describe it as being instrumental in this manner. His prescription was for a broad HRM approach to the ways in which people are treated, jobs are designed and organizations are managed. He believed that the aim should be to develop 'mutuality', a state that exists when management and employees are interdependent and both benefit from this interdependency. The importance of mutuality (the belief that management and employees share the same concerns and it is therefore in both their interests to work together) and its relationship to commitment was spelt out by Walton (1985a: 64) as follows. The new HRM model is composed of policies that promote mutuality – mutual goals, mutual influence, mutual respect, mutual rewards, mutual responsibility. The theory is that policies of mutuality will elicit commitment which in turn will yield both better economic performance and greater human development.

But a review by Guest (1991) of the mainly North American literature reinforced by the limited UK research available led him to the conclusion that: 'High organizational commitment is associated with lower labour turnover and absence, but there is no clear link to performance.' Swailes (2002: 164) confirmed that: 'Despite the best efforts of researchers ... the evidence for a strong positive link between commitment and performance remains patchy.'

It is probably unwise to expect too much from commitment as a means of making a direct and immediate impact on performance. It is not the same as motivation. It is possible to be dissatisfied with a particular feature of a job while retaining a reasonably high level of commitment to the organization as a whole. But it is reasonable to believe that strong commitment to work may result in conscientious and self-directed application to do the job, regular attendance, the need for less supervision, and a high level of discretionary effort. Commitment to the organization will certainly be related to the intention to stay with the organization.

Commitment and engagement

The notion of commitment as described above appears to be very similar, if not identical, to that of organizational engagement, which, as described in Chapter 9, focuses on attachment to or identification with the organization as a whole. Are there any differences?

Some commentators have asserted that there is a difference by referring to commitment as a distinct although closely linked entity. As cited by Buchanan (2004: 19), the US Corporate Executive Board divides engagement into two aspects of commitment: (1) rational commitment, which occurs when a job serves employees' financial, developmental, or professional self-interest; and (2) emotional commitment, which arises when workers value, enjoy and believe in what they do, and which has four times the power of its more pragmatic counterpart to affect performance. The Corporate Executive Board (2004: 1) indicated that engagement is 'the extent to which employees commit to someone or something in their organization, how hard they work, and how long they stay as a result of that commitment'. Wellins and Concelman (2005: 1) suggested that 'to be engaged is to be actively committed'. And Macey and Schneider (2008: 8–9) observed that:

> Organizational commitment is an important facet of the state of engagement when it is conceptualized as positive attachment to the larger organizational entity and measured as a willingness to exert energy in support of the organization, to feel pride as an organizational member, and to have personal identification with the organization.

Clearly, organizational engagement and commitment are closely associated, and commitment was included by the Institute for Employment Studies in their model (Chapter 9, Figure 9.1) as an element of engagement. Appelbaum et al (2000: 183) noted that: 'The willingness to exert extra effort is the aspect of organizational commitment that has been shown to be most closely related to an employee's job performance.' Robinson et al (2004: 7) suggested that the closest relationship of commitment to engagement was 'affective commitment, ie the satisfaction people get from their jobs and their colleagues and their willingness to go beyond the call of duty for the sake of the organization'. Salanova et al (2005) saw commitment as part of engagement but not equivalent to it.

The analysis of the concept of commitment as undertaken in this chapter is based on a considerable body of work exploring its nature and significance and therefore helps to illuminate the somewhat elusive notion of engagement. But there are problems with commitment, as discussed below.

Problems with the concept of commitment

A number of commentators have raised questions about the concept of commitment. These relate to three main problem areas: (1) the imprecise nature of the term; (2) its unitary frame of reference; and (3) commitment as an inhibitor of flexibility.

The imprecise nature of the term

Guest (1987: 513) raised the question of what commitment really means:

> The case for seeking high commitment among employees seems plausible but the burgeoning research on the topic has identified a number of problems. One of

these concerns the definition of the concept. The first issue is – commitment to what? Most writers are interested in commitment to the organization, but others have examined career commitment and job commitment. Once the general concept of commitment is utilized, then union commitment, workgroup commitment and family commitment should also be considered. The possibility of multiple and perhaps competing commitments creates a more complex set of issues.

Unitary frame of reference

The concept of commitment, especially as put forward by Walton, can be criticized as being simplistic, even misguided, in adopting a unitary frame of reference which assumes that organizations consist of people with shared interests. It has been suggested by people like Cyert and March (1963), Mangham (1979) and Mintzberg (1983) that an organization is really a coalition of interest groups where political processes are an inevitable part of everyday life.

Legge (1989: 38) also raises this question in her discussion of strong culture as a key requirement of HRM, which she criticized because it is said to function through 'a shared set of managerially sanctioned values… that assumes an identification of employee and employer interests'.

As Coopey and Hartley (1991: 20) put it: 'Commitment is not an all-or-nothing affair (though many managers might like it to be) but a question of multiple or competing commitments for the individual.' A pluralist perspective recognizes the legitimacy of different interests and is more realistic.

It could be argued that values concerned with performance, quality, service, equal opportunity and innovation are not necessarily wrong because they are managerial values. But pursuing a value such as innovation could work against the interests of employees by, for example, resulting in redundancies. And flexibility may sound a good idea but beyond the rhetoric, as Sisson (1994: 5) observed, the reality may mean that management can do what it wants. It would be quite reasonable for any employee encouraged to behave in accordance with a value supported by management to ask 'What's in it for me?' It can also be argued that the imposition from above of management's values on employees without their having any part to play in discussing and agreeing them is a form of coercion.

Commitment and flexibility

It was pointed out by Coopey and Hartley (1991: 21) that: 'The problem for a unitarist notion of organizational commitment is that it fosters a conformist approach which not only fails to reflect organizational reality, but can be narrowing and limiting for the organization.' They argued that if employees are expected and encouraged to commit themselves tightly to a single set of values and goals they will not be able to cope with the ambiguities and uncertainties which are endemic in organizational life in times of change. Conformity to 'imposed' values will inhibit creative problem solving, and high commitment to present courses of action will increase both resistance to change and the stress which invariably occurs when change takes place.

If commitment is related to tightly defined plans then this will become a real problem. To avoid it, the emphasis should be on overall strategic directions. These would be communicated to employees with the proviso that changing circumstances will require their amendment. In the meantime, however, everyone can at least be informed in general terms where the organization is heading and, more specifically, the part they are expected to play in helping the organization to get there. And if they can be involved in the decision-making processes on matters that affect them (which include management's values for performance, quality and customer service), so much the better.

Values need not necessarily be restrictive. They can be defined in ways which allow for freedom of choice within broad guidelines. In fact, the values themselves can refer to such processes as flexibility, innovation and responsiveness to change. Thus, far from inhibiting creative problem solving, they can encourage it. But they will not do so if they are imposed from above. Employees need to have a say in defining the values they are expected to support.

Factors affecting commitment

Kochan and Dyer (1993) indicated that the factors affecting the level of commitment in what they call mutual-commitment firms are as follows:

- strategic level: supportive business strategies, top management value commitment and effective voice for HR in strategy making and governance;
- functional (human resource policy) level: staffing based on employment stabilization, investment in training and development and contingent compensation that reinforces cooperation, participation and contribution;
- workplace level: selection based on high standards, broad task design and teamwork, employee involvement in problem solving and a climate of cooperation and trust.

The research conducted by Purcell et al (2003) identified the following key policy and practice factors that influence levels of commitment:

- received training last year;
- satisfied with career opportunities;
- satisfied with the performance appraisal system;
- think managers are good in people management (leadership);
- find their work challenging;
- think their firm helps them achieve a work–life balance;
- satisfied with communication or company performance.

Developing a commitment strategy

A commitment strategy can be based on the high-commitment model incorporating policies and practices in areas of HR such as job design, learning and development, career planning, performance management, reward management, participation, communication and employee well-being.

HR should play a major part in developing a high-commitment organization. The ten steps it can take are:

- Advise on methods of communicating the values and aims of management and the achievements of the organization so that employees are more likely to identify with it as one they are proud to work for.

- Emphasize to management that commitment is a two-way process; employees cannot be expected to be committed to the organization unless management demonstrates that it is committed to them and recognizes their contribution as stakeholders.

- Impress on management the need to develop a climate of trust by being honest with people, treating them fairly, justly and consistently, keeping its word, showing willingness to listen to the comments and suggestions made by employees during processes of consultation and participation.

- Develop a positive psychological contract (the set of reciprocal but unwritten expectations which exist between individual employees and their employers) by treating people as stakeholders, relying on consensus and cooperation rather than control and coercion and focusing on the provision of opportunities for learning, development and career progression.

- Advise on the establishment of partnership agreements with trade unions which emphasize unity of purpose, common approaches to working together and the importance of giving employees a voice in matters that concern them.

- Recommend and take part in the achievement of single status for all employees (often included in a partnership agreement) so that there is no longer an 'us and them' culture.

- Encourage management to declare a policy of employment security and ensure that steps are taken to avoid involuntary redundancies.

- Develop performance management processes which provide for the alignment of organizational and individual objectives.

- Advise on means of increasing employee identification with the company through rewards related to organizational performance (profit sharing or gainsharing) or employee share ownership schemes.

- Enhance employee job engagement (ie identification of employees with the job they are doing) through job design processes which aim to create higher levels of job satisfaction (job enrichment).

KEY LEARNING POINTS

The meaning of commitment

Commitment refers to attachment and loyalty. It is associated with the feelings of individuals about their organization.

The three characteristics of commitment identified by Mowday et al (1982) are:

- a strong desire to remain a member of the organization;
- a strong belief in and acceptance of the values and goals of the organization;
- a readiness to exert considerable effort on behalf of the organization.

The impact of high commitment

In his seminal *Harvard Business Review* article 'From Control to Commitment', Richard Walton (1985b) stated that 'eliciting employee commitment will lead to enhanced performance, the evidence shows this belief to be well founded'.

The importance of commitment was highlighted by Walton. His theme was that improved performance would result if the organization moved away from the traditional control-orientated approach to workforce management, which relies upon establishing order, exercising control and achieving efficiency. He proposed that this approach should be replaced by a commitment strategy.

Problems with the concept of commitment

There are four main problem areas: (1) the imprecise nature of the term, (2) its unitary frame of reference, (3) commitment as an inhibitor of flexibility, and (4) the extent to which high commitment does in practice result in improved organizational performance.

Engagement and commitment

Organizational engagement and commitment are closely associated.

Commitment was included by the Institute for Employment Studies in their model as an element of engagement.

But commitment is a somewhat wider concept in that it is concerned with both job engagement and organizational engagement.

The factors affecting the level of commitment (Kochan and Dyer,1993)

- strategic level: supportive business strategies, top management value commitment and effective voice for HR in strategy making and governance;
- functional (human resource policy) level: staffing based on employment stabilization, investment in training and development and contingent compensation that reinforces cooperation, participation and contribution;
- workplace level: selection based on high standards, broad task design and teamwork, employee involvement in problem solving and a climate of cooperation and trust.

HR's role in enhancing commitment

HR should play a major part in developing a high-commitment organization. The 10 steps it can take are:

- Advise on methods of communicating the values and aims of management.
- Emphasize to management that commitment is a two-way process.
- Impress on management the need to develop a climate of trust.
- Develop a positive psychological contract.
- Advise on the establishment of partnership agreements with trade unions.
- Recommend and take part in the achievement of single status for all employees.
- Encourage management to declare a policy of employment security.
- Develop performance management processes.
- Advise on means of increasing employee identification with the company.
- Enhance employee job engagement through job design processes.

References

Appelbaum, E, Bailey, T, Berg, P and Kalleberg, A L (2000) *Manufacturing Advantage: Why high-performance work systems pay off*, Ithaca NY, ILR Press

Beer M, Spector B, Lawrence P, Quinn Mills, D and Walton, R (1984) *Managing Human Assets*, New York, The Free Press

Buchanan, L (2004) The things they do for love, *Harvard Business Review*, December, pp 19–20

Coopey, J and Hartley, J (1991) Reconsidering the case for organizational commitment, *Human Resource Management Journal*, 1 (3), pp 18–31

Corporate Executive Board (2004) *Driving Performance and Retention Through Employee Engagement*, www.corporateleadershipcouncil.com/Images/CLC/PDF/CLC12KADBP.pdf (accessed 13 September 2005)

Cyert, R M and March, J G (1963) *A Behavioural Theory of the Firm*, Englewood Cliffs NJ, Prentice-Hall

Guest, D E (1987) Human resource management and industrial relations, *Journal of Management Studies*, 24 (5), pp 503–21

Guest, D E (1990) HRM and the American Dream, *Journal of Management Studies*, 27 (4), pp 377–97

Guest, D E (1991) Personnel management: the end of orthodoxy, *British Journal of Industrial Relations*, 29 (2), pp 149–76

Kochan, T A and Dyer, L (1993) Managing transformational change: the role of human resource professionals, *International Journal of Human Resource Management*, 4 (3), pp 569–90

Legge, K (1989) Human resource management: a critical analysis, in J Storey (ed) *New Perspectives in Human Resource Management*, London, Routledge, pp 19–40

Macey, W H and Schneider, B (2008) The Meaning of Employee Engagement, Industrial and Organizational Psychology, 1, pp 3–30

Mangham, L L (1979) *The Politics of Organizational Change*, London, Associated Business Press

Mintzberg, H (1983) *Power in and around Organizations*, Prentice-Hall, Englewood Cliffs, NJ

Mowday, R, Porter, L and Steers, R (1982) *Employee–Organization Linkages: The psychology of commitment, absenteeism and turnover*, London, Academic Press

Purcell, J, Kinnie, N, Hutchinson, S, Rayton, B and Swart, J (2003) *Understanding the People and Performance Link: Unlocking the black box*, London, CIPD

Robinson, D, Perryman, S and Hayday, S (2004) *The Drivers of Employee Engagement*, Brighton, Institute for Employment Studies

Salancik, G R (1977) Commitment and the control of organizational behaviour and belief, in B M Staw and G R Salancik (eds) *New Directions in Organizational Behavior*, Chicago, St Clair Press

Salanova, M, Agut, S and Peiro, J M (2005) Linking organizational resources and work engagement to employee performance and customer loyalty: The mediation of service climate, *Journal of Applied Psychology*, **90**, pp 1217–27

Sisson, K (1994) Personnel management: paradigms, practice and prospects, in K Sisson (ed) *Personnel Management*, 2nd edn, Oxford, Blackwell, pp 3–50

Swailes, S (2002) Organizational commitment; a critique of the construct and measures, *International Journal of Management Reviews*, **4** (2), pp 155–78

Walton, R E (1985a) Towards a strategy of eliciting employee commitment based on principles of mutuality, in R E Walton and P R Lawrence (eds) *HRM Trends and Challenges*, Boston MA, Harvard Business School Press, pp 35–65

Walton, R E (1985b) From control to commitment in the workplace, *Harvard Business Review*, March–April, pp 77–84

Wellins, R and Concelman, J (2005) Personal engagement: Driving growth at the see-level, www.ddiworld.com/pdf/ddipersonalengagement.ar.pdf (accessed 29 April 2005)

Questions

1 What is commitment?

2 What is mutuality?

3 What are the three characteristics of commitment?

4 Why is commitment important?

5 What impact can high levels of commitment have on performance?

6 What is the relationship between commitment and engagement?

7 What did the research conducted by Purcell et al (2003) tell us about the factors affecting commitment?

8 Is a belief in the virtues of commitment based on an unrealistic unitary view of employment relationships?

9 Do high levels of commitment result in lack of flexibility and if so, what can be done about it?

10 What are the essential features of a commitment strategy?

Change management

LEARNING OUTCOMES

On completing this chapter you should be able to define these key concepts. You should also know about:

- Types of change
- The change process
- Change models
- Reasons for resistance to change
- Overcoming resistance to change
- Implementing change
- The role of HR in leading and facilitating change

Introduction

Change management is defined as the process of achieving the smooth implementation of change by planning and introducing it systematically, taking into account the possibility of it being resisted or at least misunderstood.

However, Kotter (1996) emphasized the importance of leading change rather than simply managing it.

As described in this chapter, to manage change it is first necessary to understand the types of change and how the process works. It is important to bear in mind that while those wanting change need to be constant about ends, they have to be flexible about means. This requires them to come to an understanding of the various models of change that have been developed and of the factors that create resistance to change and how to minimize such resistance. In the light of an understanding of these models and the phenomenon of resistance to change they will be better equipped to make use of the guidelines for change set out in this chapter. The role of HR in leading and managing change is examined in the penultimate section of the chapter and the chapter ends with a set of guidelines.

Types of change

There are three types of change: transformational, strategic and operational.

Transformational change

Transformational change, sometimes referred to as gamma change, takes place when there are fundamental and comprehensive changes in structures, processes and behaviours which have a dramatic effect on the ways in which the organization functions.

Strategic change

Strategic change is concerned with broad, long-term and organization-wide issues involving change. It is about moving to a future state which has been defined generally in terms of strategic vision and scope. It will cover the purpose and mission of the organization. It will also refer to its corporate philosophy on such matters as growth, quality, innovation and values concerning employees and customers, competitive positioning and strategic goals for achieving and maintaining competitive advantage and for product–market development. These goals are supported by policies concerning marketing, sales, manufacturing, product and process development, finance and human resource management.

Strategic change takes place within the context of the external competitive, economic and social environment, and the organization's internal resources, capabilities, culture, structure and systems. Its successful implementation requires thorough analysis and understanding of these factors in the formulation and planning stages.

However, strategic change should not be treated simplistically as a linear process of getting from A to B which can be planned and executed as a logical sequence of events. Pettigrew and Whipp (1991: 31) issued the following warning based on their research into competitiveness and managing change in the motor, financial services, insurance and publishing industries:

> The processes by which strategic changes are made seldom move directly through neat, successive stages of analysis, choice and implementation. Given the powerful internal characteristics of the firm it would be unusual if they did not affect the process: more often they transform it. Changes in the firm's environment persistently threaten the course and logic of strategic changes: dilemma abounds…. We conclude that one of the defining features of the process, in so far as management action is concerned, is ambiguity; seldom is there an easily isolated logic to strategic change. Instead, that process may derive its motive force from an amalgam of economic, personal and political imperatives. Their interaction through time requires that those responsible for managing that process make continual assessments, repeated choices and multiple adjustments.

Operational change

Operational change relates to new systems, procedures, structures or technology which will have an immediate effect on working arrangements within a part of the organization. But their impact on people can be more significant than broader strategic change and they have to be handled just as carefully.

The change process

Conceptually, the change process starts with an awareness of the need for change. An analysis of this situation and the factors that have created it leads to a diagnosis of their distinctive characteristics and an indication of the direction in which action needs to be taken. Possible courses of action can then be identified and evaluated and a choice made of the preferred action. It is then necessary to decide how to get from here to there. Managing change during this transition state is a critical phase in the change process. It is here that the problems of introducing change emerge and have to be managed. These problems can include resistance to change, instability, high levels of stress, misdirected energy, conflict, and loss of momentum. Hence the need to do everything possible to anticipate reactions and likely impediments to the introduction of change.

The final stage in which the new structure, system or process is installed can also be demanding, indeed painful. As described by Pettigrew and Whipp (1991: 27), the implementation of change is an 'iterative, cumulative and reformulation-in-use process'.

The next issue is how to 'hold the gains', ie how to ensure that the change is embedded and maintained. This means continuously monitoring the effects and impact of the change and taking corrective action where necessary to ensure that it continues to work well. The change process has been described in the various change models set out below.

Change models

Change models explain the mechanisms for change and the factors that affect its success. The best-known change models are those developed by Lewin (1951) and Beckhard (1969). But other important contributions to an understanding of the mechanisms for change have been made by Thurley (1979), Bandura (1986) and Beer et al (1990).

Lewin

The basic mechanisms for managing change as set out by Lewin (1951) are:

- Unfreezing – altering the present stable equilibrium which supports existing behaviours and attitudes. This process must take account of the inherent threats change presents to people and the need to motivate those affected to attain the natural state of equilibrium by accepting change.
- Changing – developing new responses based on new information.
- Refreezing – stabilizing the change by introducing the new responses into the personalities of those concerned.

Lewin also suggested the following methodology for analysing change which he called 'field force analysis':

- Analyse the restraining or driving forces which will affect the transition to the future state – these restraining forces will include the reactions of those who see change as unnecessary or as constituting a threat.
- Assess which of the driving or restraining forces are critical.
- Take steps both to increase the critical driving forces and to decrease the critical restraining forces.

Beckhard

Beckhard (1969) proposed that a change programme should incorporate the following processes:

- Set goals and define the future state or organizational conditions desired after the change.
- Diagnose the present condition in relation to these goals.
- Define the transition state activities and commitments required to meet the future state.
- Develop strategies and action plans for managing this transition in the light of an analysis of the factors likely to affect the introduction of change.

Thurley

Keith Thurley (1979) described the following five approaches to managing change:

- Directive – the imposition of change in crisis situations or when other methods have failed. This is done by the exercise of managerial power without consultation.
- Bargained – this approach recognizes that power is shared between the employer and the employed and change requires negotiation, compromise and agreement before being implemented.
- 'Hearts and minds' – an all-embracing thrust to change the attitudes, values and beliefs of the whole workforce. This 'normative' approach (ie one which starts from a definition of what management thinks is right or 'normal') seeks 'commitment' and 'shared vision' but does not necessarily include involvement or participation.
- Analytical – a theoretical approach to the change process using models of change such as those described above. It proceeds sequentially from the analysis and diagnosis of the situation, through the setting of objectives, the design of the change process, the evaluation of the results and, finally, the determination of the objectives for the next stage in the change process. This is the rational and logical approach much favoured by consultants – external and internal. But change seldom proceeds as smoothly as this model would suggest. Emotions, power politics and external pressures mean that the rational approach, although it might be the right way to start, is difficult to sustain.
- Action based – this recognizes that the way managers behave in practice bears little resemblance to the analytical, theoretical model. The distinction between managerial thought and managerial action blurs in practice to the point of invisibility. What managers think is what they do. Real life therefore often results in a 'Ready, aim, fire' approach to change management. This typical approach to change starts with a broad belief that some sort of problem exists, although it may not be well defined. The identification of possible solutions, often on a trial or error basis, leads to a clarification of the nature of the problem and a shared understanding of a possible optimal solution, or at least a framework within which solutions can be discovered.

Bandura

The ways in which people change was described by Bandura (1986). He suggested that people make conscious choices about their behaviours. The information people use to make their choices comes from their environment and their choices are based upon the things that are important to them, the views they have about their own abilities to behave in certain ways and the consequences they think will accrue to whatever behaviour they decide to engage in.

For those concerned in change management, the implications of Bandura's concept of change (which is linked to expectancy theory; see Chapter 10) are that:

- the tighter the link between a particular behaviour and a particular outcome, the more likely it is that we will engage in that behaviour;
- the more desirable the outcome, the more likely it is that we will engage in behaviour that we believe will lead to it;
- the more confident we are that we can actually assume a new behaviour, the more likely we are to try it.

To change people's behaviour, therefore, we have first to change the environment within which they work; secondly, convince them that the new behaviour is something they can accomplish (training is important); and, thirdly, persuade them that it will lead to an outcome that they will value. None of these steps is easy.

Beer, Eisenstat and Spector

Michael Beer (1990) and his colleagues suggested in a seminal *Harvard Business Review* article, 'Why change programs don't produce change', that most such programmes are guided by a theory of change which is fundamentally flawed. This theory states that changes in attitudes lead to changes in behaviour. 'According to this model, change is like a conversion experience. Once people get religion, changes in their behaviour will surely follow.' They thought that this theory gets the change process exactly backwards and made the following comment on it (ibid: 159):

> In fact, individual behaviour is powerfully shaped by the organizational roles people play. The most effective way to change behaviour, therefore, is to put people into a new organizational context, which imposes new roles, responsibilities and relationships on them. This creates a situation that in a sense 'forces' new attitudes and behaviour on people.

They prescribe six steps to effective change which concentrate on what they call 'task alignment' – reorganizing employee's roles, responsibilities and relationships to solve specific business problems in small units where goals and tasks can be clearly defined. The aim of following the overlapping steps is to build a self-reinforcing cycle of commitment, coordination and competence:

- Mobilize commitment to change through the joint analysis of problems.

- Develop a shared vision of how to organize and manage to achieve goals such as competitiveness.
- Foster consensus for the new vision, competence to enact it, and cohesion to move it along.
- Spread revitalization to all departments without pushing it from the top – don't force the issue, let each department find its own way to the new organization.
- Institutionalize revitalization through formal policies, systems and structures.
- Monitor and adjust strategies in response to problems in the revitalization process.

Resistance to change

People resist change because it is seen as a threat to familiar patterns of behaviour as well as to status and financial rewards. Joan Woodward (1968: 80) made this point clearly:

> When we talk about resistance to change we tend to imply that management is always rational in changing its direction, and that employees are stupid, emotional or irrational in not responding in the way they should. But if an individual is going to be worse off, explicitly or implicitly, when the proposed changes have been made, any resistance is entirely rational in terms of his own best interest. The interests of the organization and the individual do not always coincide.

Hamlin and Davies (2001: 58) commented that: 'Any change creates stress and anxiety; this is because as human beings we deal individually with uncertainty in different ways.'

However, some people will welcome change as an opportunity. These need to be identified and where feasible they can be used to help in the introduction of change as change agents.

Reasons for resisting change

Specifically, the reasons for resisting change are:

- The shock of the new – people are suspicious of anything which they perceive will upset their established routines, methods of working or conditions of employment. They do not want to lose the security of what is familiar to them. They may not believe statements by management that the change is for their benefit as well as that of the organization; sometimes with good reason. They may feel that management has ulterior motives and sometimes, the louder the protestations of managements, the less they will be believed.

- Economic fears – loss of money, threats to job security.
- Inconvenience – the change will make life more difficult.
- Uncertainty – change can be worrying because of uncertainty about its likely impact.
- Symbolic fears – a small change which may affect some treasured symbol, such as a separate office or a reserved parking space, may symbolize big ones, especially when employees are uncertain about how extensive the programme of change will be.
- Threat to interpersonal relationships – anything that disrupts the customary social relationships and standards of the group will be resisted.
- Threat to status or skill – the change is perceived as reducing the status of individuals or as de-skilling them.
- Competence fears – concern about the ability to cope with new demands or to acquire new skills.

Overcoming resistance to change

Resistance to change can be difficult to overcome even when it is not detrimental to those concerned. But the attempt must be made. The starting point is an analysis of the potential impact of change by considering how it will affect people in their jobs. The reasons for resisting change set out above can be used as a checklist to establish where there might be problems, generally, with groups or with individuals.

The analysis should indicate what aspects of the proposed change may be supported generally or by specified individuals and which aspects may be resisted. So far as possible, the potentially hostile or negative reactions of people and the reasons for them should be identified. It is necessary to try and understand the likely feelings and fears of those affected so that unnecessary worries can be relieved and, as far as possible, ambiguities can be resolved. In making this analysis, the individual introducing the change – the change agent – should recognize that new ideas are likely to be suspect and should make ample provision for the discussion of reactions to proposals to ensure complete understanding of them.

Involvement in the change process gives people the chance to raise and resolve their concerns and make suggestions about the form of the change and how it should be introduced. The aim is to get 'ownership' – a feeling amongst people that the change is something that they are happy to live with because they have been involved in its planning and introduction – it has become their change.

A communication strategy to explain the proposed change should be prepared and implemented so that unnecessary fears are allayed. All the available channels as should be used but face-to-face communications direct from managers to individuals or through a team briefing system are best.

Implementing change

The problems of implementing strategic change were summed up by Lawler and Mohrman (2003: 24) as follows:

> Most strategies, like most mergers, fail not because of poor thinking, but because of poor implementation. Implementation failures usually involve the failure to acknowledge and build the needed skills and organizational capabilities, to gain support of the workforce, and to support the organizational changes and learning required to behave in new ways. In short, execution failures are often the result of poor human capital management. This opens the door for HR to add important value if it can deliver change strategies, plans, and thinking that aid in the development and execution of business strategy.

Implementing change can indeed be difficult. Research by Carnall (1991) in 93 organizations identified the following explanations for failures to implement change effectively:

- Implementation took more time than was originally allowed.
- Major problems emerged during implementation which had not been identified beforehand.
- Coordination of implementation activities was not effective enough.
- Competing activities and other crises distracted management from implementing the change decision.
- The capabilities of the employees involved were not sufficient.
- Training and instruction to lower level employees was inadequate.
- Uncontrollable factors in the external environment had an adverse effect on implementation.

The following suggestions on how to minimize such problems were produced by Nadler and Tushman (1980):

- Motivate in order to achieve changes in behaviour by individuals.
- Manage the transition by making organizational arrangements designed to assure that control is maintained during and after the transition and by developing and communicating a clear image of the future.
- Shape the political dynamics of change so that power centres develop that support the change rather than block it.
- Build in stability of structures and processes to serve as anchors for people to hold on to – organizations and individuals can only stand so much uncertainty and turbulence, hence the emphasis by Quinn (1980) on the need for an incremental approach.

The role of change agents

The change process will take place more smoothly with the help of credible internal or external change agents — people who help to manage change by providing advice and support on its introduction and management. A change agent was defined by Caldwell (2003: 139–40) as 'an internal or external individual or team responsible for initiating, sponsoring, managing and implementing a specific change initiative or complete change programme'. As described by Balogun and Hope-Hailey (2004), the role of the change agent is to lead change. Alfes et al (2010) noted that change agents establish what is required, involve people in planning and managing change, advise on how change should be implemented and communicate to people the implications of change.

Keep (2001: 89) listed the following change agent competencies:

- project management – planning and resource allocation;
- contracting with clients – defining the task, establishing relationships;
- team building – defining roles, maintaining good working relationships;
- analysis and diagnosis – data collection, problem solving, systems thinking;
- data utilization – qualitative or quantitative data, paper-based review, survey techniques;
- interpersonal skills – dealing with people, leadership;
- communication skills – speaking, written presentations/reports, listening;
- political awareness – sensitivity, influencing;
- intervention implementation – participation, involvement;
- monitoring and evaluation – criteria setting and reviewing, measuring effectiveness;
- technical skills – financial interpretation, psychometrics;
- process skills – facilitation;
- insight – reflection, awareness of key issues, critical thinking, intuition.

It is often assumed that only people from outside the organization can take on the change agent role because they are independent and do not 'carry any baggage'. They can be useful but people from within the firm who are respected and credible can do the job well. This is often the role of HR specialists but the use of line managers adds extra value.

The role of HR in leading and facilitating change

Leading and facilitating change are two of the key roles of HR professionals. In practice, they are probably the most demanding of all HR roles. If HR is concerned – as it should be – in playing a major part in the achievement of continuous improvement in organizational capability and individual perform- ance and in the HR processes that support that improvement, then it will need to be involved in facilitating change. Caldwell (2001) stated that the change agent roles that can be carried out by HR professionals are those of change champions, change adapters, change consultants and change synergists.

Leading change

Leading change involves initiating and managing culture change (the process of changing the organization's culture in the shape of its values, norms and beliefs) and the introduction of new structures, systems, working practices and people management processes. The aim is to increase organizational capability (the ability of the organization to perform well) and organiza- tional effectiveness (how well the organization performs).

Ulrich (1997: 7) observed that HR professionals should be 'as explicit about culture change as they are today about the requirements for a suc- cessful training program or hiring strategy'. He later emphasized that 'HR should become an agent of continuous transformation, shaping processes and a culture that together improve an organization's capacity for change' (Ulrich, 1998: 125).

Change leadership means:

- identifying where change is required;
- specifying what changes should take place;
- assessing the benefits of the change and what it will cost;
- establishing the consequences of the change;
- assessing any problems the change may create, eg resistance to the change, and any risks involved;
- persuading management and anyone else affected by the change that it is necessary; spelling out the benefits and indicating what will be done to deal with potential problems;
- planning how the change should be implemented; this includes nominating and briefing change agents (people responsible for achieving change); minimizing potential resistance through communication and involvement, and managing risks;
- facilitating the introduction and management of the change;
- ensuring that the change is embedded successfully – 'holding the gains'.

Facilitating change

Change management is largely about facilitation. As Hamlin and Davies (2001: 13) observed, one of the major challenges facing HR 'is how to help people through the transitions of change, and how to survive in working conditions that are in a constant state of flux'. Brown and Eisenhardt (1997: 21) noted that managers who were successful in the art of continuous change 'carefully managed the transition between the past and the future. Much like the pit stop in a car race or the baton pass in track, this transition appeared critical.'

The role of HR in facilitating change was described by Vere and Butler (2007: 34) as follows:

- The issue needs to be on the strategic business agenda and managers must see how action will improve business results: that is, there needs to be a sound business case for the initiative. HR managers need to be able to demonstrate the return on the planned investment.

- The change needs to have the active backing of those at the top of the organization, so it is for the HR director to gain the commitment of the top team and engage them in a practical way in taking the work forward.

- HR needs to engage managers in the design of change from the outset or, if this is a business-driven change, HR needs to be involved at the outset.

- The programme needs to be framed in the language of the business to have real meaning and achieve buy-in from all parties; if there is too much HR jargon, this will be a turn off.

- Project and people management skills are crucial to ensure the programme is well planned and resourced and risks are assessed and managed.

- As in all change programmes, the importance of communication is paramount to explain, engage and commit people to the programme.

- In this respect the crucial role that HR can play is to ensure that employees are fully engaged in the design and implementation of the change.

- HR needs to draw on others' experience and learning.

To do all this, Ulrich (1997: 8) pointed out that 'HR professionals need a model of change and the ability to apply the model to a specific situation.' The models as described earlier need to be understood and applied as appropriate. The other qualities required are insight – to understand the need for change – courage – to pursue change – and determination – to achieve change.

But leading and facilitating change are hard work. As Alfes et al (2010: 111) observed on the basis of their research: 'The role is generally constrained and reactive.' They also noted that: 'HR professionals may find their roles circumscribed by expectations of their role, the nature of the change process, capability and capacity' (ibid: 125).

Ulrich (1997) may emphasize that one of the key roles of HR professionals is to act as change agents, but it is a difficult role to play. Perhaps, as Thornhill et al (2000) pointed out, the main contribution HR can make is to generate and support change where a core feature is the development and alignment of HRM practices such as culture management, performance management, learning and development, reward management and employee relations.

Guidelines for change management

- The achievement of sustainable change requires strong commitment and visionary leadership from the top.
- Understanding is necessary of the culture of the organization and the levers for change which are most likely to be effective in that culture.
- Those concerned with managing change at all levels should have the temperament and leadership skills appropriate to the circumstances of the organization and its change strategies.
- Change is more likely to be successful if there is a 'burning platform' to justify it, ie a powerful and convincing reason for change.
- It is important to build a working environment which is conducive to change. Learning and development programmes can help to do this.
- It is easier to change behaviour by changing processes, structure and systems than to change attitudes or the organizational culture.
- People support what they help to create. Commitment to change is improved if those affected by change are allowed to participate as fully as possible in planning and implementing it. The aim should be to get them to 'own' the change as something they want and will be glad to live with.
- The reward system should encourage innovation and recognize success in achieving change.
- Change will always involve failure as well as success. The failures must be expected and learned from.
- Hard evidence and data on the need for change are the most powerful tools for its achievement, but establishing the need for change is easier than deciding how to satisfy it.
- There are always people in organizations who can act as champions of change. They will welcome the challenges and opportunities that change can provide. They are the ones to be chosen as change agents.
- Resistance to change is inevitable if the individuals concerned feel that they are going to be worse off – implicitly or explicitly. The inept management of change will produce that reaction.
- In an age of global competition, technological innovation, turbulence, discontinuity, even chaos, change is inevitable and necessary. The organization must do all it can to explain why change is essential and how it will affect everyone. Moreover, every effort must be made to protect the interests of those affected by change.

KEY LEARNING POINTS

Types of change

The main types are: strategic change, operational change and transformational change.

The change process

The change process starts with an awareness of the need for change. An analysis of this situation and the factors that have created it leads to a diagnosis of their distinctive characteristics and an indication of the direction in which action needs to be taken. Possible courses of action can then be identified and evaluated and a choice made of the preferred action.

Change models

The main change models are those produced by Lewin, Beckhard, Thurley, Bandura, and Beer et al.

Reasons for resistance to change

The shock of the new, economic fears, inconvenience, uncertainty, symbolic fears, threat to interpersonal relationships, threat to status or skills, competence fears.

Overcoming resistance to change

- Analyse the potential impact of change by considering how it will affect people in their jobs.
- Identify the potentially hostile or negative reactions of people.
- Make ample provision for the discussion of reactions to proposals to ensure complete understanding of them.
- Get 'ownership' – a feeling amongst people that the change is something that they are happy to live with because they have been involved in its planning and introduction.
- Prepare and implement a communication strategy to explain the proposed change.

Implementing change

Implementation failures usually involve the failure to acknowledge and build the needed skills and organizational capabilities, to gain support of the workforce, and to support the organizational changes and learning required to behave in new ways. (Lawler and Mohrman, 2003: 24)

The role of HR in leading and facilitating change

Leading and facilitating change are two of the key roles of HR professionals. In practice, they are probably the most demanding of all HR roles.

Leading change

Leading change involves initiating and managing culture change (the process of changing the organization's culture in the shape of its values, norms and beliefs) and the introduction of new structures, systems, working practices and people management processes.

Facilitating change

Change management is largely about facilitation.

References

Alfes, K, Truss, C and Gill, J (2010) The HR manager as change agent: evidence from the public sector, *Journal of Change Management*, **10** (1), pp 109–27

Balogun, J and Hope-Hailey, V (2004) *Exploring Strategic Change*, 2nd edn, London, Prentice Hall

Bandura, A (1986) *Social Boundaries of Thought and Action*, Englewood Cliffs NJ, Prentice Hall

Beckhard, R (1969) *Organization Development: Strategy and Models*, Reading MA, Addison-Wesley

Beer, M, Eisenstat, R and Spector, B (1990) Why change programs don't produce change, *Harvard Business Review*, November–December, pp 158–66

Brown, S L and Eisenhardt, K M (1997) The art of continuous change: linking complexity theory and time-paced evolution in relentlessly shifting organizations, *Administrative Science Quarterly*, **42** (1), pp 1–24

Caldwell, R (2001) Champions, adapters, consultants and synergists: the new change agents in HRM, *Human Resource Management Journal*, **11** (3), pp 39–52

Caldwell, R (2003) Models of change agency: a fourfold classification, *British Journal of Management*, **14** (2), pp 131–42

Carnall, C (1991) *Managing Change*, London, Routledge

Cummins, T G and Worley, C G (2009) *Organization Development and Change*, 9th edn, Mason OH, South Western

Hamlin, B and Davies, G (2001) Managers, trainers and developers as change agents, in B Hamlin, J Keep and K Ash (eds) *Organizational Change and Development: A reflective guide for managers, trainers and developers*, Harlow, Pearson Education, pp 39–60

Hughes, M (2010) *Managing Change*, London, CIPD

Keep, J (2001) The change practitioner: perspectives on role, effectiveness, dilemmas and challenges, in B Hamlin, J Keep and K Ash (eds) *Organizational Change and Development: A reflective guide for managers, trainers and developers*, Harlow, Pearson Education, pp 13–38

Kotter, J J (1995) Leading change, *Harvard Business Review*, March–April, pp 59–67

Kotter, J J (1996) *Leading Change*, Boston MA, Harvard University Press

Krames, J A (2004) *The Welch Way*, New York, McGraw-Hill

Lawler, E E and Mohrman, S A (2003) HR as a strategic partner: What does it take to make it happen?, *Human Resource Planning*, **26** (3), pp 15–29

Lewin, K (1951) *Field Theory in Social Science*, New York, Harper & Row

Nadler, D A and Tushman, M L (1980) A congruence model for diagnosing organizational behavior, in R H Miles (ed) *Resource Book in Macro-organizational Behavior*, Santa Monica CA, Goodyear Publishing

Pettigrew, A and Whipp, R (1991) *Managing Change for Competitive Success*, Oxford, Blackwell

Quinn, J B (1980) Managing strategic change, *Sloane Management Review*, **11** (4/5), pp 3–30

Thornhill, A, Lewis, P, Saunders, M and Millmore, M (2000) *Managing Change: A Human Resource Strategy Approach*, Harlow, Financial Times, Prentice Hall

Thurley, K (1979) *Supervision: A reappraisal*, London, Heinemann

Ulrich, D (1997) *Human Resource Champions*, Boston MA, Harvard Business School Press

Ulrich, D (1998) A new mandate for human resources, *Harvard Business Review*, January–February, pp 124–34

Vere, D and Butler, L (2007) *Fit for Business: Transforming HR in the Public Service*, London, CIPD

Woodward, J (1968) Resistance to change, *Management International Review*, 8, pp 78–93

Questions

1 What is involved in leading change?

2 What is the role of HR in facilitating change?

3 What are the main conclusions Alfes et al (2010) came to, following their research on leading and facilitating change

4 What is change management?

5 What is transformational change?

6 What is strategic change?

7 What is operational change?

8 What is the change process?

9 What are the main problems in implementing change?

10 What is Lewin's change model?

11 What is field force analysis?

12 Why do people resist change?

13 How can resistance to change be overcome?

14 What is the role of a change agent?

15 What are the key guidelines for change management?

Flexible working 13

LEARNING OUTCOMES

On completing this chapter you should be able to define these key concepts. You should also understand:

- What flexible working means
- Why flexibility matters
- The concept of the flexible firm
- How to develop a flexibility strategy

Introduction

Flexible working is a pattern of working practice or working hours which deviates from the standard or normal arrangement. The aim is to provide for greater operational flexibility, improve the use of employees' skills and capacities, increase productivity and reduce employment costs. Flexible working has become increasingly important as a means of enhancing operational effectiveness.

Flexible working means reconsidering traditional employment patterns. This could include operational flexibility, multi-skilling, developing a 'flexible firm', the use of subcontracting and outsourcing, or introducing working arrangements such as job sharing, home working and teleworking, flexible hours, and overtime and shift working.

Forms of operational flexibility

Operational flexibility refers to flexibility in the ways in which work is carried out. The term is sometimes extended to include financial flexibility.

The three forms of operational flexibility are:

- Functional flexibility so that employees can be redeployed quickly and smoothly between activities and tasks. It may require multi-skilling – workers who possess and can apply a number of skills: for example, both mechanical and electrical engineering, or multi-tasking – workers who carry out a number of different tasks in a work team.
- Structural flexibility in a 'flexible firm', where the core of permanent employees is supplemented by a peripheral group of part-time employees, employees on short- or fixed-term contracts or subcontracted workers.
- Numerical flexibility, which is associated with structural flexibility and means that the number of employees can be quickly and easily increased or decreased in line with even short-term changes in the level of demand for labour.

Financial flexibility provides for pay levels to reflect the state of supply and demand in the external labour market and also means the use of flexible pay systems which facilitate either functional or numerical flexibility.

Multi-skilling

Multi-skilling takes place when workers acquire through experience and training a range of different skills which they can apply when carrying out different tasks (multi-tasking). This means that they can be used flexibly transferring from one task to another as the occasion demands.

A muti-skilling strategy will mean providing people with a variety of experience, through, for example, job rotation and secondments, and making arrangements for them to acquire new skills through training. It typically includes setting up flexible work teams, the members of which can be deployed on all or many of the team's tasks. A flexible employee resourcing policy can then be established which enables the organization to redeploy people rapidly to meet new demands. This implies abandoning the traditional job description which prescribes the tasks to be carried out and replacing it with a role profile which specifies the range of knowledge and skills the role holder needs.

The flexible firm

Flexibility can be enhanced by developing what has come to be known as the flexible firm: one in which there is structural and operational flexibility. The concept was originated by Doeringer and Priore (1971) but was popularized by Atkinson (1984). The latter suggested that in a flexible firm the labour force is divided into increasingly peripheral, and therefore numerically flexible, groups of workers clustered around a numerically stable core group which will conduct the organization's key, firm-specific activities. This is often called the 'core–periphery' view of the firm.

At the core, the focus is on functional flexibility. However, at the periphery, numerical flexibility becomes more important. As the market grows, the periphery expands to take up slack; as growth slows, the periphery contracts. In the core, only tasks and responsibilities change; the workers here are insulated from medium-term fluctuations in the market and can therefore enjoy a measure of job security, which does not apply to those in the periphery.

Creating the flexible firm

The first step is to identify the 'core' of permanent employees who are essential to the conduct of the organization's business. The core may include managers, team leaders, professional staff, knowledge workers and technicians and other workers with relevant key skills. Employees in this core group need to be flexible and adaptable. It may mainly consist of full-time workers but core workers could be part-time.

Having identified the core group, the next step is to make the peripheral arrangements. These can include the use of temporary workers and subcontracting work to other firms. The numbers of temporary staff can be increased or reduced to match fluctuations in the level of business activity or to cover peaks.

Outsourcing of activities such as recruitment, training and payroll administration can increase operational flexibility by allowing organizations easily to adjust the amount of work outsourced as situations change.

Critical evaluation of the flexible firm concept

The concept of the flexible firm has created a lot of interest but concerns about it have been raised by Marchington and Wilkinson (1996). First, it tends to fuse together description, prediction and prescription into a self-fulfilling prophesy. Second, the evidence of a significant increase in 'flexible firms' and flexibility within firms is lacking. Third, it is not a recent phenomenon – the proportion of people working part-time has grown for decades. And fourth, there are doubts about the costs and benefits of flexibility – subcontracted workers can be expensive and part-time workers may have higher levels of absenteeism and lack commitment.

Job sharing

This is an arrangement whereby two employees share the work of one full-time position, dividing pay and benefits between them according to the time each works. Job sharing can involve splitting days or weeks or, less frequently, working alternate weeks. The advantages of job sharing include reduced employee turnover and absenteeism because it suits the needs of individuals. Greater continuity results because if one half of the job-sharing team is ill or leaves, the sharer will continue working for at least half the time. Job sharing also means that a wider employment pool can be tapped for those who cannot work full-time but want permanent employment. The disadvantages are the administrative costs involved and the risk of responsibility being divided.

Homeworking

Home-based employees can carry out such roles as consultants, analysts or designers, programmers, or undertake various kinds of administrative work. The advantages are flexibility to respond rapidly to fluctuations in demand, reduced overheads and lower employment costs if the homeworkers are self-employed. However, care has to be taken to ensure that they are regarded as self-employed for income tax and national insurance purposes.

Teleworking

Teleworkers are people working at home with a terminal which is linked to the main company or networked with other outworkers. Its aim is to achieve greater flexibility, rapid access to skills and the retention of skilled employees who would otherwise be lost to the company. Teleworkers can be used in a number of functions such as marketing, finance and management services. The arrangement does, however, depend for its success on the involvement and education of all employees (full-time and teleworkers), the careful selection and training of teleworkers, allocating adequate resources to them and monitoring the operation of the system.

Flexible hours arrangements

Flexible hours arrangements can be included in the flexibility plan in one or more of the following ways:

- Flexible daily hours – these may follow an agreed pattern day by day according to typical or expected work loads (eg flexitime systems).

- Flexible weekly hours – providing for longer weekly hours to be worked at certain peak periods during the year.
- Flexible daily and weekly hours – varying daily or weekly hours or a combination of both to match the input of hours to achieve the required output. Such working times, unlike daily or weekly arrangements, may fluctuate between a minimum and a maximum.
- Compressed working weeks in which employees work fewer than the five standard days.
- Annual hours – scheduling employee hours on the basis of the number of hours to be worked, with provisions for the increase or reduction of hours in any given period, according to the demand for goods or services.

Overtime and shift arrangements

A flexibility plan can contain proposals to reduce overtime costs by the use of flexible hours, new shift arrangements (eg twilight shifts), time off in lieu and overtime limitation agreements. The reduction of overtime is often catered for in formal deals which include a quid pro quo in the form of increased pay for the elimination of overtime payments and the introduction of flexible work patterns.

Developing a flexibility strategy

A flexibility strategy incorporates plans for increased flexibility in the use of human resources to enable the organization to make the best use of people and adapt swiftly to changing circumstances. Developing the strategy involves:

- producing workforce plans which set out present and future people requirements;
- examining the extent to which work can be outsourced, subcontracted or carried out by part-time employees;
- considering what needs to be done to develop multi-skilling;
- reviewing all working hours arrangements to establish the scope for revising shift or overtime patterns or introducing annual hours contracts;
- identifying the scope for home or teleworking.

The role of HR and L&D

The HR and L&D functions can make a significant contribution to the development of flexible working. They can take the lead in formulating and implementing a flexibility strategy. They will be closely involved in workforce planning, outsourcing work, recruiting part-time employees, advising on the working conditions of employees of subcontractors working on the premises, developing flexible working hours arrangements, advising on the terms and conditions of employment for tele- and homeworkers and providing the training required to enhance multi-skilling.

KEY LEARNING POINTS

Flexible working defined

Flexible working is any pattern of working practice or working hours which deviates from the standard or normal arrangement. The aim is to provide for greater operational flexibility, improve the utilization of employees' skills and capacities, increase productivity and reduce employment costs.

Forms of flexible working

This means considering possible forms of operational flexibility and the scope for more flexible working based on multi-skilling, developing a 'flexible firm' by identifying and employing core and peripheral employees, including the use of subcontracting and outsourcing, and introducing more flexible working arrangements including job sharing, homeworking and teleworking, flexible hours, and overtime and shift working.

The four types of operational flexibility

These are: functional flexibility, structural flexibility, numerical flexibility and financial flexibility.

Multi-skilling

Multi-skilling takes place when workers acquire through experience and training a range of different skills which they can apply when carrying out different tasks.

The flexible firm (core and periphery workers)

Flexibility can be enhanced by developing a flexible firm in which there is structural and operational flexibility and which consists of peripheral, and therefore numerically flexible, groups of workers clustered around a numerically stable core group.

Job sharing

This involves two employees sharing the work of one full-time position, dividing pay and benefits between them according to the time each works.

Teleworking

This involves people working at home with a terminal which is linked to the main company or networked with other outworkers.

Flexible hours arrangements

Flexible hours arrangements can be included in the flexibility plan in one or more of the following ways:

- flexible daily hours;
- flexible weekly hours;
- compressed working week;
- annual hours.

Flexibility strategy

A flexibility strategy incorporates plans for increased flexibility in the use of human resources to enable the organization to make the best use of people and adapt swiftly to changing circumstances.

References

Atkinson, J (1984) Manpower strategies for flexible organizations, *Personnel Management*, August, pp 28–31

Doeringer, P and Priore, M (1971) *Internal Labour Markets and Labour Market Analysis*, Lexington DC, Heath

Marchington, M and Wilkinson, A (1996) *Core Personnel and Development*, London, IPD

Questions

1 What is flexible working?
2 What are the forms of operational flexibility?
3 What is multi-skilling?
4 What is the concept of the flexible firm?
5 What are the key features of a flexibility strategy?

PART FOUR
Management skills

Managing oneself

14

Key concepts and terms

- *The 'big five'*
- *Interactionism*
- *Personality*
- *Personality traits*
- *Personality types*
- *Reference group*

LEARNING OUTCOMES

On completing this chapter you should be able to define these key concepts. You should also know about:

- Self-awareness
- Time management
- Personal organizing skills
- Managing stress
- Professional and ethical approaches to self-management at work

Introduction

Successful managers are good at managing all the resources available to them – people, money, equipment and other facilities. But they also have to be good at managing a key resource – themselves. That is what this chapter is about. The starting points in managing yourself are an understanding of individual differences as they affect your own and other people's behaviour, and an appreciation of the meaning of personality and its dimensions in terms of individual traits and types. Against this background, this chapter reviews in succession five key aspects of managing yourself, namely: self-assessment; managing another key resource – your time, the skills you need to organize yourself and your work; managing stress – in yourself and others; the need for continuing personal development; and, finally, how to adopt a professional and ethical approach to your work.

Individual differences

The development of HR processes, the design of organizations and the ways in which people manage others are often based on the belief that everyone is the same and will behave rationally when faced with change or other demands. But the behaviour of people differs because of their characteristics and individual differences and it is not always rational. When managing yourself it is equally important to know how you fit in with other people in all their variety so that, as necessary, you can adapt your behaviour.

The management of people and working with them would be much easier if everyone were the same – but they aren't. As discussed below, they are of course, different because of variations in personal characteristics – their personality, abilities and intelligence, and the influence of their background. Gender, race or disability is also considered a factor by some people, although holding this view readily leads to discrimination.

Variations in personal characteristics,

The headings under which personal characteristics can vary have been classified by Mischel (1968) as follows.

- competencies – abilities and skills;
- constructs – the conceptual framework which governs how people perceive their environment;
- expectations – what people have learned to expect about their own and others' behaviour;
- values – what people believe to be important;
- self-regulatory plans – the goals people set themselves and the plans they make to achieve them.

These are affected by environmental or situational variables, which include the type of work individuals carry out; the culture, climate and management style in the organization; the social group within which they work; and the 'reference groups' which individuals use for comparative purposes (eg comparing conditions of work or pay between one category of employee and another).

The influence of background and culture

Individual differences may be a function of people's background, which includes the environment and culture in which they have been brought up and now exist. Levinson (1978) suggested that 'individual life structure' is shaped by three types of external event:

- the sociocultural environment;
- the roles they play and the relationships they have;
- the opportunities and constraints that enable or inhibit them to express and develop their personality.

Differences arising from gender, race or disability

It is futile, dangerous and invidious to make assumptions about inherent differences between people because of their sex, race or disability. If there are differences in behaviour at work these are likely to arise from environmental and cultural factors and not from variations in fundamental personal characteristics. The work environment undoubtedly influences feelings and behaviour for all these categories. Arnold et al (1991) referred to research which established that working women as a whole 'experienced more daily stress, marital dissatisfaction, and ageing worries, and were less likely to show overt anger than either housewives or men'. Ethnic minorities may find that the selection process is biased against them, promotion prospects are poor and that they are subject to other overt or subtle forms of discrimination. The behaviour of disabled people can also be affected by the fact that they are not given equal opportunities. There is, of course, legislation against discrimination in each of those areas but this cannot prevent the more covert forms of prejudice.

Influences on behaviour at work

Behaviour at work is dependent on both the personal characteristics of individuals as considered below and the situation in which they are working. These factors interact, and this theory of behaviour is sometimes called interactionism. It is because of the process of interaction and because there are so many variables in personal characteristics and situations that behaviour is difficult to analyse and predict. James and Sells (1981) noted the following environmental influences on behaviour:

- role characteristics such as role ambiguity and conflict;
- job characteristics such as autonomy and challenge;
- leader behaviours, including goal emphasis and work facilitation;
- work group characteristics including cooperation and friendliness;
- organizational policies that directly affect individuals, such as the reward system.

It is generally assumed that attitudes determine behaviour but there is not such a direct link as most people suppose. Arnold et al (1991) commented that research evidence has shown that feelings and beliefs about someone or something seemed only loosely related to how people behaved towards the person or object of those feelings.

Dimensions of personality

Differences in the dimensions of personality between people are significant factors in explaining behaviour. That is why personality tests are often used as part of selection procedures and various forms of personality indicators or inventories such as Myers-Briggs, the 'big five' test and the 16PF questionnaire are used in leadership and management development programmes, including executive coaching.

Personality has been defined by Huczynski and Buchanan (2007: 844) as: 'The psychological qualities that influence an individual's characteristic behaviour patterns in a stable and distinctive manner.' As noted by Ivancevich et al (2008), personality appears to be organized into patterns which are, to some degree, observable and measurable and involves both common and unique characteristics – every person is different from every other person in some respects but similar to other persons in other respects. Personality is a product of both nature (heredity) and nurture (the pattern of life experience). The dimensions of personality can be described in terms of traits or types.

The trait concept of personality

Traits are predispositions to behave in certain ways in a variety of different situations. We all attribute traits to people in an attempt to understand why they behave in the way they do. It is assumed that traits describe enduring behaviour that occurs in a variety of settings. This assumption that people are consistent in the ways they express these traits is the basis for making predictions about their future behaviour. As Chell (1987) explained, traits are used to classify people in an attempt to understand how they act. There have been a number of ways of classifying traits as described below.

On the basis of exhaustive factor analysis (the statistical analysis of the interactions between the effects of random or independent variables), Cattell (1946) identified 16 factors underlying human personality, which he called 'source traits' because he believed that they provide the underlying source for the surface behaviours we think of as personality. This theory of personality is known as the 16-factor personality model. Cattell also developed an instrument to measure them, called the 16PF Questionnaire. The factors are:

- warmth;
- liveliness;
- vigilance;

- openness to change;
- reasoning;
- rule consciousness;
- abstractedness;
- self-reliance;
- emotional stability;
- social boldness;
- privateness;
- perfectionism;
- dominance;
- sensitivity;
- apprehension;
- tension.

Eysenck (1953) produced a simpler model. He identified three personality traits: extroversion–introversion, neuroticism and psychoticism, and classified people as stable or unstable extroverts or introverts. For example, a stable introvert is passive, careful, controlled and thoughtful, while a stable extrovert is lively, outgoing, responsive and sociable.

A further development, based in part on the original research by Cattell, was the 'big five' classification of trait dimensions (Digman, 1990; Costa and McRae, 1992) which has become the leading model of personality traits. The big five are:

- openness – inventive/curious or consistent/cautious;
- conscientiousness – efficient/organized or easy-going/careless;
- extroversion – outgoing/energetic or solitary/reserved;
- agreeableness – friendly/compassionate or cold/unkind;
- neuroticism – sensitive/nervous or secure/confident.

But the trait theory of personality has been attacked by people such as Mischel (1968). The main criticisms have been as follows:

- People do not necessarily express the same trait across different situations or even the same trait in the same situation. Different people may exhibit consistency in some traits and considerable variability in others.
- Classical trait theory as formulated by Cattell (1946) assumes that trait behaviour is independent of the situations and the persons with whom the individual is interacting. This assumption is questionable, given that trait behaviour usually manifests itself in response to specific situations.
- Trait attributions are a product of language – they are devices for speaking about people and are not generally described in terms of behaviour.

Type theory of personality

Type theory identifies a number of types of personality which can be used to categorize people and may form the basis of a personality test. The types may be linked to descriptions of various traits. As Huczynski and Buchanan (2007: 142) observed: 'While individuals belong to types, traits belong to individuals. You fit a type, you have a trait.'

The most familiar type theory is that of Jung (1923). He identified four major preferences of people:

- relating to other people – extroversion or introversion;
- gathering information – sensing (dealing with facts that can be objectively verified) or intuitive (generating information through insight);
- using information – thinking (emphasizing logical analysis as the basis for decision making) or feeling (making decisions based on internal values and beliefs);
- making decisions – perceiving (collecting all the relevant information before making a decision) or judging (resolving the issue without waiting for a large quantity of data).

This theory of personality forms the basis of one of the most popular personality tests – the Myers-Briggs Types Indicator. This rates personal preferences on four scales:

- introvert–extrovert;
- sensing–intuition;
- thinking–feeling;
- judging–perceiving.

Self-awareness

Self-awareness is about knowing yourself, so far as that is possible, and analysing your achievements, skills and knowledge and managerial competences. The aim is to identify strengths and weaknesses in order to make the most of the former and do what you can to overcome the latter.

Knowing yourself

The question you have to answer is 'What sort of person am I?' This is the most difficult question to answer truthfully. Try answering the following self-analysis questionnaire, which is based on Cattell's classification of primary personality factors as listed earlier in this chapter. Consider each statement under the heading 'I think I am someone who is…' and indicate

FIGURE 14.1 Self-assessment questionnaire

	I think I am someone who is	Strongly agree	Agree	Neither agree nor disagree	Disagree	Strongly disagree
1a	Outgoing, likes people					
1b	Reserved, aloof					
2a	An abstract thinker, conceptual					
2b	A concrete thinker, practical					
3a	Emotionally stable					
3b	Easily upset					
4a	Forceful, domineering					
4b	Cooperative, accommodating					
5a	Lively, enthusiastic					
5b	Serious, introspective					
6a	Conscientious, dutiful					
6b	Expedient, non-conforming					
7a	Venturesome, uninhibited					
7b	Timid, hesitant					
8a	Sensitive, intuitive					
8b	Unsentimental, objective					
9a	Distrustful, suspicious					
9b	Trusting, unsuspecting					
10a	Imaginative, creative					
10b	Prosaic, conventional					
11a	Astute, diplomatic					
11b	Guileless, forthright					
12a	Insecure, worrying					
12b	Self-assured, confident					
13a	Open to change					
13b	Traditional					
14a	Self-reliant, individualistic					
14b	Group orientated, a joiner					
15a	Exacting, a perfectionist					
15b	Flexible, unexacting					
16a	Driven					
16b	Relaxed					

in the appropriate box the extent to which you agree or disagree with it. The outcome will be a profile which you can study to identify any personality characteristics which you might need to do something about.

This analysis will help you to think about how you behave. You can't really change your personality but, given what you know about the sort of person you are, you may be able to adjust your behaviour to make it more productive and acceptable to people. However, bear in mind what Browning wrote: 'Best be yourself, imperial plain and true.' Your behaviour must be genuine, not assumed, otherwise people will see through you and the relationships will simply get worse.

An alternative questionnaire you might use is the Big Five Personality Test. This is based on the 'big five' personality characteristics, also listed earlier in this chapter. It can be downloaded from www.outofservice.com/bigfive.

Analysis of achievements, skills and knowledge

An analysis of your achievements, skills and knowledge can be conducted by answering the following questions:

- *What have I achieved so far?* Answer this question by looking back on your life and list the key events, happenings, incidents and turning points that have taken place. Whenever you have succeeded in doing something new or better than ever before, analyse the factors which contributed to that success. Was it initiative, hard work, determination, the correct application of skills and knowledge based on a searching analysis of the situation, the ability to work in a team, the exercise of leadership, the capacity to seize an opportunity (another and better word for luck) and exploit it, the ability to articulate a need and get into action to satisfy it, the ability to make things happen – or any other factor you can think of?

- *When have I failed to achieve what I wanted?* You do not want to dwell too much on failure but it can be treated positively, as long as you analyse dispassionately where you went wrong and assess what you might have been able to do to put it right.

- *What am I good or not so good at doing?* What are your distinctive competences? Consider these in terms of professional, technical or managerial know-how as well as the exercise of such skills as communicating, decision making, problem solving, team working, exercising leadership, delegating, coordinating, meeting deadlines, managing time, planning, organizing and controlling work, dealing with crises.

- *What have been my significant learning experiences?* Recall events when you have learned something worthwhile and how you made use of it.

- *How well do I know my chosen area of expertise?* Have you got or are you getting the right qualifications? Have you acquired or are you acquiring the right know-how through study, training and relevant experience?

Time management

Time management is the process of making the most of a key but limited resource: the time available to carry out your work. Shakespeare's Richard II lamented: 'I wasted time, now doth time waste me.' It's a problem many people still come up against. Even if we haven't been wasting our time, most of us recognize that there is scope for managing our time more productively. To do this you need to think systematically about how you use your time. You can then take steps to organize yourself better and to get other people to help or at least not to hinder you. To find out where there is scope for improvement, the first things you need to do are to analyse your job and how you spend your time.

Analyse your job

Start with your job – the tasks you have to carry out and the objectives you are there to achieve. Try to establish an order of priority between your tasks and among your objectives. It is more difficult to do this if you have a number of potentially conflicting areas of responsibility. You have to try and reconcile these and establish priorities.

Analyse how you spend your time

Having sorted out your main priorities, you should analyse in more detail how you spend your time. This will identify time-consuming activities and indicate where there are problems as well as possible solutions to them. The best way to analyse time is to keep a diary. You can do this electronically using Microsoft Outlook organizing software. Do this for a week, or preferably two or three weeks, as one week may not provide a typical picture. Divide the day into 15-minute sections and note down what you did in each period. Against each space, summarize how effectively you spent your time by writing V for valuable, D for doubtful and U for useless. If you want to make more refined judgements, give your ratings pluses or minuses. At the end of the week analyse your time under the following headings:

- Dealing with people (individuals or groups);
- Attending meetings;
- Sending and opening e-mails;
- Telephoning;
- Reading;
- Writing;
- Travelling;
- Miscellaneous administrative tasks;
- Other (specify).

Analyse also the V–D–U ratings of the worth of each activity under each heading and then consider how you can organize yourself more effectively.

Organize yourself

Such an analysis will usually throw up weaknesses in the way you plan your work and establish your priorities. You have to fit the tasks you must complete into the time available to complete them, and get them done in order of importance.

Some people find it difficult, if not impossible, to plan their work ahead. They find that they work best if they have to achieve almost impossible deadlines. Working under pressure concentrates the mind wonderfully, they say. But ordinary mortals, who work under a variety of conflicting pressures, cannot rely upon crisis action to get them out of logjams of work. For most of us it is better to try to minimize the need for working under exceptional pressure by a little attention to the organization of our week or day. At the very least you should use your diary for long-range planning, organizing your weekly activities in broad outline and planning each day in as much detail as possible. You can then use a daily organizer to good purpose.

Use your diary

Attempt to leave at least one day a week free of meetings and avoid filling any day with appointments. In other words, leave blocks of unallocated time for planning, thinking, reading, writing and dealing with the unexpected. Sit down at the beginning of each week with your electronic, desk or pocket diary and plan how you are going to spend your time. Assess each of your projects or tasks and work out priorities. Leave blocks of time for dealing with e-mails and other correspondence and seeing people. Try to preserve one free day, or at least half a day, if at all possible.

If it helps you, record on Microsoft Outlook organizing software or on paper what you intend to do each morning, afternoon and, if it's work, evening.

Use a daily organizer

At the beginning of each day, consult your electronic, pocket or desk diary to check on your plans and commitments. Refer to the previous day's organizer to find out what is outstanding. Inspect your pending tray, in-tray and incoming e-mails to check on what remains and what has just arrived. Then enter or write down the things to do:

- meetings or interviews;
- respond to e-mails;
- telephone calls;
- tasks in order of priority:
  - A: must be done today;
  - B: ideally should be done today but could be left till tomorrow;
  - C: can be dealt with later.

Plan broadly when you are going to fit your A and B priority tasks into the day. Tick off your tasks as they are completed. Retain the list to consult next day. You can use your electronic organizer to do this. But many successful

FIGURE 14.2 Example of a daily organizer

DAILY ORGANIZER			
	Committee/person	Where	When
Meetings and appointments			
	Person	About what	When
To e-mail			
	Person	About what	When
To telephone			
	Tasks (in order of priority)	Priority rating* A, B or C	Approximate timing
To do			

*A = must be done today   B = ideally done today   C = later

time managers are happy with a blank sheet of paper. However, you can use a simple form as illustrated in Figure 14.2.

Personal organizing skills

Effectiveness in a job is largely dependent on how well you organize yourself. Time management as discussed above is important but so are planning and prioritizing.

Planning

To plan, you need to decide on a course of action, ensure that the resources required to implement the action will be available, and schedule and prioritize the work required to achieve an end result. The aim is to enable you to complete tasks on time by making the best use of the resources available. You need to avoid crises and the high costs that they cause: to have fewer 'Drop everything and rush this' problems. Contingency or fallback plans need to be prepared if there is any reason to believe that the initial plan may fail for reasons beyond your control.

When managers plan, they may choose certain courses of action and rule out others; that is to say, they may lose flexibility. This will be a disadvantage if the future turns out differently from what was expected – which is only too likely. You should try to make plans that can be changed without undue difficulty. It is a bad plan that admits no change.

Most of the planning managers carry out is simply a matter of thinking systematically and using common sense. Every plan contains five key ingredients:

- the objective – what is to be achieved;
- the action programme – the specific steps required to achieve the objective;
- resource requirements – what resources in the shape of money, people, facilities and time will be required;
- impact assessment – determining the impact made on the organization by achieving the plan (assessed in terms of costs and benefits);
- consequence assessment – anticipating any outcomes that may arise when implementing the plan.

Prioritizing

Planning involves prioritizing work, which means deciding on the relative importance of a range of demands or tasks so that the order in which they are undertaken can be determined. But the fragmented nature of managerial work and the sudden and often conflicting demands made on your time mean that you will constantly be faced with decisions on when to do things, however carefully you have planned in advance. There may often be situations when you have to cope with conflicting priorities. This can be stressful unless you adopt a systematic approach to prioritization, which can be carried out in the following stages:

1 List all the things you have to do. These can be classified into three groups:
   - regular duties such as submitting a report, calling on customers, carrying out a performance review;
   - special requests from managers, colleagues, customers, clients, suppliers and so on, delivered orally, by e-mail, telephone or letter;
   - self-generated work such as preparing proposals on a new procedure.
2 Classify each item on the list according to:
   - the significance of the task to be done in terms of its impact on your work (and reputation) and on the results achieved by the organization, your team or anyone else involved;
   - the importance of the person requesting the work or expecting you to deliver something; less-significant tasks may well be put higher

on the priority list if they are set by the chief executive or a key
client;

- – the urgency of the tasks: deadlines, what will happen if they are
  not completed on time;
- – any scope there may be for extending deadlines: altering start and
  finish times and dates;
- – how long each task will take to complete: noting any required or
  imposed starting and completion times which cannot be changed.

3 Assess how much time you have available to complete the tasks, apart
from the routine work which you must get done. Also assess what
resources, such as your own staff, are available to get the work done.

4 Draw up a provisional list of priorities by reference to the criteria of
significance, importance and urgency listed at 2 above.

5 Assess the possibility of fitting this prioritized schedule of work into
the time available. If this proves difficult, put self-imposed priorities
on a back-burner and concentrate on the significant tasks. Negotiate
delayed completion or delivery times where you believe this is
possible, and if successful, move the task down the priority list.

6 Finalize the list of priorities and schedule the work you have to do
(or you have to get others to do) accordingly.

Managing stress

People become stressed when they experience more pressure, frustration or
a higher level of emotional or physical demands than they can handle. Pressures include achieving performance expectations, meeting deadlines, cop-
ing with an excessive workload, dealing with difficult bosses, colleagues,
clients, customers or subordinates, being bullied or subject to harassment,
achieving a satisfactory work–life balance (reconciling the demands of work
with family responsibilities or outside interests), and role ambiguity (lack
of understanding of what is expected). Pressure is fine as long as it does
not build up to too high a level. Up to a point it will motivate and improve
performance but it then turns into stress and results in a decline in performance, as illustrated in Figure 14.3.

FIGURE 14.3. How pressure becomes stress

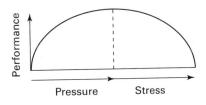

The important thing to remember is that the ability to withstand pressure varies: one person's stimulating amount of pressure is another person's stress. But this suggests that although some people may temperamentally be more prone to suffer from stress, there is some scope to manage or limit stress, bearing in mind that it is often self-imposed.

Symptoms of stress

The symptoms of stress that you can observe in others or yourself include inability to cope with the demands of the job (which creates more stress), lethargy, lack of enthusiasm and bad temper.

Managing stress – what the organization can do

Organizations can manage stress by developing policies and processes for implementation by line managers and specialist staff. These include:

- clarifying roles to reduce role ambiguity and give people more autonomy;
- setting reasonable and achievable performance standards;
- establishing performance management processes which encourage a dialogue about work and its pressures between managers and their staff;
- giving individuals the opportunity to obtain professional counselling;
- developing anti-bullying and anti-harassment policies and ensuring they are implemented (not easy);
- developing work–life balance policies which take account of the pressures on employees as parents, partners or carers, and which can include provisions such as special leave or flexible working hours.

Managing stress in others – what you can do

To manage stress in others, you need to do the following:

- Be aware of organizational policies and procedures as set out above, and be prepared to implement them for your own staff.
- Tailor your demands on people according to their capacities – it is a good idea to agree stretching targets but they must be achievable (with effort but without undue stress) by the individual concerned.
- If an individual is under stress because of undue pressure, try to adjust demands to a more reasonable level, possibly by redesigning the job or transferring duties to someone else.
- Look out for symptoms of stress and try to establish the cause as the basis for alleviating them.
- Be prepared to listen and respond to individuals who complain of being over-stressed – you don't have to accept what they say but you should certainly hear them out.

Managing your own stress

If you feel that you are unduly stressed, here are 10 things you can do:

- Try to establish why you are stressed – are there any specific causes or is it a general feeling that the work is getting on top of you?
- Talk to someone about it – your boss (if likely to be sympathetic), colleagues, HR, friends, your partner.
- If the stress is serious, ask if the organization can provide advice from a professional counsellor.
- Discuss your workloads and deadlines with your boss to see if they can be alleviated in any way.
- Consider if there is any scope to delegate more work to your staff.
- Decide what is beyond your control and put it firmly to one side. Focus on what is within your sphere of influence and get on with it.
- Take the occasional brief break in the day, if you can – relax (switch off) for a few minutes over a cup of coffee with your colleagues.
- Don't work excessive hours unless you really have to – don't work late just to impress your manager (who wants results, not just to have you around the office) or your colleagues.
- Don't take work home unless this is absolutely unavoidable.
- Take regular exercise.

Principles of continuing professional development

Continuing professional development (CPD) is the means by which members of professional associations maintain, improve and broaden their knowledge and skills and develop the personal qualities required in their professional lives. CPD is defined as a commitment to structured skills enhancement and personal or professional competence. It is about lifelong learning and development.

As defined by the CIPD, continuing professional development is the process of consciously updating professional knowledge and improving professional competence throughout a person's working life. It is a commitment to being professional, keeping up to date and continuously seeking to improve. It is the key to optimizing a person's career opportunities, both today and for the future. It enables the integration of learning with work in ways relevant to the learner, is self-directed and contributes to the learner's development needs. The benefits to the individual include becoming a better learner, profiting from learning opportunities, managing self-development, helping career advancement and improving professional standing. The benefits to the organization include better contributions by individuals to organizational goals and objectives, improved performance for the organization, and the ability to help others learn and develop themselves to enhance their work performance and their organizational commitment.

According to the CIPD, continuing professional development should be:

- continuous – professionals should always be looking for ways to improve performance;
- the responsibility of the individual learner to own and manage;
- driven by the learning needs and development of the individual;
- evaluative rather than descriptive of what has taken place;
- an essential component of professional and personal life, never an optional extra.

Professional and ethical approaches to self-management at work

A professional approach to self-management means organizing and developing yourself to carry out your work in ways which use your expertise in providing professional advice and services. An ethical approach to self-management means that what happens as a result of your activities meets defined or generally accepted standards of behaviour. The approach should be based on self-management strategies and ethical principles as considered below.

Self-management strategies

Self-management strategies should be based on self-assessment, which means assessing your own performance and identifying how you can improve. To assess your own performance you need to:

- Ensure that you are clear about what your job entails in terms of the main tasks or key result areas. If in doubt, ask your manager for clarification.
- Find out what you are expected to achieve for each of the key result areas. Expectations should be definable as objectives in the form of quantified targets or standards of performance (qualitative statements of what constitutes effective performance). Ideally they should have been discussed and agreed as part of the performance appraisal/management process but if this has not happened, ask your manager to spell out what they expect you to achieve.
- Refer to the organization's competency framework. Discuss with your manager how they interpret these as far as you are concerned.
- At fairly regular intervals, say once a month, review your progress by reference to the objectives, standards and competency headings. Take note of your achievements and, if they exist, your failures.

Ask yourself why you were successful or unsuccessful and what you can do to build on success or overcome failure. You may identify actions you can take or specific changes in behaviour you can try to achieve. Or you may identify a need for further coaching, training or experience.

- At the end of the review period and prior to the appraisal discussion with your manager, look back at each of your interim reviews and the actions you decided to take. Consider what more needs to be done in any specific area or generally. You will then be in a position to answer the following questions that might be posed by your manager before or during the appraisal discussion:

  - How do you feel you have done?
  - What are you best at doing?
  - Are there any parts of your job which you find difficult?
  - Are there any aspects of your work in which you would benefit from better guidance or further training?

Developing yourself

This assessment should identify specific areas for development or improvement. The following 10 steps can be taken to develop yourself:

- Create a development log – record your plans and action.
- State your objectives – the career path you want to follow and the skills you will need to proceed along that path.
- Develop a personal profile – what sort of person you are, your likes and dislikes about work, your aspirations.
- List your strengths and weaknesses – what you have done well so far and why you believe these were worthwhile achievements.
- List your achievements – what you have done well so far and why you believe these were worthwhile achievements.
- List significant learning experiences – recall events when you have learned something worthwhile (this can help you to understand your learning style).
- Ask other people about your strengths and weaknesses and what you should do to develop yourself.
- Focus on the present – what is happening to you now: your job, your current skills, your short-term development needs.
- Focus on the future – where you want to be in the longer term and how you are going to get these (including a list of the skills and abilities you need to develop).
- Plan your self-development strategy – how you are going to achieve your ambitions.

Ethical principles for self-management

The ethical principles you should adopt for self-management should be in accord with the principles that should govern all aspects of your work as a manager. These are:

- When deciding what to do, always consider the extent to which it can be justified in terms of your professional and your organization's codes of conduct and your own values on how people should be treated.
- Before doing something that affects people, review the likely consequences for them and asses whether this can be justified from the viewpoints of natural, procedural and distributive justice as defined in Chapter 8.
- Compete fairly – manage your career in a way which does not unfairly prejudice the rights of others. Do not take advantage of the weakness of others, especially those with disabilities or older people.
- Do not put people who are with you or under you to unreasonable pressure. Set fair targets to your staff – they can be demanding but they must be achievable.

KEY LEARNING POINTS

Managing yourself

The starting points in managing yourself are an understanding of individual differences as they affect your own and other people's behaviour, and an appreciation of the meaning of personality and its dimensions in terms of individual traits and types.

Personality

Personality has been defined by Huczynski and Buchanan (2007: 844) as: 'The psychological qualities that influence an individual's characteristic behaviour patterns in a stable and distinctive manner.'

The trait concept of personality

Traits are predispositions to behave in certain ways in a variety of different situations. Traits are used to classify people in an attempt to understand how they act. Type theory identifies a number of types of personality which can be used to categorize people and may form the basis of a personality test.

Self-awareness

Self-awareness is about knowing yourself, so far as that is possible, and analysing your achievements, skills and knowledge and managerial competences.

Time management

Time management is the process of making the most of a key but limited resource – the time available to carry out your work.

Personal organizing skills

Effectiveness in a job is largely dependent on how well you organize yourself. Time management is important but so are planning and prioritizing.

Planning

Planning involves deciding on a course of action, ensuring that the resources required to implement the action will be available and scheduling and prioritizing the work required to achieve a defined end result.

Prioritizing

Prioritizing work means deciding on the relative importance of a range of demands or tasks so that the order in which they are undertaken can be determined.

Managing stress

People become stressed when they experience more pressure, frustration, or a higher level of emotional or physical demands than they can handle.

The symptoms of stress include inability to cope with the demands of the job (which creates more stress), tiredness, lethargy, lack of enthusiasm and bad temper.

Stress can be managed at organizational level, for individuals, and for yourself.

Continuing professional development

Continuing professional development (CPD) is the means by which members of professional associations maintain, improve and broaden their knowledge and skills and develop the personal qualities required in their professional lives.

Professional and ethical approaches to self-management

A professional approach to self-management means organizing and developing yourself to carry out your work in ways which use your expertise in providing professional advice and services.

An ethical approach to self-management means that what happens as a result of your activities meets defined or generally accepted standards of behaviour.

References

Arnold, J, Robertson, I T and Cooper, C L (1991) *Work Psychology*, London, Pitman

Cattell, R B (1946) *Description and Measurement of Personality*, New York, World Books

Chell, E (1987) *The Psychology of Behaviour in Organizations*, London, Macmillan

Costa, P and McRae, R R (1992) *NEO PI-R: Professional Manual*, Odessa FL, Psychological Assessment Resources

Digman, J M (1990) Personality structure: Emergence of the five-factor model, *Annual Review of Psychology*, **41**, pp 417–40

Eysenck, H J (1953) *The Structure of Human Personality*, London, Methuen

Huczynski, A A and Buchanan, D A (2007) *Organizational Behaviour*, 6th edn, Harlow, FT Prentice Hall

Ivancevich, J M, Konopaske, R and Matteson, M T (2008) *Organizational Behaviour and Management*, 8th edn, New York, McGraw-Hill/Irwin

James, R and Sells, S B (1981) Psychological climate: theoretical perspectives and empirical research, in D Magnusson (ed) *Towards a Psychology of Situations: An interactional perspective*, Hillsdale NJ, Erlbaum

Jung, C (1923) *Psychological Types*, London, Routledge Kegan Paul

Levinson, D (1978) *The Seasons of Man's Life*, New York, Knopf

Mischel, W (1968) *Personality and Assessment*, New York, Wiley

Questions

1 What are the headings under which personal characteristics can vary?

2 What are the main environmental influences on behaviour?

3 What is personality?

4 What is the trait theory of personality?

5 What are the 'big five' personality factors?

6 What is the type theory of personality?

7 What is self-awareness?

8 What are the key questions to be answered when analysing achievements, skills and knowledge?

9 What is time management?

10 What are the main steps required to manage time?

11 What is involved in planning?

12 What is involved in prioritizing?

13 When do people become stressed?

14 What can be done to manage the stress of others? (List at least four actions.)

15 What can be done to manage one's own stress? (List at least four actions.)

16 What is continuing professional development (CPD)?

17 How should CPD take place?

18 What is a professional approach to self-management?

19 What steps can you take to develop yourself? (Name at least four.)

20 What is an ethical approach to self-management?

Managing interpersonal relationships at work

Key concepts and terms

- *Assertiveness*
- *Dominant coalition*
- *Interpersonal relationships*
- *Networks*
- *Self-managed team*

LEARNING OUTCOMES

On completing this chapter you should be able to define these key concepts. You should also understand:

- The significance of team working in organizations
- How to achieve good teamwork
- The importance of networking and how to do it
- Barriers to communication and how to overcome them
- What it means to behave assertively
- How to handle emotional behaviour
- How to manage conflict
- How to negotiate
- The meaning of political behaviour in organizations and how to deal with it
- What HR people should do about being politically astute and ethical
- How to liaise with external and internal customers

Introduction

Interpersonal relationships are those that take place between people when they associate with one another at work. As covered in this chapter, they take the form of working in teams or groups, networking, communicating, being assertive, handling emotional behaviour and conflict, negotiating, handling politics, acting in a politically astute and ethical manner to secure HR objectives, and liaising with customers.

Team working

Teams are essential to the effective functioning of organizations. They assemble the skills, experiences and insights of a number of people who work together to achieve a common purpose. Most formally constituted teams have an appointed leader. But informal teams can develop during the normal course of work in which leaders may emerge with the consent of the work group. It is also possible for both formal and informal teams to be self-managed.

Effective teams

In an effective team its members work together in order to achieve expected results. The purpose of the team is clear and its members feel the task is important, both to them and to the organization. They may not always agree on the best way to achieve the task but when they don't agree, they discuss, even argue, about their differences to resolve them.

The structure of the team is likely to be one in which the leadership and methods of operation are relevant to its purpose. People will have been grouped together in a way which ensures that they are related to each other by way of the requirements of task performance and task interdependence. Job specialization is minimized, team members operate flexibly within the group, tasks are rotated among them and they are multi-skilled.

The atmosphere in an effective team tends to be informal, comfortable and relaxed. The leader of the team does not dominate it, nor does the team defer unduly to them. The role of the team leader may be primarily to act as a facilitator – more supportive and participative than directive. There is little evidence of a struggle for power as the team operates. The issue is not who controls, but how to get the job done.

Self-managed teams

High levels of engagement and commitment and better teamwork can be achieved by a self-managed team. Such a team is highly autonomous, responsible to a considerable degree for planning and scheduling work, problem solving, developing its own performance indicators, and setting and monitoring team performance and quality standards.

Ten things to do to achieve good teamwork

- Establish urgency and direction.
- Select members based on skills and skill potential who are good at working with others but still capable of taking their own line when necessary.
- Pay particular attention to first meetings and actions.
- Set immediate performance-orientated tasks and goals, including overlapping or interlocking objectives for people who have to work together. These will take the form of targets to be achieved or projects to be completed by joint action.
- Assess people's performance not only on the results they achieve but also on the degree to which they are good team members. Recognize and reward people who have worked well in teams (using team bonus schemes where appropriate), bearing in mind that being part of a high-performance team can be a reward in itself.
- Encourage people to build networks – results are achieved in organizations, as in the outside world, on the basis of who you know as well as what you know.
- Describe and think of the organization as a system of interlocking teams united by a common purpose. Don't emphasize hierarchies. Abolish departmental boundaries if they are getting in the way, but do not be alarmed if there is disagreement – remember the value of constructive conflict.
- Hold special 'off-the-job' meetings for work teams so they can get together and explore issues without the pressures of their day-to-day jobs.
- Encourage teams to socialize and provide them with facilities and even the funds to do so.
- Use learning and development programmes to build relationships. This can often be a far more beneficial result of a course than the increase in skills or knowledge which was its ostensible purpose. Use team building and interactive skills training to supplement the other approaches. But do not rely upon them to have any effect unless the messages they convey are in line with the organization's culture and values.

Networking

Networks are loosely organized connections between people with shared interests. Increasingly in today's more fluid and flexible organizations, people get things done by networking. They exchange information, enlist support and create alliances – getting agreement with other people on a course of action and joining forces to make it happen.

To network effectively here are ten steps you can take:

- Identify people who may be able to help.
- Seize any opportunity that presents itself to get to know people who may be useful.
- Have a clear idea of why you want to network – to share knowledge, to persuade people to accept your proposal or point of view, to form an alliance.
- Know what you can contribute – networking is not simply about enlisting support, it is just as much if not more concerned with developing knowledge and understanding through 'communities of interest' and joining forces with like-minded people so that concerted effort can be deployed to get things done.
- Show interest – if you engage with people and listen to them they are more likely to want to network with you.
- Ask people if you can help them as well as asking people to help you.
- Put people in touch with one another.
- Operate informally but be prepared to call formal meetings when necessary to reach agreement and plan action.
- Make an effort to keep in touch with people.
- Follow up – check with members of the network on progress in achieving something, refer back to conversations you have had, discuss with others how the network might be developed or extended to increase its effectiveness.

Communicating

People recognize the need to communicate but find it difficult. Like Schopenhauer's hedgehogs, they want to get together; it's only their prickles that keep them apart. Words may sound or look precise, but they are not. All sorts of barriers exist between the communicator and the receiver. Unless these barriers are overcome the message will be distorted or will not get through.

Barriers to communication

The barriers to communication are:

- Hearing what we want to hear. What we hear or understand when someone speaks to us is largely based on our own experience and background. Instead of hearing what people have told us, we hear what our minds tell us they have said. We have preconceptions about what people are going to say, and if what they say does not fit into our framework of reference, we adjust it until it does.

- Ignoring conflicting information. We tend to ignore or reject communications that conflict with our own beliefs. If they are not rejected, some way is found of twisting and shaping their meaning to fit our preconceptions. When a message is inconsistent with existing beliefs, the receiver rejects its validity, avoids further exposure to it, easily forgets it and, in his or her memory, distorts what has been heard.

- Perceptions about the communicator. It is difficult to separate what we hear from our feelings about the person who says it. Non-existent motives may be ascribed to the communicator. If we like people we are more likely to accept what they say – whether it is right or wrong – than if we dislike them.

- Influence of the group. The group with which we identify influences our attitudes and feelings. What a group hears depends on its interests. Workers are more likely to listen to their colleagues, who share their experiences, than to outsiders such as managers or union officials.

- Words mean different things to different people. Essentially, language is a method of using symbols to represent facts and feelings. Strictly speaking, we can't convey meaning; all we can do is to convey words. Do not assume that because something has a certain meaning to you, it will convey the same meaning to someone else.

- Non-verbal communication. When we try to understand the meaning of what people say we listen to the words but we also use other clues which convey meaning. We attend not only to what people say but to how they say it. We form impressions from what is called body language – eyes, shape of the mouth, the muscles of the face, even posture. We may feel that these tell us more about what someone is really saying than the words he or she uses. But there is enormous scope for misinterpretation.

- Emotions. Our emotions colour our ability to convey or to receive the true message. When we are insecure or worried, what we hear seems more threatening than when we are secure and at peace with the world. When we are angry or depressed, we tend to reject what might otherwise seem like reasonable requests or good ideas. During heated argument, many things that are said may not be understood or may be badly distorted.

- Noise. Any interference to communication is 'noise'. It can be literal noise which prevents the message being heard, or figurative in the shape of distracting or confused information which distorts or obscures the meaning.

- Size. The larger and more complex the organization, the greater the problem of communication. The more levels of management and supervision through which a message has to pass, the greater the opportunity for distortion or misunderstanding.

Overcoming barriers to communication

- Adjust to the world of the receiver. Try to predict the impact of what you are going to write or say on the receiver's feelings and attitudes. Tailor the message to fit the receiver's vocabulary, interests and values. Be aware of how the information might be misinterpreted because of prejudices, the influence of others and the tendency of people to reject what they do not want to hear.
- Use feedback. Ensure that you get a message back from the receiver which tells you how much has been understood.
- Use face-to-face communication. Whenever appropriate and possible, talk to people rather than sending an e-mail or writing to them. That is how you get feedback. You can adjust or change your message according to reactions. You can also deliver it in a more human and understanding way – this can help to overcome prejudices. Verbal criticism can often be given in a more constructive manner than a written reproof, which always seems to be harsher.
- Use reinforcement. You may have to present your message in a number of different ways to get it across. Re-emphasize the important points and follow up.
- Use direct, simple language. This seems obvious. But many people clutter up what they say with jargon, long words and elaborate sentences.
- Suit the actions to the words. Communications have to be credible to be effective. There is nothing worse than promising the earth and then failing to deliver. When you say you are going to do something, do it. Next time you are more likely to be believed.
- Reduce problems of size. If you can, reduce the number of levels of management. Encourage a reasonable degree of informality in communications. Ensure that activities are grouped together to ease communication on matters of mutual concern.

Assertiveness

Assertiveness is about expressing your opinions, beliefs, needs, wants and feelings firmly and in direct, honest and appropriate ways. It means standing up for your own rights in such a way that you do not violate another person's rights. When you are being assertive you are not being aggressive, which means violating or ignoring other people's rights in order to get your own way or dominate a situation.

Behaving assertively puts you into the position of being able to influence people properly and react to them positively. Assertive statements:

- are brief and to the point;
- indicate clearly that you are not hiding behind something or someone and are speaking for yourself by using expressions such as: 'I think that…', 'I believe that…', 'I feel that…';
- are not over-weighted with advice;
- use questions to find out the views of others and to test their reactions to your behaviour;
- distinguish between fact and opinion;
- are expressed positively but not dogmatically;
- indicate that you are aware that the other people have different points of view;
- express, when necessary, negative feelings about the effects of other people's behaviour on you – pointing out in dispassionate and factual terms the feelings aroused in you by that behaviour, and suggesting the behaviour you would prefer;
- indicate to people politely but firmly the consequences of their behaviour.

Handling emotional behaviour

Emotional behaviour can include aggression, withdrawal and unreasonable actions or reactions.

Aggression

If you are faced by aggression, take a breath, count up to 10 and then:

- Ask calmly for information about what is bugging the aggressor.
- State clearly, and again calmly, the position as you see it.
- Empathize with the aggressor by making it plain that you can see their point of view, but at the same time explaining in a matter-of-fact way how you see the discrepancy between what they believe and what you feel is actually happening.
- If the aggressive behaviour persists, indicate your different beliefs or feelings, but do not cut aggressors short – people often talk, or even shout, themselves out of being aggressive when they realize that you are not reacting aggressively and that their behaviour is not getting them anywhere.
- If all else fails, suggest that you leave it for the time being and talk about it again after a cooling-off period.

Withdrawal

Withdrawal can take the form of lack of interest, uncooperative behaviour or refusing to take part in the work of a team, an activity or a project. If any of these happens and work is affected, you have to deal with it, not by confrontation but by trying to reach agreement that something is wrong (not easy; people in an emotional state are quite prepared to believe that everyone is out of step but them) and attempting to establish the cause of the behaviour.

By definition, if someone is in an emotional state it is going to be difficult to get through to them. But the attempt must be made and this is best done by being unemotional yourself and only referring to facts about the situation – what has happened or is happening. The aim is to get the person to accept that these facts are correct, although there may still be a real problem in that their view of the facts is distorted by their emotions. Of course, this could apply to you and a dispassionate pursuit of the truth may result in you readjusting your views on the matter. If, and it can be a big if, you get to the root of the problem, you can try to get the individual to propose what actions should be taken by them or by you. Try to get them to suggest solutions; don't impose your own ideas.

Unreasonable actions or reactions

If someone seems to be acting unreasonably, the first reaction of many people is: 'I must make them see reason.' But you can't make people see reason; they have to be convinced that an alternative way of behaviour or reaction is more reasonable than the one they have adopted. The best approach is the one suggested above for dealing with withdrawal. You have to question to get the facts and listen to what is said. You have to establish the reasoning behind the behaviour (assuming there is any – it could be no more than an immediate emotional reaction) so that agreement can be reached as to what can be done about it. However, if it is unreasonable and unacceptable this must be spelt out so that the individual knows what is expected and is aware of the possible consequences (eg disciplinary action) if the behaviour persists.

Handling conflict

Conflict is inevitable in organizations because they function by means of adjustments and compromises among competitive elements in their structure and membership. Conflict also arises when there is change, because it may be seen as a threat to be challenged or resisted, or when there is frustration – this may produce an aggressive reaction: fight rather than flight. Conflict is not to be deplored. It results from progress and change and it can and should be used constructively. Bland agreement on everything would be unnatural and enervating. There should be clashes of ideas about tasks and projects, and disagreements should not be suppressed. They should come out into the open because that is the only way to ensure that the issues are explored and conflicts are resolved.

There is such a thing as creative conflict – new or modified ideas, insights, approaches and solutions can be generated by a joint re-examination of the different points of view as long as this is based on an objective and rational exchange of information and ideas. But conflict becomes counterproductive when it is based on personality clashes, or when it is treated as an unseemly mess to be hurriedly cleared away, rather than as a problem to be worked through. Conflict resolution can be concerned with conflict between groups or conflict between individuals (interpersonal conflict).

Handling inter-group conflict

There are three principal ways of resolving inter-group conflict: peaceful coexistence, compromise and problem solving.

Peaceful coexistence

The aim here is to smooth out differences and emphasize the common ground. People are encouraged to learn to live together, there is a good deal of information, contact and exchange of views, and individuals move freely between groups (for example, between headquarters and the field, or between sales and marketing).

This is a pleasant ideal, but it may not be practicable in many situations. There is much evidence that conflict is not necessarily resolved by bringing people together. Improved communications and techniques such as briefing groups may appear to be good ideas but are useless if management has nothing to say that people want to hear. There is also the danger that the real issues, submerged for the moment in an atmosphere of superficial bonhomie, will surface again later.

Compromise

The issue is resolved by negotiation or bargaining and neither party wins or loses. This concept of splitting the difference is essentially pessimistic. The hallmark of this approach is that there is no 'right' or 'best' answer. Agreements only accommodate differences. Real issues are not likely to be solved.

Problem solving

An attempt is made to find a genuine solution to the problem rather than just accommodating different points of view. This is where the apparent paradox of 'creative conflict' comes in. Conflict situations can be used to advantage to create better solutions.

If solutions are to be developed by problem solving, they have to be generated by those who share the responsibility for seeing that the solutions work.

The sequence of actions is: first, those concerned work to define the problem and agree on the objectives to be attained in reaching a solution; second, the group develops alternative solutions and debates their merits; and third, agreement is reached on the preferred course of action and how it should be implemented.

Handling interpersonal conflict

Handling conflict between individuals can be even more difficult than resolving conflicts between groups. Whether the conflict is openly hostile or subtly covert, strong personal feelings may be involved. However, interpersonal conflict, like inter-group conflict, is an organizational reality which is not necessarily good or bad. It can be destructive, but it can also play a productive role.

The reaction to interpersonal conflict may be the withdrawal of either party, leaving the other one to hold the field. This is the classic win–lose situation. The problem has been resolved by force, but this may not be the best solution if it represents one person's point of view which has ignored counterarguments, and has, in fact, steamrollered over them. The winner may be triumphant but the loser will be aggrieved and either demotivated or resolved to fight again another day. There will have been a lull in, but not an end to, the conflict.

Another approach is to smooth over differences and pretend that the conflict does not exist, although no attempt has been made to tackle the root causes. Again, this is an unsatisfactory solution. The issue is likely to re-emerge and the battle will recommence.

Yet another approach is bargaining to reach a compromise. This means that both sides are prepared to lose as well as win some points and the aim is to reach a solution acceptable to both sides. Bargaining, however, involves all sorts of tactical and often counterproductive games, and the parties are often more anxious to seek acceptable compromises than to achieve sound solutions.

Personal counselling is an approach which does not address the conflict itself but focuses on how the two people are reacting. It gives people a chance to release pent-up tensions and may encourage them to think about new ways of resolving the conflict. But it does not address the essential nature of the conflict, which is the relationship between two people. That is why constructive confrontation offers the best hope of a long-term solution.

Constructive confrontation is a method of bringing the individuals in conflict together with a third party whose function is to help build an exploratory and cooperative climate. Constructive confrontation aims to get each party involved to understand and explore the other's perceptions and feelings. It is a process of developing mutual understanding to produce a win–win situation. The issues will be confronted but on the basis of a joint analysis, with the help of the third party, of facts relating to the situation and the actual behaviour of those involved. Feelings will be expressed but they will be analysed by reference to specific events and behaviours rather than inferences or speculations about motives. Third parties have a key role in this process, and it is not an easy one. They have to get agreement to the ground rules for discussions aimed at bringing out the facts and minimizing hostile behaviour. They must monitor the ways in which negative feelings are expressed and encourage the parties to produce new definitions of the problem and its cause or causes and new motives to reach a common solution. Third parties must avoid the temptation to support or appear to support either of those in contention. They should adopt a counselling approach, as follows:

- Listen actively.
- Observe as well as listen.
- Help people to understand and define the problem by asking pertinent, open-ended questions.
- Recognize feelings and allow them to be expressed.
- Help people to define problems for themselves.
- Encourage people to explore alternative solutions.
- Get people to develop their own implementation plans but provide advice and help if asked.

To conclude, conflict, as has been said, is in itself not to be deplored: it is an inevitable concomitant of progress and change. What is regrettable is the failure to use conflict constructively. Effective problem solving and constructive confrontation both resolve conflicts and open up channels of discussion and cooperative action.

Many years ago one of the pioneering and most influential writers on management, Mary Parker Follett (1924), wrote something on managing conflict which is as valid today as it was then. She said that differences can be made to contribute to the common cause if they are resolved by integration rather than domination or compromise.

Resolving conflict between team members

To resolve conflict between team members the following actions can be taken:

- Obtain an overview of the situation from your own observations.
- Find out who is involved.
- Talk to each of the parties to the conflict to obtain their side of the story.
- Talk to other members of the group to get their views, being careful to be dispassionate and strictly neutral.
- Evaluate what you hear from both parties and other people against your knowledge of what has been happening, any history of conflict and the dispositions and previous behaviour of the people involved.

- Reach preliminary conclusions on the facts, the reasons for the dispute and the extent to which either of the parties or both of them are to blame (but keep these to yourself at this stage).

- Bring the parties together to discuss the situation. The initial aim of this meeting would be to bring the problem out into the open, get the facts and defuse any emotions that may prejudice a solution to the problem. Both parties should be allowed to have their say but as the facilitator of this meeting, you should do your best to ensure that they stick to the facts and explain their point of view dispassionately. You should not even remotely give the impression that you are taking sides.

- Try to defuse the situation so that a solution can be reached which on the whole will be acceptable to all concerned. Ideally, this should be an integrated solution reached by agreement on the basis of collaboration along the lines of 'Let's get together to find the best solution on the basis of the facts.' It may be necessary to reach a compromise or accommodation – something everyone can live with.

- Only if all else fails or the parties are so recalcitrant in holding an untenable position that no integrated, compromise or accommodating solution can be reached should you resort to direct action – instructing one or other or both the parties to bury their differences and get on with their work. If the worse comes to the worst, this may involve disciplinary action beginning with a formal warning.

Negotiating

Negotiating takes place when two parties meet to reach an agreement on the price of something, on the terms and conditions of a contract or employment or a pay claim. Negotiation can be convergent when both parties are equally keen to reach a win–win agreement (in commercial terms a willing buyer–willing seller arrangement). It can be divergent when one or both of the parties aim to win as much as they can from the other while giving away as little as possible. This can become a zero-sum game where the winner takes all and the loser gets nothing.

Negotiations in an industrial relations setting differ from commercial negotiations in the respects set out below.

Negotiations take place in an atmosphere of uncertainty. Neither side knows how strong the other side's bargaining position is or what it really wants and will be prepared to accept.

Negotiating and bargaining skills

The skills required to be effective in negotiations and bargaining are:

- analytical ability – the capacity to assess the factors that affect the negotiating stance and tactics of both parties;

TABLE **15.1** Differences between industrial relations negotiations and commercial negotiations

Industrial relations negotiations	Commercial negotiations
• Assume an ongoing relationship – negotiators cannot walk away. • The agreement is not legally binding. • Conducted on a face-to-face basis. • Carried out by representatives responsible to constituents. • Make frequent use of adjournments. • May be conducted in an atmosphere of distrust or even hostility.	• Negotiators can walk away. • The contract is legally binding. • May be conducted at a distance. • Carried out directly with the parties being responsible to a line manager. • Usually conducted on a continuing basis. • Usually conducted on a 'willing buyer/willing seller' basis.

- empathy – the ability to put oneself in the other party's shoes;
- interactive skills – the ability to relate well to other people;
- communicating skills – the ability to convey information and arguments clearly, positively and logically;
- keeping cards close to the chest – not giving what you really want or are prepared to concede until you are ready to do so (in the marketplace it is always easier for sellers to drive a hard bargain with buyers who have revealed somehow that they covet the article);
- flexible realism – the capacity to make realistic moves during the bargaining process to reduce the claim or increase the offer, which will demonstrate that the bargainer is seeking a reasonable settlement and is prepared to respond appropriately to movements from the other side.

Organizational politics

To be politic, according to the *Concise Oxford English Dictionary*, you can be sagacious, prudent, judicious, expedient, scheming or crafty. Organizational politics involves various kinds of desirable and undesirable behaviour designed to get outcomes which are sought by an individual or a group. The behaviour may consist of overt, or, more probably, covert, pressures on individuals in positions of power or on interest groups to agree to or obstruct a course of action. Influence may be exerted outside the usual channels to get things done or to undo things; for example, the opinions of committee members might be influenced by lobbying them outside the committee. This could be justified by the politician as the best way of achieving something. But it could be undesirable if it consists of perverting the normal open and transparent processes of decision making, especially when it is perpetrated simply to pursue the organizational politician's own ends.

Political behaviour is inevitable in organizations because they consist of individuals who, while they are ostensibly there to achieve a common purpose, will, at the same time, be driven by their own needs to achieve their own goals. Effective management is the process of harmonizing individual endeavour and ambition to the common good. Some individuals will genuinely believe that using political means to achieve their goals will benefit the organization as well as themselves. Others will rationalize this belief. Yet others will unashamedly pursue their own ends. They may use all their powers of persuasion to legitimize these ends to their colleagues, but self-interest remains the primary drive. These are the corporate politicians whom the *Oxford English Dictionary* describes as 'shrewd schemers, crafty plotters or intriguers'. Politicians within organizations can be like this. They manoeuvre behind people's backs, blocking proposals they do not like. They advance their own reputation and career at the expense of other people's. They can be envious and jealous and act accordingly. They are bad news.

But it can also be argued that a political approach to management is inevitable and even desirable in any organization where the clarity of goals is not absolute, where the decision-making process is not clear cut and where the authority to make decisions is not evenly or appropriately distributed. And there can be few organizations where one or more of these conditions do not apply.

Political sensitivity

Organizational politicians exert hidden influence to get their way, and 'politicking' in some form takes place in most organizations. If you want to progress, a degree of political sensitivity is desirable – knowing what is going on so that influence can be exerted. This means that you have to:

- know 'how things are done around here';
- know how decisions are made;
- understand the factors that are likely to affect decisions;
- know where the power base is in the organization (sometimes called the dominant coalition) – who makes the running, who the people are who count when decisions are taken;
- be aware of what is going on behind the scenes;
- know who is a rising star, and whose reputation is fading;
- identify any 'hidden agendas' – try to understand what people are really getting at, and why, by obtaining answers to the question: 'Where are they coming from?'

- find out what other people are thinking and seeking;
- network – identifying the interest groups and keeping in contact with them.

Dangers

The danger of politics, however, is that it can be carried to excess and can then seriously harm the effectiveness of an organization. The signs of excessive indulgence in political behaviour include:

- backbiting;
- buck passing;
- secret meetings and hidden decisions;
- feuds between people and departments;
- e-mail or paper wars between armed camps – arguing by e-mail or memorandum is always a sign of distrust;
- a multiplicity of snide comments and criticisms;
- excessive and counterproductive lobbying;
- the formation of cabals – cliques which spend their time intriguing.

Dealing with organizational politicians

One way to deal with this sort of behaviour is to find out who is going in for it and openly confront them with the damage they are doing. They will, of course, deny that they are behaving politically (they wouldn't be politicians if they didn't), but the fact that they have been identified might lead them to modify their approach. It could, of course, only serve to drive them further underground, in which case their behaviour will have to be observed even more closely and corrective action taken as necessary.

A more positive approach to keeping politics operating at an acceptable level is for the organization to manage its operations as openly as possible. The aims should be to ensure that issues are debated fully, that differences of opinion are dealt with frankly and that disagreements are depersonalized, so far as this is possible. Political processes can then be seen as a way of maintaining the momentum of the organization as a complex decision-making and problem-solving entity.

Meeting HR aims in a politically astute and ethical manner

HR practitioners are inevitably involved in organizational politics and they are more likely to survive and thrive if they handle these astutely. But they also have to behave ethically, whether they are politicking or going about their daily business of providing advice and services.

On being politically astute

Politically astute behaviour on the part of HR practitioners means that they have to identify the key decision makers when they are involved in developing new approaches and getting things done. Before coming to a final conclusion and launching a fully fledged proposal at a committee or in a memorandum, it makes good sense to test opinion and find out how other people may react. This testing process enables them to anticipate counterarguments and modify their proposals either to meet legitimate objections or, when there is no alternative, to accommodate other people's requirements. All this requires political sensitivity, as described in the previous section of this chapter.

Ethical considerations

Making deals as described above may not appear to be particularly desirable, although it does happen, and HR practitioners can always rationalize this type of behaviour by reference to the end result. This is in effect utilitarianism as described in Chapter 8 – the belief that the greatest good to the greatest number allows people to be treated as means to an end, ie it is to the advantage of the majority. Actions should be judged in terms of their consequences. This is sometimes interpreted as supporting the dubious principle that the ends justify the means.

Politicking is unethical if it means adopting a devious approach to getting things done. For example, withholding information is not legitimate behaviour, but people do indulge in it in recognition of the fact that knowledge is power. Judicious withdrawal may also seem to be questionable, but most people prefer to live to fight another day rather than launch a doomed campaign. It may be unethical to abandon beliefs in an effort to achieve results. But it is worth remembering what Benjamin Franklin presented to the meeting held on Monday, 17 September 1787 in Pennsylvania State House to debate the draft Constitution of the United States of America. His words were:

> For having lived long, I have experienced many instances of being obliged
> by better Information, or fuller Consideration, to change Opinions even on
> important Subjects, which I once thought right, but found to be otherwise.
> That people believe themselves to be right is no proof that they are; the only
> difference between the Church of Rome and the Church of England is that the
> former is infallible while the latter is never wrong.

This is a particular case. In general, ethical behaviour by HR practitioners means that HR specialists need to take account of the dignity and rights of employees when taking employment decisions. These include having clear, fair terms and conditions of employment, healthy and safe working conditions, fair remuneration, promoting equal opportunities and employment diversity, encouraging employees to develop their skills, and not discriminating against or harassing employees. The ethical frameworks for judging HR practices are basic rights, organizational justice, respecting individuals, and community of purpose.

Liaising with customers

Liaising with customers, whether external or internal, is a matter of establishing their wants and needs and then meeting them in a way that will create and maintain good relationships. With external customers this results in repeat sales and an enhancement of the company's reputation in the marketplace, and with internal customers it means furthering the objectives of the organization and fostering a cooperative attitude between those involved. It is necessary to define what is required from all concerned in liaising with external or internal customers. It is also necessary to remember that relationships with internal customers are also important.

Defining customer service requirements

The requirements for effectively liaising with customers can be defined in terms of attitudes, skills, knowledge and behaviours.

Attitudes

Customer service excellence is achieved by people whose attitudes can be summed up in the sentence: 'Put the customer first.' They must believe that they exist because customers exist and that being responsive to customer needs and expectations is a vital part of their role.

Skills

The main skills required are:

- interpersonal skills – ability to relate well to people during person-to-person contacts;
- listening skills – ability to pay attention to people, absorb what they are saying and react appropriately;
- communication skills – ability to explain matters to customers clearly and with conviction and to handle telephone conversations;
- complaints handling skills – ability to deal with complaints and handle angry customers.

Knowledge

Knowledge will be required of the product or service offered. For external customers, this could be quite advanced knowledge enabling individuals to identify and deal with faulty equipment or provide technical advice. It will also be necessary to understand the customer service systems and procedures used in the organization. For internal customers it is necessary to understand what the departments or individuals need and how to satisfy those needs.

Behaviours

When liaising with customers the behaviours required are:

- taking time to understand the specific needs, requirements and any current pressures the customer may be under;
- looking for ways to delight the customer;
- being honest about the product or service offered and what can be done to help the customer;
- generating a range of solutions to address a difficulty.

Internal customers

An internal customer is anyone who makes use of the outputs or services provided by other departments or individuals in the organization. This means everyone – all employees are customers of other employees and they all provide services to other employees. Some departments, such as HR, IT and facilities management, provide professional or technical services directly to other departments. Other departments exist to produce outputs upon which other departments rely to achieve their objectives. Research and development has to deliver products which can be promoted and sold by marketing and sales departments. Production or operating departments exist to deliver the products or services that are required by sales to meet customer demands. Marketing and sales departments produce the information on forecast demand which enables production and operating departments to plan their activities.

It can be argued that meeting the needs of internal customers is a prerequisite for meeting the needs of external customers. If, for example, marketing gets its sales forecasts wrong or manufacturing fails to meet the requirements specified by sales, then it is the level of service to external customers that suffers and this has a negative impact on satisfaction and loyalty.

The basic approach to creating high standards of service for internal customers is to define how the different parts of the organization interrelate and spell out who serves whom and who receives service from whom. It is then necessary to ensure that all the parties concerned know the importance of good service to internal customers and what is expected of them from their internal customers. This can be defined formally as a service level agreement, which sets out the levels of service to be provided.

For example, an agreement for an HR service centre could set out standards in the following areas:

- speed of response to requests for help or guidance in areas such as recruitment, training, handling disciplinary cases and grievances, and health and safety;

- the time taken to prepare and agree role profiles, fill job vacancies or conduct a job evaluation exercise;
- the quality of candidates submitted for job vacancies;
- the proportion of discipline or grievance issues settled at the first time HR is involved;
- the number of appeals (successful and unsuccessful) against job grading decisions;
- the results of evaluations of training carried out by participants in training programmes;
- the outcome of employee attitude surveys.

KEY LEARNING POINTS

Interpersonal relationships

Interpersonal relationships are those that take place between people when they associate with one another at work.

Teamwork

Teams are essential to the effective functioning of organizations.

In an effective team its members work together in order to achieve expected results. The purpose of the team is clear and its members feel the task is important, both to them and to the organization. The structure of the team is likely to be one in which the leadership and methods of operation are relevant to its purpose. The atmosphere in an effective team tends to be informal, comfortable and relaxed. The leader of the team does not dominate it, nor does the team defer unduly to them.

Networks

Networks are loosely organized connections between people with shared interests. Increasingly in today's more fluid and flexible organizations, people get things done by networking. They exchange information, enlist support and create alliances – getting agreement with other people on a course of action and joining forces to make it happen.

Communicating

People recognize the need to communicate but find it difficult. Words may sound or look precise, but they are not. All sorts of barriers exist between the communicator and the receiver. Unless these barriers are overcome, the message will be distorted or will not get through.

Assertiveness

Assertiveness is about expressing your opinions, beliefs, needs, wants and feelings firmly and in direct, honest and appropriate ways.

Emotional behaviour

Emotional behaviour can include aggression, withdrawal and unreasonable actions or reactions.

Conflict

Conflict is inevitable in organizations because they function by means of adjustments and compromises among competitive elements in their structure and membership. There are three principal ways of resolving inter-group conflict: peaceful coexistence, compromise and problem solving.

Interpersonal conflict can be handled by constructive confrontation.

Negotiating and bargaining skills

The skills required to be effective in negotiations and bargaining are analytical ability, empathy, interactive skills, communicating skills, keeping cards close to the chest and flexible realism.

Organizational politics

Political behaviour is inevitable in organizations because they consist of individuals who, while they are ostensibly there to achieve a common purpose, will, at the same time, be driven by their own needs to achieve their own goals.

Organizational politics involves various kinds of desirable and undesirable behaviour designed to get outcomes which are sought by an individual or a group.

HR practitioners are inevitably involved in organizational politics and they are more likely to survive and thrive if they handle these astutely.

But they also have to behave ethically, whether they are politicking or going about their daily business of providing advice and services.

Liaising with customers

Liaising with customers, whether external or internal, is a matter of establishing their wants and needs and then meeting those wants and needs.

The requirements for effectively liaising with customers can be defined in terms of attitudes, skills, knowledge and behaviours.

Reference

Follett, M P (1924) *Creative Experience*, New York, Longmans Green

Questions

1 What are interpersonal relationships?
2 What is the significance of teams in organizations?

3 What makes a team effective?

4 How can good team working be achieved? (List at least four approaches.)

5 What are networks in organizations?

6 What steps can be taken to improve networking? (List at least four.)

7 What are the main barriers to communication?

8 How can those barriers be overcome?

9 What is assertiveness?

10 What are the characteristics of assertive behaviour?

11 How can aggression be handled?

12 What are the three main ways of handling inter-group conflict?

13 How should counselling be handled when dealing with interpersonal conflict?

14 What is the process of negotiating?

15 What are the most important negotiating and bargaining skills? (Name at least four.)

16 What is the role of political behaviour in organizations?

17 What do you have to do to be politically sensitive? (Name at least four actions.)

18 What is politically astute behaviour on the part of HR practitioners?

19 What are the skills required when liaising with customers?

20 What is a service level agreement?

Influencing people

Key concepts and terms

- *Added value*
- *Business case*
- *Change agent*
- *Culture change*
- *Facilitating*
- *Organizational capability*
- *Organizational effectiveness*
- *Return on investment*

LEARNING OUTCOMES

On completing this chapter you should be able to define these key concepts. You should also understand:

- What supervisors do
- How to provide direction
- How to motivate people
- How to delegate
- How to persuade and make a business case
- Chairing meetings
- Facilitating and coordinating discussion

Introduction

Managers in their capacity as leaders are in the business of influencing people. As Stodgill (1950: 3) pointed out, leadership is an 'influencing process aimed at goal achievement'. HR specialists are particularly involved in influencing senior management, line managers and employees generally in order to persuade them to accept their advice or proposals. Influencing, as considered in this chapter, is associated with the supervision of people and providing direction. It involves the processes of motivation, delegation and persuasion, chairing meetings and facilitating discussion.

Effective supervision – providing direction

Effective supervision is the process of ensuring that the work gets done. It means influencing and as necessary directing people. In the language used by John Adair (1973), supervisors or team leaders are concerned with meeting the needs of the task. They define the task, provide direction – making it clear what the group and its individual members are expected to do and what results are to be achieved, and supervise the work to ensure that it is done as required. To do this the supervisor has to answer the following questions:

- What results have to be achieved, why and by when?
- What needs to be done to achieve those results?
- What are the priorities?
- What resources (people, money and equipment) are needed and where can they be obtained?
- How do I ensure that the team members are motivated?
- How do I ensure that the team members work well together?
- What problems do we face?
- To what extent are these problems straightforward?
- How are we going to overcome the difficult problems?
- Is there a crisis situation?
- What has to be done now to deal with the crisis?
- What pressures are likely to be exerted to get results?

Effective supervisors will provide clear answers to these questions, which will guide their actions and the behaviour of the group. But in motivating people and generating engagement and cooperation, they will have to focus on developing and applying their influencing skills as considered below.

How to motivate people

If you want to motivate your people more effectively, the first thing you should do is understand the basic principles of leadership and motivation as described in Chapters 1 and 10 of this book. Against this background the following are a further 10 steps you can take to achieve higher levels of motivation:

- Exercise authentic leadership as described in Chapter 1.
- Get to know individual team members to understand what is likely to motivate them.
- Set and agree demanding but achievable goals.
- Provide feedback on performance.
- Create expectations that certain behaviours and outputs will produce worthwhile rewards when people succeed.
- Design jobs which enable people to feel a sense of accomplishment, to express and use their abilities and to exercise their own decision-making powers.
- Provide appropriate financial incentives and rewards for achievement (pay for performance).
- Provide appropriate non-financial rewards such as recognition and praise for work well done.
- Select and train team leaders who will exercise effective leadership and have the required motivating skills.
- Give people guidance and training which will develop the knowledge, skills and competencies they need to improve their performance.

Delegating

You can't do everything yourself, so you have to delegate. It is one of the most important things you do. At first sight delegation looks simple. Just tell people what you want them to do and then let them get on with it. But there is more to it than that. It is not easy. It requires courage, patience and skill. And it is an aspect of your work in which you have more freedom of choice than in any other of your activities. What you choose to delegate, to whom and how, is almost entirely at your discretion.

What is delegation?

Delegation is not the same as handing out work. There are some things that your team members do that go with the territory. They are part of their normal duties and all you have to do is to define what those duties are and allocate work accordingly.

Delegation is different. It takes place when you deliberately give someone the authority to carry out a piece of work which you could have decided to keep and carry out yourself. Bear in mind that what you are doing is allocating authority to carry out a task and make the decisions this involves. You are still accountable for the results achieved. It is sometimes said that you cannot delegate responsibility but this is misleading if responsibility is defined, as it usually is, as what people are expected to do – their work, their tasks and their duties. What you cannot do is delegate accountability. In the last analysis you as the manager or team leader always carry the can. What managers have to do is to ensure that people have the authority to carry out their responsibilities. A traffic warden without the power to issue tickets would have to be exceptionally persuasive to have any chance of dealing with parking offences.

What are the advantages of delegation?

The advantages of delegation are that:

- It enables you to focus on the things that really matter in your job – those aspects which require your personal experience, skill and knowledge.
- It relieves you of less critical and routine tasks.
- It frees you from being immersed in detail.
- It extends your capacity to manage.
- It reduces delay in decision making – as long as authority is delegated close to the scene of action.
- It allows decisions to be taken at the level where the details are known.
- It empowers and motivates your staff by extending their responsibilities and authority and providing them with greater autonomy.
- It develops the knowledge and skills of your staff and increases their capacity to exercise judgement and make decisions.

What are the difficulties of delegation?

The advantages of delegation are compelling, but there are difficulties. The main problem is that delegation often involves risk. You cannot be absolutely sure that the person to whom you have delegated something will carry out the work as you would wish. The temptation therefore is to over-supervise, breathe down people's necks and interfere. This inhibits their authority, makes them nervous and resentful and destroys their confidence, thus dissipating any advantages the original act of delegation might have had. Another difficulty is that many managers are reluctant to delegate because they cannot let go – they want to keep on top of everything. They really think they know best and cannot trust anyone else to do it as well, never mind better. Finally, some managers are reluctant to delegate simply because they enjoy what they are doing and cannot bear the possibility of giving it away to anyone else.

FIGURE 16.1 The sequence of delegation

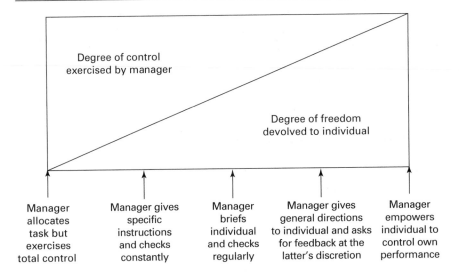

| Manager allocates task but exercises total control | Manager gives specific instructions and checks constantly | Manager briefs individual and checks regularly | Manager gives general directions to individual and asks for feedback at the latter's discretion | Manager empowers individual to control own performance |

Approaches to delegation

To a degree, overcoming these difficulties is a matter of simply being aware of them and appreciating that if there are any disadvantages, these are outweighed by the advantages. But approaches to delegation such as those discussed below help. You need to understand the process of delegation, when to delegate, what to delegate, how to choose people to whom you want to delegate, how to give out the work and how to monitor performance.

The sequence of delegation

Delegation is a sequential process which starts from the point when total control is exercised (no freedom of action for the individual to whom work has been allocated) to full devolution (the individual is completely empowered to carry out the work). This sequence is illustrated in Figure 16.1.

When to delegate

You should delegate when you:

- have more work than you can carry out yourself;
- cannot allow sufficient time for your priority tasks;
- want to develop a member of your team;
- believe that it will increase someone's engagement with their job;
- think that the job can be done adequately by the individual or the team to whom you delegate.

What to delegate

The tasks you delegate are the routine and repetitive tasks which you cannot reasonably be expected to do yourself – as long as you use the time you have won productively. You are not just ridding yourself of the difficult, tedious or unrewarding tasks. Neither are you trying simply to win for yourself an easier life. In some ways delegation will make your life more difficult, but also more rewarding.

You can delegate specialist tasks to those who have the skills and know-how to do them. You cannot be expected to do it all yourself. Neither can you be expected to know it all yourself.

You can sometimes delegate tasks which are designed to stretch and develop the individual you ask to carry them out.

Giving out the work

When you delegate you should ensure that the individuals or team concerned understand:

- why the work needs to be done;
- what they are expected to do;
- the date by which they are expected to do it;
- the end results they are expected to achieve;
- the authority they have to make decisions;
- the problems they must refer back;
- the progress or completion reports they should submit;
- any guidance and support that will be available to them.

You have to consider how much guidance will be required on how the work should be done. You don't want to give directions in such laborious detail that you run the risk of stifling initiative. Neither do you want to infuriate people by explaining everything needlessly. As long as you are reasonably certain that they will do the job to your satisfaction without embarrassing you or seriously upsetting people, exceeding the budget or breaking the law, let them get on with it.

Persuading people

HR professionals are very much in the business of influencing thinking and decision making on the part of others. They must know about persuading people and case presentation.

Persuading people

A manager's job is 60 per cent getting it right and 40 per cent putting it across. Managers spend a lot of time persuading other people to accept their ideas and suggestions. Persuasion is just another word for selling. You may feel that good ideas should sell themselves, but life is not like that. People resist change and anything new is usually treated with suspicion. Here are 10 rules for effective persuasion:

- Define your objective and get the facts. If you are persuading someone to agree to a proposal, first decide what you want to achieve and why. Assemble all the facts you need to support your case. Eliminate emotional arguments so that you and others can judge the proposition on the facts alone.

- Define the problem. If there is a problem to resolve and you are trying to persuade someone to accept your views on what should be done about it, first decide whether the problem is a misunderstanding (a failure to understand each other accurately) or a true disagreement (a failure to agree even when both parties understand one another). It is not necessarily possible to resolve a true disagreement by understanding each other better. People generally believe that an argument is a battle to understand who is correct. More often, it is a battle to decide who is more stubborn.

- Find out what the other party wants. The key to all persuasion is to see your proposition from the other person's point of view. Find out how they look at things. Establish what they need and want.

- Accentuate the benefits. Present your case in a way that highlights the benefits to the other party or at least reduces any objections or fears.

- Predict the other person's response. Everything we say should be focused on that likely response. Anticipate objections by asking yourself how the other party might react negatively to your proposition and thinking up ways of responding to them.

- Create the person's next move. It is not a question of deciding what we want to do but what we want the other person to do.

- Convince people by reference to their own perceptions. People decide on what to do on the basis of their own perceptions, not yours.

- Prepare a simple and attractive proposition. Make it as straightforward as possible. Present the case 'sunny side up', emphasizing its benefits. Break the problem into manageable pieces and deal with them one step at a time.

- Make the other person a party to your ideas. Get them to contribute. Find some common ground so that you can start with agreement. Don't try to defeat them in an argument – you will only antagonize them.

- Clinch and take action. Choose the right moment to clinch the proposal – don't prolong the discussion and risk losing it. But follow up promptly.

Case presentation

Persuasion frequently means presenting a case. You will often have to make out a case for what you think should be done. You have to persuade people to believe in your views and accept your recommendations. To do this, you must have a clear idea of what you want, and you have to show that you believe in it yourself. Above all, the effectiveness of your presentation will depend upon the care with which you have prepared it.

Thorough preparation is vital. You must think through not only what should be done and why, but also how people will react. Only then can you decide how to make your case: stressing the benefits without underestimating the costs, and anticipating objections. The steps you should take are:

- Show that your proposal is based on a thorough analysis of the facts and that the alternatives were properly evaluated before the conclusion was reached. If you have made assumptions, you must demonstrate that these are reasonable on the basis of relevant experience and justifiable projections, which allow for the unexpected. Bear in mind that a proposal is only as strong as its weakest assumption.

- Spell out the benefits – to the company and the individuals to whom the case is being made. Wherever possible, express benefits in financial terms. Abstract benefits, such as customer satisfaction or workers' morale, are difficult to sell. But don't produce 'funny numbers' – financial justification which will not stand up to examination.

- Reveal costs. Don't try to disguise them in any way. And be realistic. Your proposition will be destroyed if anyone can show that you have underestimated the costs.

- Remember, senior management decision makers want to know in precise terms what they will get for their money. Most are likely to be cautious, being unwilling and often unable to take much risk. For this reason, it can be difficult to make a case for experiments or pilot schemes unless the decision maker can see what the benefits and the ultimate bill will be.

Making a business case

You may be asked specifically to produce a business case. This will set out the reasons why a proposed course of action will benefit the business, how it will provide that benefit and how much it will cost. A business case is a particular form of persuasion and all the points made above apply to its preparation and presentation. But there are some special features about business cases as described below.

A business case is typically made either in added value terms (ie the income generated by the proposal will significantly exceed the cost of implementing it), or on the basis of the return on investment (ie the cost of the investment, say in training, is justified by the financial returns in such areas as increased productivity). Clearly, a business case is more convincing when it is accompanied by realistic projections of added value or return on investment. The case for capital expenditure can be made by an analysis of the cash flows associated with the investment and appraisals of the benefits that are likely to arise from them. The object is to demonstrate that in return for paying out a given amount of cash today, a larger amount will be received over a period of time. A number of investment appraisal techniques are available, such as payback, the accounting rate of return, discounted cash flow and net present value.

A business case will be enhanced if:

- data is available on the impact the proposal is likely to make on key areas of the organization's operations, eg customer service levels, quality, shareholder value, productivity, income generation, innovation, skills development, talent management;

- it can be shown that the proposal will increase the business's competitive edge, for example enlarging the skill base or multi-skilling to ensure that it can achieve competitive advantage through innovation and/or reducing time to market;

- there is proof that the innovation has already worked well within the organization (perhaps as a pilot scheme) or represents 'good practice' which is likely to be transferable to the organization;

- it can be implemented without too much trouble, for example not taking up a lot of managers' time or not meeting with strong opposition from line managers, employees or trade unions (it is as well to check the likely reaction before launching a proposal);

- it will add to the reputation of the company by showing that it is a 'world class' organization, ie what it does is as good as, if not better than, the world leaders in the sector in which the business operates (a promise that publicity will be achieved through articles in professional journals, press releases and conference presentations, will help);

- it will enhance the 'employer brand' of the company by making it a 'best place to work';

- the proposal is brief, to the point and well argued – it should take no more than five minutes to present orally and should be summarized in writing on the proverbial one side of one sheet of paper (supplementary details can be included in appendices).

Making the business case is obviously easier where management is preconditioned to agree to the proposition. For example, it is not hard to convince top managers that performance-related pay is a good thing – they may well be receiving bonus payments themselves and believe, rightly or wrongly, that because it motivates them it will motivate everyone else. Talent management is another process where top management needs little persuasion that things need to be done to enhance and preserve the talent flow, although they will have to be convinced that in practice, innovations will achieve that aim. Performance management may be slightly more difficult because it is hard to demonstrate that it can produce measurable improvements in performance, but senior managers are predisposed towards an approach which at least promises to improve the level of performance.

The toughest area for justification in added value terms can be expenditure on learning and development programmes. This is where a return on investment (ROI) approach is desirable. The business case for learning and development should demonstrate how learning, training and development programmes will meet business needs. Kearns and Miller (1997) go as far as to claim that: 'If a business objective cannot be cited as a basis for designing training and development, then no training and development should be offered.'

Chairing meetings

Most managers, including those in HR, will find themselves required to chair a meeting from time to time, and meetings provide major arenas for exerting influence. The success or failure of a meeting largely depends on the effectiveness with which it is chaired. If you are chairing a meeting, this is what you must do.

Prepare for the meeting

Before the meeting starts, ensure that it has proper terms of reference and that the members are briefed on what to expect and what they should be prepared to contribute. Plan the agenda to ensure that all the issues will be dealt with in a logical order. Prepare and issue briefing papers which will structure the meeting and spell out the background, thus saving time going into detail or reviewing purely factual information during the meeting.

Conduct the meeting

Start by clearly defining the objective of the meeting, setting a timescale which you intend to keep.

Go through each item of the agenda in turn, ensuring that a firm conclusion is reached and recorded.

Initiate the discussion on each item by setting the scene very briefly and asking for contributions – ask for answers to specific questions (which you should have prepared in advance) or you may refer the matter first to a member of the meeting who can make the best initial contribution (ideally, you should have briefed that individual in advance).

Invite contributions from other members of the meeting, taking care not to allow anyone to dominate the discussions.

Bring people back to order if they drift from the point.

If there is too much talk, remind members that they are there to make progress.

Encourage the expression of different points of view and avoid crushing anyone too obviously if they have not made a sensible comment.

Allow disagreement between members of the meeting but step in smartly if the atmosphere becomes too contentious.

Chip in with questions or brief comments from time to time, but do not dominate the discussion.

At appropriate moments during the meeting, summarize the discussion, express views on where the meeting has got to and outline your perception of the interim or final decision that has been made. Then check that the meeting agrees, amending the conclusion as necessary, and ensuring that the decision is recorded exactly as made.

Summarize what has been achieved at the end of the meeting, indicating who has to do what by when.

If a further meeting is needed, agree the purpose of the meeting and what has to be done by those present before it takes place.

Facilitating and coordinating discussions

More frequently than chairing meetings, HR specialists will be involved in facilitating and coordinating discussions.

Facilitating

Facilitating is the process of helping a group reach conclusions in the shape of ideas and solutions. Facilitators do not exist to 'chair' the meeting in the sense of controlling the discussion and pressurizing the group to agree to a course of action. The group is there to make up its own mind and the facilitator helps it to do so. The help is provided by asking questions which encourage the group members to think for themselves. These can be challenging and probing questions but the facilitator does not provide the answers – that is the role of the group. Neither do facilitators allow their own opinions to intrude – they are there to help the group marshal its opinions, not to enforce their own ideas. However, by using questioning techniques carefully, facilitators can ensure that the group does thoroughly discuss and analyse the issues and reaches conclusions by consensus rather than allowing anyone to dominate the process.

Facilitators ensure that everyone has their say and that they are listened to. They step in quickly to defuse unproductive arguments. They see that the group defines and understands its objectives and any methodology they might use. They summarize from time to time the progress made in achieving the objectives without bringing their own views to bear. Facilitators are there to ensure that the group makes progress and does not get stuck in fruitless or disruptive argument. But they encourage the group rather than drive it forward.

The aim of the facilitator is to guide the group's thinking. The facilitator may, therefore, be more concerned with shaping attitudes than convincing people about what to do or imparting new knowledge. The facilitator has unobtrusively to stimulate people to talk, guide the discussion along predetermined lines (there must be a plan and an ultimate objective), and provide interim summaries and a final summary.

Coordinating discussions

Coordinating discussions is a matter of getting active participation and then ensuring that the discussion informs people of the issues related to the subject and leads to a conclusion which satisfies the participants. The following techniques can be used to get active participation and coordinate the process:

- Ask for contributions by direct questions.
- Use open-ended questions which will stimulate thought.
- Check understanding; make sure that everyone is following the argument.
- Encourage participation by providing support rather than criticism.
- Prevent domination by individual members of the group by bringing in other people and asking cross-reference questions.
- Avoid dominating the group yourself. The leader's job is to guide the discussion, maintain control and summarize from time to time. If necessary, 'reflect' opinions expressed by individuals back to the group to make sure they find the answer for themselves. The leader is there to help the group reach a conclusion, not to do it for them.
- Maintain control – ensure that the discussion is progressing along the right lines towards a firm conclusion.

KEY LEARNING POINTS

Effective supervision

Effective supervision is the process of directing people to ensure that they get the work done.

Supervisors define the task, provide direction – making it clear what the group and its individual members are expected to do and what results are to be achieved – and ensure that the work is done as required.

Motivating people

Exercise visionary and inspiring leadership, establish what is likely to motivate team members, set demanding but achievable goals and provide feedback, clarify potential rewards, design jobs that will motivate, and provide financial and non-financial rewards.

Delegation
Delegation takes place when you deliberately give someone the authority to carry out a piece of work which you could have decided to keep and carry out yourself.

Leading change
Leading change involves initiating and managing culture change (the process of changing the organization's culture in the shape of its values, norms and beliefs) and the introduction of new structures, systems, working practices and people management processes.

Facilitating change
Facilitating change is the process of making change happen.

Influencing people
HR professionals are often involved in influencing thinking and decision making on the part of others. They must know about persuading people and case presentation.

Chairing meetings
Most managers, including those in HR, will find themselves required to chair a meeting. The success or failure of a meeting largely depends on the effectiveness with which it is chaired.

Facilitating
Facilitating is the process of helping a group reach conclusions in the shape of ideas and solutions.

Coordinating discussions
Coordinating discussions is a matter of getting active participation and then ensuring that the discussion informs people of the issues related to the subject and leads to a conclusion which satisfies the participants.

References

Adair, J (1973) *The Action Centred Leader*, London, McGrawHill

Hamlin, B (2001) A review and synthesis of context and practice, in B Hamlin, J Keep and K Ash (eds) *Organizational Change and Development: A reflective guide for managers, trainers and developers*, Harlow, Pearson Education, pp 13–38

Kearns, P and Miller, T (1997) *Measuring the impact of training and development on the bottom line*, FT Management Briefings, London, Pitman

Stogdill, R M (1950) Leaders, membership and organization, *Psychological Bulletin*, 25, pp 1–14

Ulrich, D (1997) Judge me more by my future than my past, *Human Resource Management*, 36 (1), pp 5–8

Ulrich, D (1998) A new mandate for human resources, *Harvard Business Review*, January–February, pp 124–34

Questions

1 What is effective supervision?

2 What are the main steps you should take to motivate people?

3 What is delegation?

4 What are the advantages of delegation?

5 When should you delegate?

6 How should you delegate?

7 What are the most important rules for effective persuasion?

8 What are the key steps required for effective case presentation?

9 How should a business case be made?

10 What steps should you take before chairing a meeting?

11 What are the most important actions required to chair a meeting successfully?

12 What is facilitating?

13 How should facilitation be carried out?

14 How should discussions be coordinated?

People management skills

- *Competency*
- *Competency-based interview*
- *Criteria-referenced interview*
- *Open-ended question*
- *Person specification*

LEARNING OUTCOMES

On completing this chapter you should be able to define these key concepts. You should also understand:

- How to conduct a selection interview
- How to conduct a performance review meeting (an appraisal interview)
- How to ensure that people learn and develop
- How to make an effective presentation
- How to manage projects
- How to manage poor performance
- How to conduct a discipline meeting

Introduction

This chapter covers a number of the key people management skills used by managers and HR specialists.

How to conduct a selection interview

One of the most important people management tasks carried out by managers and HR specialists is to conduct a selection interview. The aim of such interviews is to provide answers to three fundamental questions:

- Can the individual do the job? Is the person capable of doing the work to the standard required?
- Will the individual do the job? Is the person well motivated?
- How is the individual likely to fit into the team? Will I and other team members be able to work well with this person?

Form of the selection interview

A selection interview should take the form of a conversation with a purpose. It is a conversation because candidates should be given the opportunity to talk freely about themselves and their careers. But the conversation has to be planned, directed and controlled to achieve your aims in the time available.

Your task as an interviewer is to draw candidates out to ensure that you get the information you want. Candidates should be encouraged to do most of the talking – one of the besetting sins of poor interviewers is that they talk too much. But you have to plan the structure of the interview to achieve its purpose and decide in advance the questions you need to ask – questions which will give you what you need to make an accurate assessment.

A selection interview has three sections:

- Beginning. At the start of the interview candidates are put at their ease. They need to be encouraged to talk freely in response to questions.
- Middle. This is where interviewers find out what they need to know about candidates to establish the extent to which they meet the requirements of the job as set out in a person or job specification. This indicates what experience, qualifications and competencies (characteristics of a person that result in effective job performance) are required. This part should take at least 80 per cent of the time, leaving, say, 5 per cent at the beginning and 15 per cent at the end.
- End. At the end of the interview candidates are given the opportunity to ask about the job and the company. More details about the job can be given to promising candidates who are told what the next step will be.

Preparing for the interview

Your first step in preparing for an interview is to familiarize or re-familiarize yourself with the person specification and candidate's CV, application form or letter. General questions should be prepared which will be put to all candidates, as well as specific questions for individuals about their career or qualifications.

Structuring the interview

The best approach is one that is criteria referenced, using competencies as the criteria (this is often called a competency-based interview). The competencies required should be set out in the person specification and the interviewer 'targets' these key criteria, having decided on what questions should be asked to draw out from candidates information about their competencies (knowledge, skills capabilities and personal qualities) which can be compared with the criteria to assess the extent to which candidates meet the specification.

Planning the interview

A biographical approach is probably the most popular because it is simple to use and logical. The interview can be sequenced chronologically, starting with the first job or even before that at school and, if appropriate, college or university. The succeeding jobs, if any, are then dealt with in turn, ending with the present job on which most time is spent if the candidate has been in it for a reasonable time. But using the chronological method for someone who has had a number of jobs can mean spending too much time on the earlier jobs, leaving insufficient time for the most important recent experiences. To overcome this problem, an alternative biographical approach is to start with the present job, which is discussed in some depth. The interviewer then works backwards, job by job, but only concentrating on particularly interesting or relevant experience in earlier jobs.

Interviewing techniques – asking questions

The interviewer's job is to draw the candidate out, at the same time ensuring that the information required is obtained. To this end it is desirable to ask a number of open-ended questions – questions which cannot be answered by yes or no and which promote a full response. But a good interviewer will have an armoury of other types of questions to be asked when appropriate, such as:

- Probing questions which ask for further details and explanations to ensure that the interviewer is getting all the facts.
- Closed questions which aim to clarify a point of fact and therefore require a single answer.

- Hypothetical questions to test how candidates would approach a typical problem.
- Behavioural event questions to get candidates to tell the interviewer how they would behave in situations which have been identified as critical to successful job performance.
- Capability questions to establish what candidates know, the skills they possess and use and their competencies – what they are capable of doing. These questions can be open, probing or closed but they will always be focused as precisely as possible on the contents of the person specification referring to knowledge, skills and competences.
- Continuity questions to keep the flow going in an interview and encourage candidates to enlarge on what they said, within limits.
- Playback questions to test understanding of what candidates have said by putting to them a statement of what it appears they have told the interviewer and asking them if they agree or disagree with the interviewer's version.

Avoid any questions that could be construed as being biased on the grounds of sex, sexual orientation, race, disability or age.

Ten useful questions

- What are the most important aspects of your present job?
- What do you think have been your most notable achievements in your career to date?
- What sort of problems have you successfully solved recently in your job?
- What have you learned from your present job?
- What has been your experience in…?
- What do you know about…?
- What particularly interests you in this job and why?
- Now you have heard more about the job, would you please tell me which aspects of your experience are most relevant?
- What do you think you can bring to this job?
- Is there anything else about your career which hasn't come out yet in this interview but you think I ought to hear?

Dos and don'ts of selection interviewing

TABLE 17.1 Dos and don'ts of selection interviewing

Do	Don't
• Plan the interview. • Give yourself sufficient time. • Use a structured interview approach wherever possible. • Create the right atmosphere. • Establish an easy and informal relationship – start with open questions. • Encourage the candidate to talk. • Cover the ground as planned, ensuring that you complete a prepared agenda and maintain continuity. • Analyse the candidate's career to reveal strengths, weaknesses and patterns of interest. • Make use of open questions which invite people to talk. • Ensure that questions are clear and unambiguous. • Get examples and instances of the successful application of knowledge, skills and the effective use of capabilities. • Make judgements on the basis of the factual information you have obtained about candidates' experience and attributes in relation to the person specification. • Keep control over the content and timing of the interview.	• Start the interview unprepared. • Plunge too quickly into demanding (probe) questions. • Ask multiple or leading questions. • Pay too much attention to isolated strengths or weaknesses. • Allow candidates to gloss over important facts. • Talk too much or allow candidates to ramble on. • Allow your prejudices to get the better of your capacity to make objective judgements. • Fall into the halo effect trap, ie drawing conclusions about a person on the basis of one or two good points, leading to the neglect of negative indicators. Or into the horns trap – focusing too much on one or two weak points. • Ask questions or make remarks that could be construed as in any way discriminatory. • Attempt too many interviews in a row.

How to conduct a performance review meeting

Performance review or appraisal meetings are a key part of a performance management system. Although performance management is a continuous process, it is still necessary to have a formal review once or twice yearly. This provides a focal point for the consideration of key performance and development issues. The performance review meeting is the means through which the five primary performance management elements of agreement, measurement, feedback, positive reinforcement and dialogue can be put to good use. It leads to the completion of the performance management cycle by informing performance and development agreements. It involves some form of assessment, often ratings. The term 'performance review' is better than 'performance appraisal' as the latter implies that the interview is just about telling people how well or badly they are doing. Performance review meetings are much more positive.

Purpose of the meeting

In a sense, a performance review meeting is a stock-taking exercise answering the questions 'Where have we got to?' and 'How did we get here?' But there is more to it than that. It is not just an historical affair, dwelling on the past and taking the form of a post mortem. The true purpose of the review is to answer the question 'Where do we go from here?' which means looking forward to what needs to be done by people to achieve the overall purpose of their jobs, to meet new challenges, to make even better use of their skills, knowledge and abilities and to develop their skills and competencies to further their career and increase their employability, within and outside the organization.

Conducting a constructive meeting

A constructive review meeting is most likely to take place if the manager or team leader:

- encourages individuals to do most of the talking; the aim should be to conduct the meeting as a dialogue rather than using it to make 'top down' pronouncements on what the manager thinks;
- listens actively to what the other person says;
- allows scope for reflection and analysis;
- provides feedback which analyses performance, not personality – concentrating on what individuals have done and achieved, not the sort of people they are;
- keeps the whole period under review, not concentrating on isolated or recent events;

- adopts a 'no surprises' approach – performance problems should have been identified and dealt with at the time they occurred;
- recognizes achievements and reinforces strengths;
- discusses any work or performance problems, how they have arisen and what can be done about them;
- ends the meeting positively with any necessary agreed action plans (learning and development and performance improvement).

How to ensure that people learn and develop

Ensuring that people learn and develop is an important responsibility of managers or team leaders, who need skilled, knowledgeable and competent people in their department or team. To improve the performance of their team members they must not only ensure that individuals learn the basic skills they need but also that they develop those skills to enable them to perform even better when faced with new demands and challenges. The HR or learning and development department also has the important responsibility of advising and helping line managers carry out their employee development role but additionally is likely to be responsible for the delivery of training.

Most learning happens at the place of work, although it can be supplemented by such activities as e-learning (the delivery of learning opportunities and support via computer, networked and web-based technology) and formal 'off-the-job' training courses. It is up to managers and team leaders to ensure that favourable conditions for learning on the job exist generally in their area. They may do this through coaching or mentoring or straightforward instruction as described in Chapter 3.

Line managers can also help people to develop through performance management. The performance planning part of the process involves agreement between the manager and the individual on what the latter needs to do to achieve objectives, raise standards, improve performance and develop the required competencies. It also establishes priorities – the key aspects of the job to which attention has to be given.

How to make an effective presentation

The three keys to delivering an effective presentation are:

- thorough preparation;
- good delivery;
- overcoming nervousness.

Thorough preparation

Allow yourself ample time for preparation. You will probably need at least 10 times as much as the duration of your talk. The main stages are:

1   Make yourself informed. Collect and assemble all the facts and arguments you can get hold of.

2   Decide what to say. Define the main messages you want to get across. Limit the number to three or four – few people can absorb more than this number of new ideas at any one time. Select the facts, arguments and examples that support your message.

3   Structure your talk into the classic beginning, middle and end:

    –   Start thinking about the middle first, with your main messages and the supporting facts, arguments and illustrations.
    –   Arrange your points so that a cumulative impact and a logical flow of ideas are achieved.
    –   Then turn to the opening of your talk. Your objectives should be to create attention, arouse interest and inspire confidence. Give your audience a trailer to what you are going to say. Underline the objective of your presentation – what they will get out of it.
    –   Finally, think about how you are going to close your talk. First and last impressions are very important. End on a high note.

4   Think carefully about length. Never talk for more than 40 minutes at a time. Twenty or 30 minutes is better.

5   Aim to keep the audience's attention throughout. Prepare interim summaries which reinforce what you are saying and, above all, hammer home your key points at intervals throughout your talk.

6   Ensure continuity. You should build your argument progressively until you come to a positive and convincing conclusion. Provide signposts, interim summaries and bridging sections which lead your audience naturally from one point to the next.

7   Prepare your notes. In the first place, write out your introductory and concluding remarks in full and set out in some detail the main text of your talk. It is not usually necessary to write everything down. You should then boil down your text to the key headings to which you will refer in your talk. Your aim should be to avoid reading your speech if you possibly can as this can remove any life from what you have to say. So as not to be pinned down behind a lectern, it is better to write your summarized points on lined index cards to which you can refer easily as you go along.

8   Prepare and use visual aids. As your audience will only absorb one-third of what you say, if that, reinforce your message with visual aids. Appeal to more than one sense at a time. PowerPoint slides provide good back-up, but don't overdo them and keep them simple. Too many

visuals can be distracting (use no more than 15 or so in a half-hour presentation) and too many words or an over-elaborate presentation will divert, bore and confuse your audience. As a rule of thumb, try not to put more than five or six bullet points on a slide. Ideally each point should contain no more than 10 words. Audiences dislike having to read a lot of small print on an over-busy slide. Breaking this rule is sometimes unavoidable when it is essential to convey a certain amount of information on the slide. If this is inevitable, go through the points very carefully and wherever possible issue the slide as a handout in advance. Use diagrams and charts wherever possible to break up the flow of words and illustrate points. If you want the members of your audience to read something fairly elaborate, distribute the material as a handout and take them through it

9 Rehearse. Rehearsal is vital. It instils confidence, helps you to get your timing right, and enables you to polish your opening and closing remarks and coordinate your talk and visual aids. Rehearse the talk to yourself several times and note how long each section takes. Get used to expanding on your notes without waffling. Practise giving your talk out loud – standing up, if that is the way you are going to present it. Get someone to hear you and provide constructive criticism. It may be hard to take but it could do you a world of good. But remember the Zen saying: 'Practise the performance, then forget the practice when you perform.'

10 Check arrangements in the room. Ensure that your projector works and you know how to operate it. Check also on focus and visibility. Before you begin your talk, check that your notes and visual aids are in the right order and to hand.

Good delivery

To deliver a presentation effectively the following approaches should be used:

- Talk audibly and check that you can be heard at the back. Your task is to project your voice. It's easier when there is a microphone, but even then you have to think about getting your words across.
- Vary the pace (not too fast, not too slow), pitch and emphasis of your delivery. Use pauses to make a point.
- Try to be conversational and as informal as the occasion requires (but not too casual).
- Convey that you truly believe in what you are saying. Audiences respond well to enthusiasm.
- Avoid a stilted delivery. That is why you must not read your talk. If you are your natural self, people are more likely to be on your side. They will forgive the occasional pause to find the right word.

- Light relief is a good thing but don't drag in irrelevant jokes or, indeed, make jokes at all if you are no good at telling them. You do not have to tell jokes.

- Use short words and sentences.

- Keep your eyes on the audience, moving from person to person to demonstrate that you are addressing them all, and also to gauge their reactions to what you are saying. Worry a little if they look at their watches. Worry even more if they shake their watches to find out if they have stopped.

- If you can manage without elaborate notes (your slides or a few cards may be sufficient), come out from behind the desk or lectern and get close to your audience. It is best to stand up so that you can project what you say more effectively unless it is a smallish meeting round a table.

- Use hands for gesture and emphasis in moderation (don't put them in your pocket – if you have one).

- Don't fidget.

- Stand naturally and upright.

- You can move around the platform a little to add variety – you don't want to look as if you are clutching the lectern for much-needed support. But avoid pacing up and down like a caged tiger.

Overcoming nervousness

Some nervousness is a good thing. It makes you prepare, makes you think and makes the adrenaline flow, thus raising performance. But excessive nervousness ruins your effectiveness and must be controlled.

The common reasons for excessive nervousness are: fear of failure, fear of looking foolish, fear of breakdown, a sense of inferiority and dread of the isolation of the speaker. To overcome nervousness you should:

- Practise. Take every opportunity you can get to speak in public. The more you do it, the more confident you will become. Solicit constructive criticism and act on it.

- Know your subject. Get the facts, examples and illustrations which you need to put across.

- Know your audience. Who is going to be there? What are they expecting to hear? What will they want to get out of listening to you?

- Know your objective. Make sure that you know what you want to achieve. Visualize, if you can, each member of your audience going away having learned something new which they are going to put to practical use.

- Prepare. If you know that you have prepared carefully, you will be much more confident on the day.
- Rehearse. This is an essential method of overcoming nervousness.

How to manage projects

HR professionals are involved in project management when they lead or take part in the introduction of a new HR system or process such as job evaluation, performance management or performance-related pay or, on a wider scale, when they are involved in an organization development programme. Project management is the planning, supervision and control of any activity or set of activities which leads to a defined outcome at a predetermined time and in accordance with specified performance or quality standards at a budgeted cost. It is concerned with deliverables – getting things done as required or promised. While delivering results on time is important, it is equally important to deliver them to meet the specification and within the projected cost.

Project management involves action planning – deciding what work is to be done, why the work needs to be done, who will do the work, how much it will cost, when the work has to be completed (totally or stage by stage) and where the work will be carried out. The three main project management activities are project planning, setting up the project and project control.

Project planning

Project planning starts with a definition of the objectives of the project, which is presented as a business case. This means answering three basic questions: (1) Why is this project needed? (2) What benefits are expected from the project? (3) How much will it cost? The answers to these questions should be quantified. The requirement could be spelt out in such terms as new systems, processes or facilities to meet defined business needs, new plant required for new products or to improve productivity or quality. The benefits are expressed as revenues generated, productivity, quality or performance improvements, added value, costs saved and return on investment.

Project planning involves deciding what resources are required – money and people. This is an investment process and investment appraisal techniques are used to ensure that the company's criteria on return on investment are satisfied. Cost–benefit analysis may be used to assess the degree to which the benefits justify the costs, time and number of people required by the project. This may mean identifying opportunity costs, which establish if a greater benefit would be obtained by investing the money or deploying the people on other projects or activities.

A performance specification is required which indicates what the expected outcome of the project is – how it should perform – and describes how it will operate. This leads to a project plan, which sets out:

- the major operations in sequence – the main stages of the project;
- a breakdown where appropriate of each major operation into a sequence of subsidiary tasks;
- an analysis of the interrelationships and interdependencies of major and subsidiary tasks;
- an estimate of the time required to complete each major operation or stage;
- a procurement plan to obtain the necessary materials, systems and equipment;
- a workforce resource plan which defines how many people will be allocated to the project with different skills at each stage and who is to be responsible for controlling the project as a whole and each of the major stages or operations.

Setting up the project

Setting up the project involves:

- obtaining and allocating resources;
- selecting and briefing the project management team;
- finalizing the project programme – defining each stage;
- defining and establishing control systems and reporting procedures (format and timing of progress reports);
- identifying key dates, stage by stage, for the project (milestones) and providing for milestone meetings to review progress and decide on any actions required.

Controlling the project

The three most important things to control are:

- time – achievement of project plan as programme;
- quality – achievement of project specifications;
- cost – containment of costs within budget.

Project control is based on progress reports showing what is being achieved against the plan. The planned completion date, actual achievement and forecast completion date for each stage or operation are provided. The likelihood of delays, overruns or bottlenecks is thus established so that corrective action can be taken in good time. Control can be achieved by the use of Gantt or bar charts and by reference to network plans or critical path analyses.

How to manage poor performance

The three major aspects of poor performance that need to be managed are absenteeism, poor timekeeping and incompetence (underperformers).

Absenteeism

A frequent people problem you probably have to face is that of dealing with absenteeism. The Chartered Institute of Personnel and Development established that absence levels in 2009 averaged 7.4 days per year per person. Your own organization should have figures which indicate average absence levels. If the levels in your department are below the average for the organization or, in the absence of that information, below the national average, you should not be complacent – you should continue to monitor the absence of individuals to find out whose absence levels are above the average and why. . If your department's absence figures are significantly higher than the norm, you may have to take more direct action such as discussing with individuals whose absence rates are high the reasons for their absences, especially when these have been self-certificated. You may have to deal with recurrent short-term (one or two days) absence or longer-term sickness absence

Recurrent short-term absence

Dealing with people who are repeatedly absent for short periods can be difficult to handle. This is because it may be hard to determine when occasional absence becomes a problem or whether it is justifiable, perhaps on medical grounds.

So what do you do about it? Many organizations provide guidelines to managers on the 'trigger points' for action (the amount of absence which needs to be investigated), perhaps based on analyses of the incidence of short-term absence and the level at which it is regarded as acceptable (in some organizations software exists to generate analyses and data which can be made available direct to managers through a self-service system). If guidelines do not exist, managers should be able to obtain advice from an HR specialist, if one is available. In the absence of either of these sources of help and in particularly difficult cases, it may be advisable to recommend to higher management that advice is obtained from an employment law expert.

But this sort of guidance may not be available and you may have to make up your own mind on when to do something and what to do. A day off every other month may not be too serious – although if it happens regularly on a Monday (after weekends in Prague, Barcelona, etc?) or a Friday (before such weekends?), you may feel like having a word with the individual, not as a warning but just to let them know that you are aware of what is going on. There may be a medical or other acceptable explanation. Return-to-work interviews can provide valuable information. You see the individual and find out why the time was taken off, giving them ample opportunity to explain the absence.

After an unauthorized absence, you can conduct an informal return-to-work interview, simply asking why the absence took place and indicating, if appropriate, that the reasons given are insufficient and that similar behaviour should not be repeated. In persistent cases of absenteeism you should hold an absence review meeting. Although this would be more comprehensive than a return-to-work interview, it should not at this stage be presented as part of a disciplinary process. The meeting should be positive and constructive. If absence results from a health problem, you can find out what the employee is doing about it and if necessary suggest that their doctor should be consulted. Or absences may be caused by problems facing a parent or a carer. In such cases you should be sympathetic but you can reasonably discuss with the individual what steps can be taken to reduce the problem or you might be able to agree on flexible working if that can be arranged. The aim is to get the employee to discuss as openly as possible any factors affecting their attendance and to agree any constructive steps.

If after holding an attendance review meeting and, it is to be hoped, agreeing the steps necessary to reduce absenteeism, short-term absence persists without a satisfactory explanation, then another meeting can be held which emphasizes the employee's responsibility for attending work. Depending on the circumstances (each case should be dealt with on its merits), at this meeting you can link any positive support with an indication that following the provision of support you expect absence levels to improve over a defined timescale (an improvement period). If this does not happen, the individual can expect more formal disciplinary action.

To summarize, the steps you can take are to:

- study any organizational guidelines on the 'trigger points' for action (the amount of absence which needs to be investigated);

- analyse data on absence levels and discuss with individuals whose absence rates are high the reasons for their absences, especially when these have been self-certificated;

- conduct return-to-work interviews to find out why the time was taken off, giving the employee ample opportunity to explain the absence;

- in persistent cases of absenteeism, hold an absence review meeting in which an agreement is reached on how to improve absence levels over a defined timescale (an improvement period). Indicate that if this does not happen, the individual can expect more formal disciplinary action.

Dealing with long-term absence

Dealing with long-term absence can be difficult. The aim should be to facilitate the employee's return to work at the earliest reasonable point while recognizing that in extreme cases the person may not be able to come back. In that case they can fairly be dismissed for lack of capability as long as:

- the employee has been consulted at all stages;
- contact has been maintained with the employee – this is something you can usefully do as long as you do not appear to be pressing them to return to work before they are ready;
- appropriate medical advice has been sought from the employee's own doctor; but the employee's consent is needed and employees have the right to see the report, and it may be desirable to obtain a second opinion;
- all reasonable options for alternative employment have been reviewed as well as any other means of facilitating a return to work.

The decision to dismiss should only be taken if these conditions are satisfied. It is a tricky one and you should seek advice before taking it.

Handling poor timekeeping

If you are faced with persistent lateness, the first step is to issue an informal warning to the individual concerned. If this has little effect, you may be forced to invoke the disciplinary procedure. If timekeeping does not improve, this could go through the successive stages of a recorded oral warning, a written warning and a final written warning. If the final warning does not work, disciplinary action would have to be taken; in serious cases this would mean dismissal.

Note that this raises the difficult question of time limits when you give a final warning that timekeeping must improve by a certain date: the improvement period. If it does improve by that date, and the slate is wiped clean, it might be assumed that the disciplinary procedure starts again from scratch if timekeeping deteriorates again. But it is in the nature of things that some people cannot sustain efforts to get to work on time for long, and deterioration often occurs. In these circumstances, do you have to keep on going through the warning cycles time after time? The answer ought to be no, and the best approach is to avoid stating a finite end date to a final warning period which implies a 'wipe the slate clean' approach. Instead, the warning should simply say that timekeeping performance will be reviewed on a stated date. If it has not improved, disciplinary action can be taken. If it has, no action will be taken, but the employee is warned that further deterioration will make them liable to disciplinary action which may well speed up the normal procedure, perhaps by only using the final warning stage and by reducing the elapsed time between the warning and the review date. There will come a time if poor timekeeping persists when you can say 'Enough is enough' and initiate disciplinary action.

Dealing with underperformers

You may have someone who is underperforming in your team. If so, what can you do about it? Essentially, you have to spot that there is a problem, understand the cause of the problem, decide on a remedy and make the remedy work.

Poor performance can be the fault of the individual but it could arise because of poor leadership or problems in the system of work. In the case of an individual, the reason may be that they fall into one or more of the following categories:

- Could not do it – ability.
- Did not know how to do it – skill.
- Would not do it – attitude.
- Did not fully understand what was expected of them.

Inadequate leadership from managers can be a cause of poor performance by individuals. It is the manager's responsibility to specify the results expected and the levels of skill and competence required. As likely as not, when people do not understand what they have to do, it is their manager who is to blame.

Performance can also be affected by the system of work. If this is badly planned and organized or does not function well, individuals cannot be blamed for the poor performance that results. This is the fault of management and they must put it right.

If inadequate individual performance cannot be attributed to poor leadership or the system of work, the following are the seven steps you can take to deal with underperformers:

- Identify the areas of underperformance – be specific.
- Establish the causes of poor performance.
- Agree on the action required.
- Ensure that the necessary support (coaching, training, extra resources, etc) is provided to ensure the action is successful.
- Monitor progress and provide feedback.
- Provide additional guidance as required.
- As a last resort, invoke the capability or disciplinary procedure, starting with an informal warning.

How to conduct a discipline meeting

If you have good reason to believe that disciplinary action is necessary, you need to take the following steps when planning and conducting a disciplinary interview:

- Get all the facts in advance, including statements from people involved.

- In writing, invite the employee to the meeting, explaining why it is being held and that they have the right to have someone present at the meeting on their behalf.
- Ensure that the employee has reasonable notice (ideally at least two days).
- Plan how you will conduct the meeting.
- Line up another member of management to attend the meeting with you to take notes (these can be important if there is an appeal) and generally provide support.
- Start the interview by stating the complaint to the employee and referring to the evidence.
- Give the employee plenty of time to respond and state their case.
- Take a break as required to consider the points raised and to relieve any pressure arising in the meeting.
- Consider what action is appropriate, if any. Actions should be staged, starting with a recorded oral warning, followed, if the problem continues, by a first written warning, then a final written warning and lastly, if the earlier stages have been exhausted, disciplinary action, which would be dismissal in serious cases.
- Deliver the decision, explaining why it has been taken and confirm it in writing.

KEY LEARNING POINTS

Selection interviewing

The aim of a selection interview is to provide answers to three fundamental questions: (1) Can the individual do the job? (2) Will the individual do the job? (3) How is the individual likely to fit into the team?

A selection interview should take the form of a conversation with a purpose. It has three sections:

- Beginning. At the start of the interview, candidates are put at their ease.
- Middle. This is where interviewers find out what they need to know about candidates to establish the extent to which they meet the requirements of the job as set out in a person or job specification.
- End. At the end of the interview, candidates are given the opportunity to ask about the job and the company. More details about the job can be given to promising candidates who are told what the next step will be.

Your first step in preparing for an interview is to familiarize or re-familiarize yourself with the person specification and candidate's CV, application form or letter.

The best approach to structuring the interview is one that is criteria and target based, using competencies as the criteria (this is often called a competency-based interview).

A biographical approach is probably the most popular because it is simple to use and appears to be logical.

The interviewer's job is to draw the candidate out, at the same time ensuring that the information required is obtained. To this end it is desirable to ask a number of open-ended questions – questions which cannot be answered by yes or no and which promote a full response. But a good interviewer will have an armoury of other types of questions to be asked when appropriate – probing, hypothetical, behaviour event and continuity.

Performance review meetings

The performance review meeting is the means through which the five primary performance management elements of agreement, measurement, feedback, positive reinforcement and dialogue can be put to good use.

A performance review meeting is a stock-taking exercise answering the questions 'Where have we got to?' and 'How did we get here?'

A constructive review meeting is most likely to take place if the manager or team leader encourages individuals to do most of the talking and listens actively to what they say, allows scope for reflection and analysis, provides feedback, analyses performance, not personality, keeps the whole period under review, adopts a 'no surprises' approach, recognizes achievements and reinforces strengths, discusses any work or performance problems, how they have arisen and what can be done about them, and ends the meeting positively with any necessary agreed action plans (learning and development and performance improvement).

How to ensure that people learn and develop

To improve the performance of their team members, managers must not only ensure that individuals learn the basic skills they need but also that they develop those skills to enable them to perform even better when faced with new demands and challenges.

The HR or learning and development department also has the important responsibility of advising and helping line managers carry out their employee development role but additionally is likely to be responsible for the delivery of training.

Presentations

The three keys to delivering an effective presentation are thorough preparation, good delivery and overcoming nervousness.

Project management

Project management is the planning, supervision and control of any activity or set of activities which leads to a defined outcome at a predetermined time and in accordance with specified performance or quality standards at a budgeted cost.

The three main project management activities are project planning, setting up the project and project control.

Handling absenteeism

You should continue to monitor the absence of individuals to find out whose absence levels are above average and why. If your department's absence figures are significantly higher than the norm, you may have to take more direct action such as discussing with individuals whose absence rates are high the reasons for their absences, especially when these have been self-certificated. You may have to deal with recurrent short-term (one or two days) absence or longer-term sickness absence.

Handling poor timekeeping

If you are faced with persistent lateness and your informal warnings to the individual concerned seem to have little effect, you may be forced to invoke the disciplinary procedure. If timekeeping does not improve, this could go through the successive stages of a recorded oral warning, a written warning and a final written warning. If the final warning does not work, disciplinary action would have to be taken; in serious cases this would mean dismissal.

Handling poor performance

These are the seven steps you can take to deal with underperformers:

- Identify the areas of underperformance – be specific.
- Establish the causes of poor performance.
- Agree on the action required.
- Ensure that the necessary support (coaching, training, extra resources, etc) is provided to ensure the action is successful.
- Monitor progress and provide feedback.
- Provide additional guidance as required.
- As a last resort, invoke the capability or disciplinary procedure, starting with an informal warning.

How to conduct a discipline meeting

If you have good reason to believe that disciplinary action is necessary, you need to get all the facts in advance, plan how you will conduct the meeting, line up another member of management to attend the meeting with you to take notes, start the interview by stating the complaint to the employee and referring to the evidence, give the employee plenty of time to respond and state their case, consider what action is appropriate, if any, and deliver the decision, explaining why it has been taken, and confirm it in writing.

Reference

Chartered Institute of Personnel and Development (2009) *Survey of Absence Management*, London, CIPD

Questions

1 What are the aims of a selection interview?

2 What is the form of a selection interview?

3 What are the sections in a selection interview?

4 How should an interview be structured?

5 In what ways can interviews be planned?

6 What approach is required in asking questions?

7 What is an open question?

8 What is a closed question?

9 What are the key 'dos' in selection interviews?

10 What are the main 'don'ts' in selection interviews?

11 What is the purpose of a performance management review meeting?

12 What are the most important approaches to conducting a constructive performance management review meeting?

13 What can line managers do to help people learn and develop?

14 What are the main requirements for an effective presentation?

15 How should you prepare a presentation?

16 What are the key points to remember when delivering a presentation?

17 How can you overcome nervousness in making a presentation?

18 What is project management?

19 What is involved in project planning?

20 What is involved in setting up a project?

21 What are the three most important things to control in conducting a project?

22 How should you handle absenteeism?

23 How do you handle poor timekeeping?

24 How do you deal with poor performance?

Problem solving and decision making

18

LEARNING OUTCOMES

On completing this chapter you should be able to define these key concepts. You should also understand:

- How to improve problem-solving skills
- How to solve a problem
- Creative thinking
- Team-based decision making
- Ethical decision making
- How to communicate and justify decisions

Introduction

Problem solving and decision making are closely associated processes which are a constant feature of life in organizations and elsewhere. A logical approach is desirable but this is not easy – the situations where problems have to be solved and decisions made are often messy, with conflicting evidence, lack of data, and political and emotional issues affecting those involved. But even if it is not possible to apply neat logical and sequential methods, the principles remain the same: getting and analysing what information is available, considering alternatives and making the best choice based on the evidence, and analysis of the context and an assessment of the possible consequences.

Problem solving

Problem solving is the process of analysing and understanding a problem, diagnosing its cause and deciding on a solution which solves the problem and prevents it being repeated. You will often have to react to problems as they arise but as far as possible a proactive approach is desirable, which involves anticipating potential problems and dealing with them in advance by taking preventative action using the normal approaches to problem solving set out below. Proactive problem solving may require creative thinking as considered later in this section.

Problems and opportunities

It is often said that 'There are no problems, only opportunities.' This is not universally true, of course, but it does emphasize the point that a problem should lead to positive thinking about what is to be done now, rather than to recriminations. If a mistake has been made, the reasons for it should be analysed, to ensure that it does not happen again.

Improving your skills

How can you improve your ability to solve problems? There are a few basic approaches you should use.

Improve your analytical ability

A complicated situation can often be resolved by separating the whole into its component parts. Such an analysis should relate to facts, although, as Peter Drucker (1955) points out, when trying to understand the root causes of a problem you may have to start with an opinion. Even if you ask people to search for the facts first, they will probably look for those facts that fit the conclusion they have already reached.

Opinions are a perfectly good starting point as long as they are brought out into the open at once and then tested against reality. Analyse each hypothesis and pick out the parts which need to be studied and tested.

Mary Parker Follett's (1924) 'law of the situation' – the logic of facts and events – should rule in the end.

Being creative

A strictly logical answer to the problem may not be the best one. Use creative thinking to get off your tramlines and dream up an entirely new approach.

Keep it simple

One of the basic principles of problem solving is known as Occam's razor. It states that 'Entities are not to be multiplied without necessity.' That is, always believe the simplest of several explanations.

Focus on implementation

A problem has not been solved until the decision has been implemented. Think carefully not only about how a thing is to be done (by whom, with what resources and by when) but also about its likely consequences – its impact on the organization and the people concerned and the extent to which they will cooperate. You will get less cooperation if you impose a solution. The best method is to arrange things so that everyone arrives jointly at a solution freely agreed to be the one best suited to the situation (the law of the situation again).

Further consideration to the processes of evaluating evidence and options and to the consulting skills used in problem solving is given in the next chapter.

Twelve problem-solving steps

The 12 steps of problem solving are:

1 Define the situation – establish what has gone wrong or is about to go wrong.

2 Specify objectives – define what is to be achieved now or in the future to deal with an actual or potential problem or a change in circumstances.

3 Develop hypotheses – develop hypotheses about what has caused the problem.

4 Get the facts – find out what has actually happened and contrast this with an assessment of what ought to have happened. This is easier said than done. Insidious political factors may have contributed to the problem and could be difficult to identify and deal with. The facts may not be clear cut. They could be obscured by a mass of conflicting material. There may be lots of opinions but few verifiable

facts. Remember that people will see what has happened in terms of their own position and feelings (their framework of reference). Try to understand the political climate and the attitudes and motivation of those concerned. Bear in mind that, as Jeffrey Pfeffer (1996: 36) commented, 'Smart organizations occasionally do dumb things.' Obtain information about internal or external constraints that affect the situation.

5 Analyse the facts – determine what is relevant and what is irrelevant. Diagnose the likely cause or causes of the problem. Do not be tempted to focus on symptoms rather than root causes. Test any assumptions. Distinguish between opinions and facts. Dig into what lies behind the problem.

6 Identify possible courses of action – spell out what each involves.

7 Evaluate alternative courses of action – assess the extent to which they are likely to achieve the objectives, the cost of implementation, any practical difficulties that might emerge and the possible reactions of stakeholders. Critical evaluation techniques as described in Chapter 19 can be used for this purpose.

8 Weigh and decide – determine which alternative is likely to result in the most practical and acceptable solution to the problem. This is often a balanced judgement.

9 Decide on objectives – set out goals for implementation of the decision.

10 Adopt a 'means–end' approach where appropriate – in complicated situations with long-term implications it may be useful to identify the steps required and select an action at each step which will move the process closer to the goal.

11 Plan implementation – prepare timetable and identify and assemble the resources required.

12 Implement – monitor progress and evaluate success. Remember that a problem has not been solved until the decision has been implemented. Always work out the solution to a problem with implementation in mind.

Decision making

Decision making is about analysing and defining the situation or problem, identifying possible courses of action, weighing them up and defining a course of action. Buchanan and Huczynski (2007) distinguished between structured and unstructured decisions. Structured decisions are programmable and can be resolved using decision rules. These are the day-to-day decisions, such as how much stock to order, which are standardized and uncontroversial. Unstructured decisions are unprogrammable and cannot be reached using standard rules and procedures. The latter are the more common.

Peter Drucker (1955) produced the following words of wisdom on the subject, which have not been bettered since:

> Management is always a decision-making process. (p 310)
>
> The important and difficult job is never to find the right answer; it is to find the right question. (p 311)
>
> The first job in decision making is… to find the real problem and to define it. (p 312)
>
> To take no action is a decision fully as much as to take specific action. (p 319)
>
> No decision can be better than the people who carry it out. (p 321)
>
> A manager's decision is always a decision concerning what other people should do. (p 322)

In 1967 (p 120) he added: 'A decision is a judgement. It is a choice between alternatives. It is rarely a choice between right and wrong. It is at best a choice between almost right and probably wrong – but much more often a choice between two courses of action neither of which is probably more nearly right than the other.'

Limitations of a logical approach to decision making

A claim that logical decision making based on the problem-solving sequence referred to above is the obvious and most valid approach is convincing. After all, who would advocate an illogical approach? But there are limitations to the power and applicability of pure logic in the real world inhabited by managers. Purcell (1999: 37) argued that we should 'avoid being trapped in the logic of rational choice'. Mabey et al (1998: 524) observed that: 'From what we know of the role of existing structures, cultures, mindsets and politics on managers' thinking, there are serious grounds for questioning the rationality of management decision making.'

As Buchanan and Huczynski (2007: 819) commented: 'The number of decisions that can be reached unambiguously using information, analysis and logical reasoning tends to be small… Most of the significant decisions in organizations, and virtually all at senior management levels, tend to be unstructured. They cannot be based on reason and logic alone, but involve in some way the values and prejudices of key organizational members… Such unstructured decisions often have to be made in a period of change and uncertainty during which an organization is unlikely to have a single, unambiguous, clearly defined objective with which all members agree.'

This situation is an important cause of the political behaviour endemic in any organization subject to change, which means most if not all organizations. Political behaviour is driven by the pursuit of power and influence, not the desire to make logical decisions and achieve optimum solutions to problems. Mintzberg (1983) identified the four political games people play in organizations: authority games, power base games, rivalry games and change games. Decisions may be made for political reasons rather than being based on logical analysis.

What is decided is influenced by the context in which it is decided. Cultural, social and political factors influence perceptions and judgements, and the extent to which people behave rationally is limited by their capacity to understand the complexities of the situation they are in and by their emotional reactions to it – the concept of bounded rationality as expressed by Simon (1957). As Harrison (2009: 331) explained: 'Some of the factors that militate against a purely "rational" approach include confused, excessive, incomplete or unreliable data, incompetent processing or communicating of information, pressures of time, human emotions, and differences in individuals' cognitive processes, mental maps and reasoning capacity.'

All this means that it is necessary to recognize that there are no simple solutions, no universal prescriptions, no sequences of actions that will inevitably lead to the one and only right conclusion. Short-term fixes may become long-term problems. Logical determinism – the belief that human actions can be governed by external forces in the shape of prescribed formulae – won't work. There is always choice. We may favour the idea of going from A to D via B and C but sometimes we have to start in the middle because our circumstances compel us to do so. We have to make the best of the situation in which we find ourselves and proceed from that point.

But we need to know what that situation is – what's right and what's wrong about it. We need to know about the social and political factors affecting the situation. We need then to understand what approaches are available to address the particular issues emerging from the situation.

Decisions will have to be made on the basis of obscure or conflicting evidence or no reliable evidence at all. What has happened in the past or is happening now may be shrouded in mystery. The future is uncertain. The consequences of decisions can only be guessed and unpredictable events will derail the actions resulting from the decision. This is the uncertainty principle applied to decision making – it is impossible to simultaneously measure the present position and determine the future position. There will always be a choice.

But the existence of all these barriers to logical decision making does not preclude the use of systematic processes to assemble and analyse the evidence in order to reach the best conclusion possible in the circumstances. It is still important to be decisive.

Ten approaches to being decisive

- Analyse and understand the context – bear in mind that while a logical approach such as that described earlier for problem solving is desirable, there are all sorts of factors that will affect the decision which have to be taken into account.

- Avoid procrastination – it is easy to put an e-mail demanding a decision into the 'too difficult' section of your actual or mental in-tray. Avoid the temptation to fill your time with trivial tasks so that the evil moment when you have to address the issue is postponed. Make a start. Once you get going you can deal with the unpleasant task of making a decision in stages. A challenge often becomes easier once we have started dealing with it. Having spent five minutes on it, we don't want to feel they were wasted, so we carry on and complete the job.

- Expect the unexpected – you are then in the frame of mind needed to respond decisively to a new situation.

- Think it through – decisive people use their analytical ability to come to swift conclusions about the nature of the situation and what should be done about it.

- Be careful about assumptions – we have a tendency to leap to conclusions and seize on assumptions that support our case and ignore the facts that might contradict it.

- Learn from the past – build on your experience in decision making; what approaches work best? But don't rely too much on precedents. Situations change. The right decision last time could well be the wrong one now.

- Be systematic – adopt a problem-solving approach as described above. It won't guarantee that a brilliant decision will emerge but at least it will have been based on an attempt to understand the circumstances rather than guesswork.

- Talk it through – before you make a significant decision talk it through with someone who is likely to disagree so that any challenge they make can be taken into account (but you have to canvass opinion swiftly).

- Leave time to think it over – swift decision making is highly desirable but you must avoid knee-jerk reactions. Pause, if only for a few minutes, to allow yourself time to think through the decision you propose to make. And confirm that it is justified.

- Consider the potential consequences – McKinsey call this 'consequence management'. Every decision has a consequence and you should consider very carefully what that might be and how you will manage it. You won't be able to anticipate everything but it is worth making the attempt. When making a decision, it is a good idea to start from where you mean to end – define the end result and then work out the steps needed to achieve it.

As described above, decision making can be a logical process following a problem-solving approach but it can benefit from creative thinking. It can also benefit from involving other people. Attention has to be paid to ethical considerations and communicating the decision.

Creative thinking

Creative thinking is imaginative thinking. It produces new ways of looking at things and innovative decisions. It relates things or ideas which were previously unrelated. It is discontinuous and divergent. Edward de Bono (1971) invented the phrase 'lateral thinking' for it and this term has stuck; it implies sideways leaps in the imagination rather than a continuous progression down a logical chain of reasoning.

Creative thinking is not superior to logical thinking. It's just different. The best managers are both creative and logical. Eventually, irrespective of how creative they have been, they have to make a decision. And logical thinking helps to ensure that it is the right decision. Creative thinking involves breaking away from any restrictions and opening up your mind to generate new ideas.

Breaking away

To break away from the constraints on your ability to generate new ideas you should:

- identify the dominant ideas influencing your thinking;
- define the boundaries (ie past experience, precedents, policies, procedures, rules) within which you are working and try to get outside them by asking questions such as: Are the constraints reasonable? Is past experience reliable? What's new about the present situation? Is there another way?
- bring your assumptions out into the open and challenge any which restrict your freedom to develop new ideas;
- reject 'either/or' propositions – ask, 'Is there really a simple choice between alternatives?'
- keep on asking 'Why?' (but bear in mind that if you do this too bluntly to other people you can antagonize them).

Generating new ideas

To generate new ideas you have to open up your mind. If you have removed some of the constraints as suggested above you will be in a better position to look at the situation differently, exploring all possible angles. You should list as many alternative approaches as possible without seeking the 'one best way' (there is no such thing).

In de Bono's words, it is also necessary to 'arrange discontinuity' by:

- deliberately setting out to break the mould by such means as free thinking (allowing your mind to wander over alternative and in many cases apparently irrelevant ways of looking at the situation);

- exposing yourself to new influences in the form of people, articles, books, indeed anything which could give you a different insight, even though it might not be immediately relevant;
- switching yourself or other people from problem to problem, arranging for the cross-fertilization of ideas with other people;
- 'reframing' – placing the problem in a different context to generate new insights.

Involving people in decision making

As Drucker (1955: 323) noted: 'People who have to carry out the decision should always participate in the work of developing alternatives... This is also likely to improve the quality of the final decision by revealing points the manager may have missed, spotting hidden difficulties and uncovering available but unused resources.'

The advantages of involving teams in decision making are that more minds will be brought to bear on the problem to generate better ideas for its solution. Those taking part are likely to 'own' the solution and should therefore be more likely to welcome it and willingly take part in its implementation.

Work teams can be involved in collectively dealing with problems, or special problem-solving groups can be formed which can resemble the once fashionable quality circles. Charles Handy (1985: 160) pointed out that:

> Groups produce less (sic) ideas, in total than the individuals of those groups working separately. So much for the stereotyping of brainstorming! But groups, though producing less ideas in total, produce better ideas in the sense that they are better evaluated, more thought through... We tend to behave more adventurously in groups than in private, where we do not have to live up to any public standard.

Group problem solving and problem solving will be most effective when:

- the problem to be solved – the task of the group – is clearly defined by a briefing or by the group itself;
- the members of the group interact with one another cooperatively;
- between them, members of the group have the knowledge and skills required, including problem-solving and decision-making skills;
- the group has access to the information it needs;
- the problem-solving processes are enhanced by a skilled facilitator;
- the group is able to communicate its findings to an appropriate authority;
- the group can take part in planning and executing the decision.

You should not expect or even welcome a bland consensus view. The best decisions emerge from conflicting viewpoints. You can benefit from a clash of opinion to prevent people falling into the trap of starting with the conclusion and then looking for the facts that support it.

Ethical decision making

Answers to the following questions should be obtained to provide guidance on whether or not a proposed decision is ethical:

- Is the proposed decision consistent with the principles of natural, procedural or distributive justice and the requirements of the organization's ethical code (if there is one)?
- Can the decision be justified on the basis of the benefits it will provide to the organization and its employees?
- Will the decision be harmful to the individual affected or to employees generally in any way and if so how?
- Will the decision harm the organization's reputation for fair dealing?

Communicating and justifying decisions

Decisions affecting people should be communicated to all concerned. The communication should spell out what the decision was, why the decision was made, who made the decision, who will be affected by the decision and the right of anyone affected to raise questions or concerns about the decision.

KEY LEARNING POINTS

Problem solving and decision making are closely associated processes which are a constant feature of life in organizations and elsewhere.

Problem solving

Problem solving is the process of analysing and understanding a problem, diagnosing its cause and deciding on a solution which solves the problem and prevents it being repeated.

Decision making

Decision making is about analysing the situation or problem, identifying possible courses of action, weighing them up and defining a course of action. However, the extent to which it can be entirely logical is limited by social, political and contextual factors.

Creative thinking

Creative thinking is imaginative thinking. It produces new ideas, new ways of looking at things and innovative decisions.

Involving teams

The advantages of involving reams in decision making are that more minds will be brought to bear on the problem to generate more ideas for its solution, and those taking part are likely to 'own' the solution and should therefore be more likely to welcome it and willingly take part in its implementation.

Ethical considerations

Decisions affecting people should take account of ethical principles and be communicated to all concerned.

References

Buchanan, D and Huczynski, A (2007) *Organizational Behaviour*, Harlow, FT Prentice-Hall

de Bono, E (1971) *Lateral Thinking for Managers*, London, McGraw-Hill

Drucker, P (1955) *The Practice of Management*, London, Heinemann

Drucker, P (1967) *The Effective Executive*, London, Heinemann

Follett, M P (1924) *Creative Experience*, New York, Longmans Green

Handy, C (1985) *Understanding Organizations*, 3rd edn, Harmondsworth, Penguin Books

Harrison, R (2009) *Learning and Development*, 5th edn, London, CIPD

Mabey, C, Salaman, G and Storey, J (1998) *Human Resource Management: A strategic introduction*, Oxford, Blackwell

Mintzberg, H (1983) *Power in and Around Organizations*, Englewood Cliffs NJ, Prentice-Hall

Pfeffer, J (1996) When it comes to 'best practices', why do smart organizations occasionally do dumb things?, *Organizational Dynamics*, Summer, pp 33–44

Purcell, J (1999) Best practice or best fit: chimera or cul-de-sac?, *Human Resource Management Journal*, 9 (3), pp 26–41

Simon, H (1957) *Administrative Behaviour*, New York, Macmillan

Questions

1 What is the nature of problem solving?

2 What is the purpose of analysis in problem solving?

3 What are the key steps that should be taken in problem solving?

4 What is the nature of decision making?

5 What are the limitations of a logical approach to decision making?

6 What are the key steps to effective decision making?

7 What is creative thinking?

8 How can you best generate new ideas?

9 What are the advantages of involving people in decision making?

10 What are the key questions you should answer when deciding on the degree to which a decision is ethical?

Analytical, critical and consultancy skills

- *Analysis*
- *Critical evaluation*
- *Critical thinking*
- *Evidence-based management*
- *Fallacy*
- *Logical reasoning*

LEARNING OUTCOMES

On completing this chapter you should be able to define these key concepts. You should also understand:

- The meaning of evidence-based management
- The use of analytical skills
- The nature of logical reasoning
- The nature of critical thinking
- The nature of critical evaluation
- The skills required by external and internal consultants

Introduction

The processes of problem solving and decision making depend largely on effective analysis, critical thinking and evaluation and the use of consultancy skills as covered in this chapter. The basis of all these is provided by evidence-based management as discussed below.

Evidence-based management

Evidence-based management is a method of informing decision making by making use of appropriate information derived from the analysis of policy and practices and surveys of employee opinion within the organization, systematic benchmarking and the messages delivered by relevant research.

The following comments on evidence-based management were made by Pfeffer and Sutton (2006: 70):

> Nurture an evidence-based approach immediately by doing a few simple things that reflect the proper mind-set. If you ask for evidence of efficacy every time a change is proposed, people will sit up and take notice. If you take the time to pursue the logic behind that evidence, people will become more disciplined in their own thinking. If you treat the organization like an unfinished prototype and encourage trial programs, pilot studies, and experimentation – and reward learning from these activities, even when something new fails – your organization will begin to develop its own evidence base.

A five-step approach was recommended by Briner et al (2009: 23):

1 Practitioners or managers gain understanding of the problem or issue.
2 Internal evidence is gathered about the issue or problem, leading, possibly, to a reformulation of the problem to make it more specific.
3 External evidence is gathered from published research.
4 The views of stakeholders are obtained.
5 All the sources of information are examined and critically appraised.

It should be emphasized that what is done in organizations with the evidence depends largely on the context in which it is done. Cultural, social and political factors influence perceptions and judgements and the extent to which people behave rationally is limited by their capacity to understand the complexities of the situation they are in and by their emotional reactions to it – the concept of bounded rationality as expressed by Simon (1957).

But we need to understand the context – its impact on what is happening and how things are done. We need then to understand what actions can be taken to address the issues emerging from the situation. We need evidence which tells us what is going on within the organization, what has worked well elsewhere which might fit our requirements and what research has revealed about policies and practices which will guide us in making our decisions. And we need to use that evidence as the basis for our choice of the actions we intend to take. In other words, we need to practice evidence-based management using the analytical, critical thinking and consultancy skills described in the rest of this chapter.

Analytical skills

Analysis is the process of breaking down a condition or state of affairs into its constituent parts and establishing the relationships between them. In the Aristotelian sense, analysis involves discerning the particular features of a situation.

Analytical skills are used to gain a better understanding of a complex situation or problem. They involve the ability to visualize, articulate and solve complex problems and concepts and make decisions based on available information. Analytical skills include the capacity to evaluate that information to assess its significance, and the ability to apply logical and critical thinking to the situation. They provide the basis for a diagnosis of the cause or causes of a problem and therefore for its solution.

Logical reasoning

If you say people are logical, you mean that they draw reasonable inferences – their conclusions can be proved by reference to the facts used to support them – and they avoid ill-founded and tendentious arguments, generalizations and irrelevancies. Logical reasoning is the basis of critical thinking and evaluation. It takes place when there is a clear relationship (a line of reasoning) between the premise (the original proposition) and the conclusion which is supported by valid and reliable evidence and does not rely on fallacious or misleading argument. Logical reasoning is what Susan Stebbing (1959) called 'Thinking to some purpose'. Clear thinking is required to establish the validity of a proposition, concept or idea.

It is necessary to spot fallacious and misleading arguments. A fallacy is an unsound form of argument leading to an error in reasoning or a misleading impression. The most common form of fallacies which need to be discerned in other people's arguments or avoided in one's own can be summarized as:

- Affirming the consequent – leaping to the conclusion that a hypothesis is true because a single cause of the consequence has been observed.
- Begging the question – taking for granted what has yet to be proved.
- Chop logic – 'Contrariwise,' continued Tweedledee, 'if it was so, it might be, and if it were so, it would be; but as it isn't it ain't. That's logic.' Chop logic may not always be as bad as that, but it is about

drawing false conclusions and using dubious methods of argument. For example: selecting instances favourable to a contention while ignoring those that are counter to it, twisting an argument used by an opponent to mean something quite different from what was intended, diverting opponents by throwing on them the burden of proof for something they have not maintained, ignoring the point in dispute, changing the question to one that is less awkward to answer, and reiterating what has been denied and ignoring what has been asserted. Politicians know all about chop logic.

- Confusing correlation with causation – assuming that because A is associated with B it has caused B. It may or may not have done.
- False choice – a situation in which only two alternatives are considered, when in fact there are additional options.
- Potted thinking – using slogans and catch phrases to extend an assertion in an unwarrantable fashion.
- Reaching false conclusions – forming the views that because some are, then all are. An assertion about several cases is twisted into an assertion about all cases. The conclusion does not follow the premise. This is what logicians call the 'undistributed middle'.
- Selective reasoning – selecting instances favourable to a contention while ignoring those which conflict with it.
- Sweeping statements – oversimplifying the facts.
- Special pleading – focusing too much on one's own case and failing to see that there may be other points of view.

Critical thinking

Critical thinking is the process of analysing and evaluating the quality of ideas, theories and concepts in order to establish the degree to which they are valid and supported by the evidence and the extent to which they are biased. It involves reflecting on and interpreting data, drawing warranted conclusions and recognizing ill-defined assumptions.

'Critical' in this context does not mean disapproval or being negative. There are many positive uses of critical thinking, for example testing a hypothesis, proving a proposition or evaluating a concept, theory or argument. Critical thinking can occur whenever people weigh up evidence and make a judgement, solve a problem or reach a decision. The aim is to come to well-reasoned conclusions and solutions and test them against relevant criteria and standards. Critical thinking calls for the ability to:

- recognize problems and establish ways of dealing with them;
- gather and marshal pertinent (relevant) information;
- identify unstated assumptions and values;

- interpret data, to appraise evidence and evaluate arguments;
- recognize the existence (or non-existence) of logical relationships between propositions;
- draw warranted conclusions and make valid generalizations;
- test assertions, conclusions and generalizations;
- reconstruct ideas or beliefs by examining and analysing relevant evidence.

Critical evaluation

Critical evaluation is the process of making informed judgements about the validity, relevance and usefulness of ideas and arguments. It uses critical thinking. Critical evaluation means not taking anything for granted and, where necessary, challenging propositions. It involves making informed judgements about the value of ideas and arguments. It uses critical thinking by analysing and evaluating the quality of theories and concepts in order to establish the degree to which they are valid and supported by the evidence (evidence based) and the extent to which they are biased. It means reflecting on and interpreting data, drawing warranted conclusions and identifying faulty reasoning, assumptions and biases. The arguments for and against are weighed and the strength of the evidence on both sides is assessed. On the basis of this assessment a conclusion is reached on which proposition or argument is to be preferred. Critical evaluation is required when testing propositions and evaluating the outcomes of research.

Testing propositions

Propositions based on research investigations and evidence can be tested by using the following checklist:

- Was the scope of the investigation sufficiently comprehensive?
- Are the instances representative or are they selected simply to support a point of view?
- Are there contradictory instances that have not been looked for?
- Does the proposition conflict with other propositions for which there are equally good grounds?
- If there are any conflicting beliefs or contradictory items of evidence, have they been put to the test against the original proposition?
- Could the evidence lead to other equally valid conclusions?
- Are there any other factors that have not been taken into account which may have influenced the evidence and, therefore, the conclusion?

Critically evaluating research

Putting the outcomes of research as, for example, published in academic journals, to the test requires critical evaluation and the following checklist can be used:

- Is the research methodology sufficiently rigorous and appropriate?
- Are the results and conclusions consistent with the methodology used and its outcomes?
- Is the perspective adopted by the researchers stated clearly?
- Have hypotheses been stated clearly and tested thoroughly?
- Do there appear to be any misleading errors of omission or bias?
- Are any of the arguments tendentious?
- Are inferences, findings and conclusions derived from reliable and convincing evidence?
- Has a balanced approach been adopted?
- Have any underlying assumptions been identified and justified?
- Have the component parts been covered in terms of their interrelationships and their relationship with the whole?
- Have these component parts been disaggregated for close examination?
- Have they been reconstructed into a coherent whole based on underlying principles?

It is worth repeating that critical evaluation does not necessarily mean negative criticism; it means reaching a judgement based on analysis and evidence, and the judgement can be positive as well as negative.

Developing and justifying original arguments

An argument as an aspect of critical thinking consists of a presentation of reasons which support a contention. It consists of:

- a proposition or statement which expresses a point of view or belief;
- the reasoning which makes a case for the proposition or point of view;
- a discussion, the aim of which is to get the reader or listener to agree with the case that has been made;
- a conclusion which sums up the argument and its significance.

Developing an argument

An argument is based (predicated) on a premise (the proposition) which sets out the underpinning assumption. There may be more than one proposition or assumption. It could be phrased something like this: 'The argument is that A is the case. It is predicated on the assumption that B and C apply.' In a sense this suggests what conclusion the argument is intended to reach but it also indicates that this conclusion depends on the validity of the assumptions, which will have to be proved (there are such things as false premises).

Justifying an argument

The argument continues by supplying reasons to accept the proposition or point of view. These reasons have to be supported by evidence which should be based on valid research, rigorous observation, or relevant and verifiable experience, not on hearsay. It involves logical reasoning which avoids the fallacies referred to earlier and requires critical thinking which as described above means coming to well-reasoned conclusions and solutions and testing them against relevant criteria and standards. It also demands critical evaluation which, as mentioned earlier, means reflecting on and interpreting data, drawing warranted conclusions and identifying faulty reasoning, assumptions and biases. Assumptions have to be tested rigorously and research evidence has to evaluated. The check lists set out in the previous section of this chapter can be used for this purpose.

Consultancy skills

External management consultants who provide advice and help in introducing new structures and systems and solving problems need certain skills to carry out their often demanding jobs effectively. So do internal consultants who carry out a similar role within the organization. The skills required are:

- analysis and diagnosis;
- problem solving;
- critical thinking and evaluation;
- interpersonal – establishing and maintaining productive relationships with clients;
- interviewing – obtaining information and views from people;
- persuading people to adopt a course of action;
- case presentation;
- written communications, especially report writing;
- oral communications – making presentations and leading discussions;
- facilitating meetings and group discussions;
- planning and running learning and development events;
- coaching;
- project management.

KEY LEARNING POINTS

The processes of problem solving and decision making depend largely on effective analysis, critical thinking and evaluation and the use of consultancy skills.

Evidence-based management

Evidence-based management is a method of informing decision making by making use of appropriate information derived from the analysis of HR policy and practices and surveys of employee opinion within the organization, systematic benchmarking and the messages delivered by relevant research.

Analytical skills

Analysis is the process of gaining a better understanding of a complex situation or problem by breaking it down into its constituent parts and establishing the relationships between them.

Logical reasoning

This involves clear thinking to establish the validity of a proposition, concept or idea.

Critical thinking

Critical thinking clarifies goals, examines assumptions, discerns hidden values, evaluates evidence, accomplishes actions and assesses conclusions.

Critical evaluation

Critical evaluation involves making informed judgements about the value of ideas and arguments.

Developing and justifying original arguments

An argument as an aspect of critical thinking consists of a presentation of reasons which support a contention.

Consultancy skills

External management consultants providing advice and help in introducing new structures and systems and solving problems need certain skills to carry out their often demanding jobs effectively. So do internal consultants who carry out a similar role within the organization.

References

Briner, R B, Denyer, D and Rousseau, D M (2009) Evidence-based management: concept clean-up time?, *Academy of Management Perspectives*, September, pp 19–32
Pfeffer, J and Sutton, R I (2006) Evidence-based management, *Harvard Business Review*, January, pp 62–74.
Simon, H (1957) *Administrative Behaviour*, New York, Macmillan
Stebbing, S (1959) *Thinking to Some Purpose*, Harmondsworth, Penguin Books

Questions

1 What is evidence-based management?

2 What does analysis involve?

3 What is logical reasoning?

4 What is a fallacy? (Give examples of three typical fallacies.)

5 What does critical thinking involve?

6 What is critical evaluation?

7 What approaches can be used to test propositions?

8 How do you critically evaluate research?

9 What does argument consist of?

10 How do you develop an argument?

11 How do you justify an argument?

12 What are the key consultancy skills?

Information handling skills

20

Key concepts and terms

- *Average*
- *Causality*
- *Chi-squared test*
- *Correlation*
- *Dispersion*
- *e-HRM*
- *Enterprise resource planning (ERP) system*
- *Frequency*
- *Frequency distribution*
- *Functionality*
- *HR information system*
- *HR portal*
- *Human capital management*
- *Intranet*
- *Line of best fit*
- *Lower quartile*
- *Mean*
- *Median*
- *Mode*
- *Multi-regression analysis*
- *Multivariate analysis*
- *Regression*
- *Reverse causation*
- *Scattergram*
- *Self-service*
- *Significance*
- *Standard deviation*
- *Statistics*
- *Trend line*
- *Upper quartile*
- *Vanilla system*
- *Variance*

LEARNING OUTCOMES

On completing this chapter you should be able to define these key concepts. You should also know about:

- The meaning and purpose of information
- How to handle information
- Reasons for using an HRIS
- Functions of an HRIS
- Features of an HRIS
- Introducing an HRIS
- The use of statistics
- Frequency analysis
- Measures of central tendency
- Measures of dispersion
- Correlation
- Regression
- Tests of significance
- Tests of hypotheses

Introduction

Information, as Drucker (1988: 46) observed, is 'data endowed with meaning and purpose'. The significance of evidence-based management, as discussed in the last chapter, is that it is based on information. Human capital management as a major HR activity is the process of informing HRM decisions by obtaining, analysing and reporting on data and information relating to employees. Evaluation of the effectiveness of learning and development and other HR activities is only possible by reference to relevant data.

HR specialists must therefore possess the knowledge required to commission and manage computerized systems to provide them and line managers with information covering such matters as employee records, absenteeism, employee turnover, rates of pay and employee benefits. Such systems also help with the administration of HR activities such as recruitment, performance management and reward. In addition, HR people need skills in using statistics to record and present information.

This chapter starts with a review of information handling skills in general, continues with an examination of the use of HR information systems (e-HRM) and is completed with an outline of the main statistical methods that can be used in HRM.

Handling information

To handle information it is necessary to:

- decide what information is required for decision making and management purposes;
- identify the relevant data that is readily available and where and how it can be obtained;
- identify where any data at present unavailable can be obtained and decide whether the value of the data justifies the effort and cost of getting it;
- take steps to convert the raw data that has been made available into information which has 'meaning and purpose' in accordance with specified requirements;
- establish how best to record, analyse and present the information in ways which ensure that it serves a useful purpose.

These actions inform the development of a computerized system for providing information as well as carrying out various administrative tasks as described below. They also provide guidance on the statistical methods which can be used to analyse and present the information.

HR information systems

An HR information system (HRIS) is a computer-based information system for managing the administration of HR processes and procedures and for providing HRM data. The process is sometimes called 'e-HRM'.

HRIS functions

A list of possible HRIS functions (its 'functionality') is given below. The functions cover almost every aspect of HRM.

- HR surveys and audits
  - Conducting opinion and engagement surveys
  - Conducting employee entrance and exit surveys
  - Measuring diversity issues
  - Knowledge management
  - Producing HRM metrics
- HR administration
  - Employee record maintenance
  - Self-service systems – enabling managers and employees to inspect and update records
  - Absence management – recording, analysing and distributing data

- Equal opportunity modelling
- Employee communications via an intranet
- Expenses
- Working time analysis (overtime, shifts, etc)

● HR planning

- Preparing and monitoring workforce plans
- Forecasting staffing levels
- Generating organizational charts
- Tracking labour costs
- Preparing and monitoring succession plans

● Resourcing

- Submitting job requisition information
- Requisition processing
- Handling internal referrals
- Posting job vacancies within the organization
- Online recruitment
- Processing job applications
- Storing CVs
- Tracking applicants through the recruitment process
- Pre-screening job applicants
- Testing candidates
- Recording outcome of interviews
- Processing correspondence with applicants

● Performance management

- Online performance management systems
- Providing and analysing 360-degree feedback data
- Producing performance management documentation
- Recording employee appraisals and 360-degree feedback

● Learning and development

- Assessing training needs
- Preparing and updating skills inventories
- Handling training requests
- Scheduling training sessions
- Developing instructional material
- Delivering course material to diverse locations
- E-learning – preparation and presentation of learning material
- Recording employee training
- Recording and analysing training costs
- Evaluating training effectiveness

● Reward management and administration

- Conducting job evaluations
- Conducting pay surveys
- Modelling pay structures
- Administering incentive pay schemes

- Modelling pay reviews and costs
- Conducting equal pay audits
- Maintaining payroll data
- Transferring employee data between HR and outside payroll systems
- Allowing managers and employees to access pay data information
- Total reward statements
- Employee benefits
  - Creating access to an employee handbook
  - Providing employees with retirement planning information
  - Giving employees access to their own benefit information
  - Providing answers to employee benefits questions
  - Providing information on flexible benefits scheme
  - Assisting employees in their benefits selection
  - Enrolling employees in benefit plans
  - Letting employees make changes to their own benefits records
- Health and safety
  - Analysing workplace incidents
  - Capturing statistical information on each incident
  - Reporting incidents
  - Health and safety prevention planning
- Employee well-being
  - Online service delivery of employee assistance programmes

The 2007 CIPD survey found that the 10 most popular uses to which respondents put their HRIS were:

- absence management;
- training and development;
- rewards;
- managing diversity;
- recruitment and selection;
- other (usually payroll);
- appraisal/performance management;
- HR planning;
- knowledge management;
- expenses.

Reasons for introducing an HRIS

The top 10 reasons for introducing an HRIS, established by the CIPD in 2007, were:

1 to improve quality of information available;
2 to reduce administrative burden on the HR department;

3 to improve speed at which information is available;

4 to improve flexibility of information to support business planning;

5 to improve services to employees;

6 to produce HR metrics;

7 to aid human capital reporting;

8 to improve productivity;

9 to reduce operational costs;

10 to manage people's working time more effectively.

Features of an HRIS

The features of particular interest in an HRIS system are the use of software, integration with other IT systems in the organization, use of the intranet and provisions for self-service.

Use of software

It is customary to buy software from an external supplier. There is a choice between buying a 'vanilla system' (ie an 'off-the-shelf' system without any upgrades) and customizing the supplier's system to meet specified business requirements. Extensive customization can make future upgrades problematic and expensive, so it is important to limit it to what is absolutely necessary.

If an external supplier is used, the choice should be made as follows:

- Research HR software market through trade exhibitions and publications.
- Review HR processes and existing systems.
- Produce a specification of system requirements.
- Send an invitation to tender to several suppliers.
- Invite suppliers to demonstrate their products.
- Obtain references from existing customers, including site visits.
- Analyse and score the product against the specification.

Integration

Enterprise resource planning (ERP) systems integrate all the data and processes of an organization into a unified system with the same database. HR systems are not frequently integrated to this extent although they often link payroll administration with other HR functions. Integration of the HR system with IT systems in the wider organization so that they can 'talk to one another' will aid human capital reporting, comply with supply-chain partner requirements, improve profitability, reduce headcount and deliver against economic criteria. However, many HR departments retain stand-alone systems because they believe that integration would compromise their own system and that there was potential lack of confidentiality. They may also be concerned with the costs and perceived risks involved.

Intranet

An intranet system is one where computer terminals are linked so that they can share information within an organization or within part of an organization. The scope of the information that can be shared across terminals can be limited to preserve confidentiality and this security can be enhanced by using passwords. HR intranet systems can be used for purposes such as updating personal details, applications for internal jobs online, requests for training, access to e-learning, administration of queries and communications.

Self-service

A human resource self-service system (HRSS) allows managers and employees access to information and the facility to interact with the system to input and obtain information. Access and the range of information covered are tightly controlled. This can operate through an HR portal (a site that functions as a point of access to information on the intranet) which may be specially designed to produce a brand image of the HR function. This is sometimes referred to as a business-to-employees (B2E) portal.

For managers, self-service means that they can access information immediately. This might be HR metrics (human capital reporting measures) in such areas as absenteeism, personal details, performance management data, learning and development progress, and pay (as a basis for pay reviews). They can also input data on their staff. This facilitates the devolution of responsibility to line managers and reduces the administrative burden on HR.

Employees can also access information, input data about themselves, request training and apply for jobs online.

Introducing an HRIS

The steps required are illustrated in Figure 20.1.

The following are six tips on introducing an HRIS:

- Make sure you really know what you need now, and what you are likely to need in the near future so you can give clear guidelines to the software provider.
- Involve end users and other stakeholders in the decision-making process.
- Include a member of staff with IT expertise on the decision-making team, even if they're not an HR professional.
- Go for something clear and straightforward that adds value. Don't go for all the 'bells and whistles'; they may cost more, take more time to administer and you will probably end up not using them anyway.

FIGURE 20.1 Introducing an HRIS

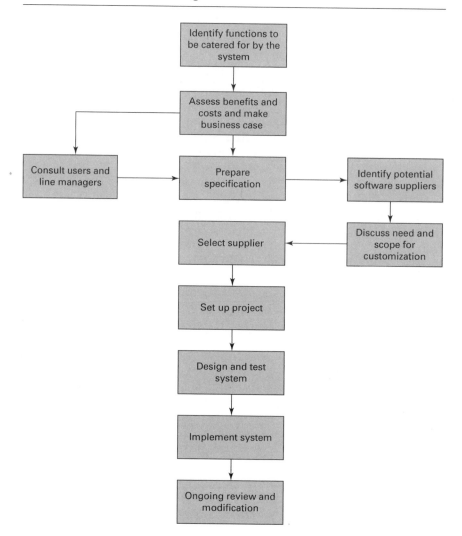

- Evaluate the range of systems on offer in terms of how they report and how easy and quick it is to produce the types of report you need on a regular basis. Look at how reports are presented; can you download them into an Excel spreadsheet so that you can manipulate the data yourself? How easy is it to do mail merge with the information reported?

- When buying an off-the-shelf system, don't customise it unless it's critical. Each time the system is upgraded, it's these modifications that may cause you difficulties. If you do have modifications, budget for these to be managed on an ongoing basis.

Using statistics

Statistics describe and summarize data relating to a 'population', ie a homogeneous set of items with variable individual values. This involves measuring frequencies, central tendencies and dispersion. Statistics can also measure the relationships between variables (correlation and regression), establish the relation between cause and effect (causality), assess the degree of confidence that can be attached to conclusions (tests of significance) and test hypotheses (the chi-squared test and null-hypothesis testing). A wide variety of software is available to conduct the more sophisticated analyses.

Statistics are used extensively in human resource management to analyse and present quantitative information in order to guide decisions and monitor outcomes. They are an essential element in human capital management and are also important in such fields as performance management (the analysis of appraisal results and levels of performance) and reward management (the analysis of market rates, pay reviews, the distribution of pay and equal pay). Statistics play a major part in the analysis of surveys and research evidence.

HR professionals seldom have to use advanced statistics unless they are conducting or taking part in detailed research projects. The main statistics they will use regularly are concerned with the analysis of the incidence of events or activities (frequencies), the use of averages (measures of central tendency), how items in a population are distributed (dispersion) and the relationship between two variables (regression). But they should also be familiar with the concepts of correlation, causation and at least understand the meaning of more advanced statistical techniques used by researchers such as the tests of significance, the chi-squared test and null-hypothesis testing.

Frequency

Frequency is the number of times individual items in a population or set occur. It is represented in frequency distributions expressed in tabular form or graphically. Commonly used graphs are illustrated in Figure 20.2.

FIGURE 20.2 Examples of charts

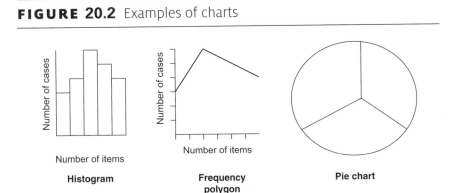

Histogram   Frequency   Pie chart
                 polygon

Measures of central tendency

Measures of central tendency identify the middle or centre of a set of data. There are three types:

- Arithmetic average or mean – the total of items or scores in a set divided by the number of individual items in the set. It may give a distorted picture because of large items at either end of the scale.
- Median – the middle item in a range of items (often used in pay surveys when the arithmetic mean is likely to be distorted).
- Mode – the most commonly occurring item in a set of data.

Measures of dispersion

It is often useful to measure the extent to which the items in a set are dispersed or spread over a range of data. This can be done in five ways:

- By identifying the upper quartile or lower quartile of a range of data. The strict definition of an upper quartile is that it is the value which 25 per cent of the values in the distribution exceed, and the lower quartile is the value below which 25 per cent of the values in a distribution occur. More loosely, especially when looking at pay distributions, the upper and lower quartiles are treated as ranges rather than points in a scale and represent the top and the bottom 25 per cent of the distribution respectively.
- By presenting the total range of values from top to bottom, which may be misleading if there are exceptional items at either end.
- By calculating the inter-quartile range, which is the range between the value of the upper quartile and that of the lower quartile. This can present more revealing information on the distribution than the total range.
- By calculating the standard deviation which is used to indicate the extent to which the items or values in a distribution are grouped together or dispersed in a normal distribution, ie one which is reasonably symmetrical around its average. As a rule of thumb, two-thirds of the distribution will be less than one standard deviation from the mean, 95 per cent of the distribution will be less than two standard deviations from the mean, and less than one per cent of the distribution is more than three standard deviations from the mean.
- By calculating variance, which is the square of a standard deviation.

Correlation

Correlation represents the relationship between two variables. If they are highly correlated they are strongly connected to one another and vice versa. In statistics, correlation is measured by the coefficient of correlation, which varies between −1 and +1 to indicate totally negative and totally positive

FIGURE 20.3 A scattergram with regression (trend) line

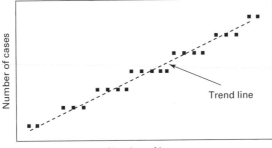

Number of items

correlations respectively. A correlation of zero means that there is no relationship between the variables. Establishing the extent to which variables are correlated is an important feature of HRM research, for example assessing the degree to which a performance management system improves organizational performance. But correlations do not indicate causal relationships. They can only show that X is associated with Y but this does not mean necessarily that X causes Y. Multiple correlation looks at the relationship between more than two variables.

Regression

Regression is another way of looking at the relationship between variables. It expresses how changes in levels of one item relate to changes in levels of another. A regression line (a trend line or line of best fit) can be traced on a scattergram expressing values of one variable on one axis and values of the other variable on another axis, as shown in Figure 20.3.

A trend line like this can be drawn by hand as a line of best fit but it can be calculated mathematically with greater accuracy. The distances of points from the trend line (the residuals) can be calculated as a check on the reliability of the line.

Multiple regression analysis can be conducted with the aid of a computer to express how changes in the levels of a number of items relate to changes in levels of other items.

Causality

Causality is the representation of cause and effect, ie the link between independent and dependent variables. To establish causality is to explain how one thing leads to another. Causality is a major issue in research, especially in the HRM field. It may be relatively easy to establish correlations in the shape of a demonstration that X is associated with Y; it is much more difficult and sometimes impossible to prove that X causes Y. There are a number of reasons for this, of which the two set out below are the most important.

First, complications arise because of the phenomenon of multiple causation. There may be a number of factors contributing to a result. Researchers pursuing the holy grail of trying to establish what HRM contributes to firm performance are usually confronted with a number of reasons why a firm has done well in addition to adopting 'best practice' HRM, whatever that is. Statistical methods can be used to 'control' some variables, ie eliminate them from the analysis, but it is difficult, if not impossible, to ensure that HRM practices have been completely isolated and that their direct impact on firm performance has been measured. Multivariate analysis is used where there is more than one dependent variable and where the dependent variables cannot be combined.

Secondly, there is the phenomenon of reverse causation, when a cause may be predated by an effect – A might have caused B but alternatively, B may have come first and be responsible for A. For example, it is possible to demonstrate that firms with effective performance management schemes do better than those without. But it might equally be the case that it is high-performing firms that introduce effective performance management. It can be hard to be certain.

Tests of significance

Significance as a statistical concept refers to the degree to which an event could have occurred by chance. At the heart of statistical science lies a simple idea, which is that the chance or probability of various patterns of events can be predicted. When a particular pattern is observed it is possible to work out what the chances of its occurrence may be, given our existing state of knowledge or by making certain assumptions. If something has been observed which is unlikely to have occurred by chance, this occurrence can be accepted as significant. The problem is that any attempt to reach general conclusions may have to rely on fragmentary data. It is usually necessary to rely on samples of the population being studied, and all sampling is subject to experimental error – the result can only be expressed in terms of probability, and confidence limits will have to be placed on it. These can be calculated in terms of the standard error that might be expected from a sample. A standard error is the estimated standard deviation of a sample mean from a true mean. This implies that on approximately 95 per cent of occasions the estimate of the mean provided by the sample will be within two standard errors of the true mean.

Testing hypotheses

The chi-squared test uses a statistical formula to assess the degree of agreement between the data actually obtained and that expected under a particular hypothesis.

A null hypothesis is a method of testing a hypothesis, frequently used by researchers, in which it is assumed that there is no relationship between two or more variables. It asks the question: 'Could the hypothetical relationship have been caused by chance?' If the answer is no, then the hypothesis is worth pursuing. However, it does not prove that the hypothesis is correct; it only indicates that something is worth pursuing. It can be associated with the chi-squared test.

KEY LEARNING POINTS

The need

HR specialists must possess the knowledge required to set up and manage computerized systems to provide them and line managers with information covering such matters as employee records, absenteeism, employee turnover, rates of pay and employee benefits. Such systems also help with the administration of HR activities such as recruitment, performance management and reward. In addition, HR people need skills in using statistics to record and present information.

Handling information

To handle information it is necessary to:

- decide what is required ;
- identify the relevant data that is available or can be made available;
- take steps to convert the raw data that has been made available into information which has 'meaning and purpose';
- establish how best to record, analyse and present the information.

HRIS defined

An HRIS is a computer-based information system for managing the administration of HR processes and procedures and for providing HRM data. The process is sometimes called 'e-HRM'.

Reasons for using an HRIS

Top five reasons are:

- to improve quality of information available.
- to reduce administrative burden on the HR department.
- to improve speed at which information is available.
- to improve flexibility of information to support business planning.
- to improve services to employees.

Functions of an HRIS

Top five uses of an HRIS:

- absence management;
- training and development;

- rewards;
- managing diversity;
- recruitment and selection.

Features of an HRIS

The features of particular interest in an HRIS system are the use of software, integration with other IT systems in the organization, use of the intranet and provisions for self-service.

Introducing an HRIS

See Figure 20.1.

Use of statistics

Statistics are used to describe and summarize data relating to a 'population', ie a homogeneous set of items with variable individual values. This involves measuring frequencies, central tendencies and dispersion.

They are also used to measure the relationships between variables (correlation and regression), to establish the relation between cause and effect (causality), to assess the degree of confidence that can be attached to conclusions (tests of significance) and to test hypotheses (the chi-squared test and null-hypothesis testing).

Statistics are used extensively in human resource management to analyse and present quantitative information which can be used to guide decisions and monitor outcomes.

Measures of central tendency

Measures of central tendency identify the middle or centre of a set of data. There are three types: arithmetic average or mean, median and mode.

Measures of dispersion

It is useful to measure the extent to which the items in a set are dispersed or spread over a range of data.

Correlation

Correlation represents the relationship between two variables. If they are highly correlated they are strongly connected to one another and vice versa.

Regression

Regression is another way of looking at the relationship between variables. It expresses how changes in levels of one item relate to changes in levels of another.

Causality

Determining the link between independent and dependent variables (cause and effect) is a major issue in research, especially in the HRM field. It may be relatively easy to establish correlations in the shape of a demonstration that X is associated with Y; it is much more difficult and sometimes impossible to prove that X causes Y.

Tests of significance

Significance as a statistical concept refers to the degree to which an event could have occurred by chance.

References

Chartered Institute of Personnel and Development (2007) *HR and Technology: Impact and advantages*, London, CIPD

Drucker, P (1988) The coming of the new organization, *Harvard Business Review*, January–February, pp 45–53

Questions

1 What is the meaning of information?

2 What are the main reasons for having a comprehensive human resource information system?

3 What are the five most popular applications of an HRIS?

4 What is an enterprise resource planning (ERP) system?

5 What is an intranet?

6 What is self-service and why is it important?

7 What are the main considerations to be taken into account in developing an HRIS?

8 How are statistics used?

9 What use of statistics is made by HR specialists?

10 What is frequency in statistics?

11 What are the three measures of central tendency?

12 What is dispersion and how is it measured?

13 What is correlation?

14 What is regression?

15 What is causality?

16 What are the problems of establishing causation?

17 What is a test of significance?

18 How can hypotheses be tested?

Business and financial skills

21

Key concepts and terms

- Absorption costing
- The acid test
- Activity-based costing
- Assets
- Balance sheet
- Budgetary control
- Budgets
- Business model
- Cash flow
- Cash flow statement
- Core competency
- Costing
- Current liabilities
- Direct costs
- Earnings per share
- Economic value added (EVA)
- Gearing
- Gross margin
- Gross profit
- Indirect costs

- Key performance indicator
- Liquidity analysis
- Marginal costing
- Net profit
- Operating or trading profit
- Overheads
- Over-trading
- Price/earnings ratio (P/E)
- Profit
- Profit before taxation
- Profit and loss account
- Profitability
- The resource-based view
- Return on capital employed
- Return on equity
- Shareholder value
- Standard costing
- Trading statement or account
- Working capital
- The working capital ratio

LEARNING OUTCOMES

On completing this chapter you should be able to define these key concepts. You should also understand:

- What it means to be businesslike
- How to interpret a balance sheet
- How profits are classified
- The purpose of trading and profit and loss statements
- The meaning of profitability and the key profitability ratios
- How budgeting and budgetary control work
- The purpose of cash management
- Methods of costing

Introduction

To make an effective contribution, HR professionals must possess business and financial skills. They need to understand what their business model is – how their organization delivers value to its customers and how the business achieves competitive advantage and makes money. They need to understand and be able to use the language of the business and, because this will generally be expressed in monetary terms, they need to appreciate how the financial systems of the business work. Equipped with this knowledge, HR professionals can develop the skills needed to interpret the organization's business or corporate strategies, to contribute to the formulation of those strategies and to develop integrated HR strategies.

This requirement was spelt out by Ulrich (1997: 7) when he wrote that: 'HR professionals must know the business, which includes a mastery of finance, strategy, marketing, and operations.' Research by the CIPD (2010: 5) led to the following conclusion:

> It is also evident that for some HR functions, they see HR as an applied business discipline first and a people discipline second. The ability to understand the business agenda in a deep way means that they are then able to help the business see how critical objectives can only truly be delivered if the people and cultural issues are fully factored in – insight into what it would take to truly deliver. In these places HR has a real share of voice and credibility... Where HR is grounded in the business and delivering the fundamentals well, then it is able to engage in higher value-adding 'OD' and talent-related activities that speak to the critical challenges faced in that organization.

Business skills

Business skills are required to adopt a businesslike approach to management – one which focuses on allocating resources to business opportunities and making the best use of them to achieve the required results. Managers who are businesslike understand and act upon:

- the business imperatives of the organization: its mission and its strategic goals;
- the organization's business model – the basis upon which its business is done (how its mission and strategic goals will be achieved);
- the organization's business drivers – the characteristics of the business which move it forward;
- the organization's core competencies – what the business is good at doing;
- the factors which will ensure the effectiveness of its activities, including specific issues concerning profitability, productivity, financial budgeting and control, costs and benefits, customer service and operational performance;
- the key performance indicators (KPIs) of the business (the results or outcomes which are identified as being crucial to the achievement of high performance), which can be used to measure progress towards attaining goals;
- the factors which will ensure that the firm's resources, especially its human resources, create sustained competitive advantage because they are valuable, imperfectly imitable and non-substitutable (the resource-based view).

Financial skills

A businesslike approach means using financial skills to know how to analyse and interpret balance sheets, cash flow and trading statements and profit and loss accounts, and to understand and make use of the financial techniques of budgeting and budgetary control, cash budgeting and costing.

Interpreting balance sheets

A balance sheet is a statement on the last day of the accounting period of the company's assets and liabilities and the share capital or shareholder's investment in the company. Balance sheet analysis assesses the financial strengths and weaknesses of the company, primarily from the point of view of the shareholders and potential investors, but also as part of management's task to exercise proper stewardship over the funds invested in the company and the assets in its care. The analysis focuses on the balance sheet equation, considers the make-up of the balance sheet in terms of assets and liabilities, and examines the liquidity position (how much cash or easily realizable assets are available) and capital structure with the help of balance sheet ratios.

The balance sheet equation

The balance sheet equation is: capital + liabilities = assets. Capital plus liabilities show where the money comes from, and assets indicate where the money is now.

Make-up of the balance sheet

The balance sheet contains four major sections:

- Assets or capital in use, divided into long-term or fixed assets (eg land, buildings and plant) and short-term or current assets, which include stocks of goods and materials, work in progress, debtors, bank balances and cash.
- Current liabilities, which are the amounts which will have to be paid within 12 months of the balance sheet date.
- Net current assets or working capital, which are current assets less current liabilities. Careful control of working capital lies at the heart of efficient business performance.
- Sources of capital, which comprise share capital, reserves including retained profits and long-term loans.

Liquidity analysis

Liquidity analysis is concerned with the extent to which the organization has an acceptable quantity of cash and easily realizable assets to meet its needs. The analysis may be based on the ratio of current assets (cash, working capital, etc) to current liabilities (the working capital ratio). Too low a ratio may mean that the liquid resources are insufficient to cover short-term payments. Too high a ratio might indicate that there is too much cash or working capital and that this is therefore being badly managed. The working capital ratio is susceptible to 'window dressing', which is the manipulation of the working capital position by accelerating or delaying transactions near the year end.

Liquidity analysis also uses the 'quick ratio' of current assets minus stocks to current liabilities. This concentrates on the more realizable of the current assets and therefore provides a stricter test of liquidity than the working capital ratio. It is therefore called 'the acid test'.

Capital structure analysis

Capital structure analysis examines the overall means by which a company finances its operations, which are partly by the funds of their ordinary shareholders (equity) and partly by loans from banks and other lenders (debt). The ratio of long-term debt to ordinary shareholder's funds indicates 'gearing'.

A company is said to be highly geared when it has a high level of loan capital as distinct from equity capital.

Classification of profits

Profit is basically the amount by which revenues exceed costs. It is classified in trading statements and profit and loss accounts in the following four ways:

- Gross profit – the difference between sales revenue and the cost of goods sold. This is also referred to as gross margin, especially in the retail industry.
- Operating or trading profit – gross profit less sales, marketing and distribution costs, administrative costs and research and development expenditure.
- Profit before taxation – operating profit plus invested income minus interest payable.
- Net profit – profit before taxation minus corporation tax.

Trading statements

Trading statements or accounts show the cost of goods manufactured, the cost of sales, sales revenue and the gross profit which is transferred to the profit and loss account.

Profit and loss accounts

Profit and loss accounts provide the information required to assess a company's profitability – the measure of the return in the shape of profits that shareholders obtain for their investment in the company. This is the primary aim and best measure of efficiency in competitive business. Profit and loss accounts show:

1 the gross profit from the trading account;
2 selling and administration expenses;
3 the operating profit (1 minus 2);
4 investment income;
5 profit before interest and taxation (3 plus 4);
6 profit before taxation (5 minus loan interest);
7 taxation;
8 net profit (6 minus 7).

Profitability analysis ratios

Profitability is expressed by the following ratios:

- Return on equity – profit after interest and preference dividends before tax in relation to ordinary share capital, reserves and retained profit.

This focuses attention on the efficiency of the company in earning profits on behalf of its shareholders; some analysts regard it as the best profitability ratio.

- Return on capital employed – trading or operating profit to capital employed. This measures the efficiency with which capital is employed.
- Earnings per share – profit after interest, taxation and preference dividends in relation to the number of issued ordinary shares. This is an alternative to return on equity as a measure of the generation of 'shareholder value' (the value of the investment made by shareholders in the company in terms of the return they get on that investment). Its drawback is that it depends on the number of shares issued, although it is often referred to within companies as the means by which their obligations to shareholders should be assessed.
- Price/earnings (P/E) ratio – market price of ordinary shares in relation to earnings per share. This ratio is often used by investment analysts.
- Economic value added (EVA) – post-tax operating profit minus the cost of capital invested in the business. This measures how effectively the company uses its funds.

Financial budgeting

Budgets translate policy into financial terms. They are statements of the planned allocation and use of the company's resources. They are needed to (1) show the financial implications of plans, (2) define the resources required to achieve the plans, and (3) provide the means of measuring, monitoring and controlling results against the plans.

The procedure for preparing financial budgets consists of the following steps:

- Budget guidelines are prepared which have been derived from the corporate plan and forecasts. They will include the activity levels for which budgets have to be created and the ratios to be achieved. The assumptions to be used in budgeting are also given. These could include rates of inflation and increases in costs and prices.
- Initial budgets for a budget or cost centre are prepared by departmental managers with the help of budget accountants.
- Departmental budgets are collated and analysed to produce the master budget, which is reviewed by top management, who may require changes at departmental level to bring it into line with corporate financial objectives and plans.
- The master budget is finally approved by top management and issued to each departmental (budget centre) manager for planning and control purposes.

Budgetary control

Budgetary control ensures that financial budgets are met and that any variances are identified and dealt with. Control starts with the budget for the cost centre, which sets out the budgeted expenditure under cost headings against activity levels. A system of measurement or recording is used to allocate expenditures to cost headings and record activity levels achieved. The actual expenditures and activity levels are compared and positive and negative variances noted. Cost centre managers then act to deal with the variances and report their results to higher management.

Cash management

Cash management involves forecasting and controlling cash flows (inflows and outflows of cash to and from the company). It is an important and systematic process of ensuring that problems of liquidity are minimized and that funds are managed effectively. The aim is to ensure that the company is not over-trading, ie that the cost of its operations does not significantly exceed the amount of cash available to finance them. The old adage is that, whatever else is done, ensure that 'Cash in exceeds cash out.'

Cash flow statements report the amounts of cash generated and cash used for a period. They are used to provide information on liquidity (the availability of cash), solvency and financial adaptability.

Cash budgeting

An operating cash budget deals with budgeted receipts (forecast cash flows) and budgeted payments (forecast cash outflows). It includes all the revenue expenditure incurred in financing current operations, ie the costs of running the business in order to generate sales.

Costing

Costing techniques provide information for decision making and control. They are used to establish the total cost of a product for stock valuation, pricing and estimating purposes and to enable the company to establish that the proposed selling price will enable a profit to be made.

Costing involves measuring the direct costs of material and labour plus the indirect costs (overheads) originating in the factory (factory overheads) and elsewhere in the company (sales, distribution, marketing, research and development and administration).

Overheads are charged to cost units to provide information on total costs – this process is called overhead recovery. There are four main methods of doing this:

- Absorption costing – this involves allocating all fixed and variable costs to cost units and is the most widely used method, although it can be arbitrary.

- Activity-based costing – costs are assigned to activities on the basis of an individual product's demand for each activity.
- Marginal costing – this segregates fixed costs and apportions the variable or marginal costs to products.
- Standard costing – this is the preparation of predetermined or standard costs which are compared with actual costs to identify variances. It is used to measure performance.

KEY LEARNING POINTS

To make an effective contribution, HR professionals must have business and financial skills. They need to understand what the business model is – how the organization delivers value to its customers and, in commercial organizations, how the business achieves competitive advantage and makes money.

Business skills

Business skills are required to adopt a businesslike approach to management – one which focuses on allocating resources to business opportunities and making the best use of them to achieve the required results.

Financial skills

A businesslike approach means using financial skills to know how to analyse and interpret balance sheets, cash flow and trading statements and profit and loss accounts, and to understand and make use of the financial techniques of budgeting and budgetary control, cash budgeting and costing.

Interpreting balance sheets

A balance sheet is a statement on the last day of the accounting period of the company's assets and liabilities and the share capital or reserves or shareholder's investment in the company.

Balance sheet analysis assesses the financial strengths and weaknesses of the company primarily from the point of view of the shareholders and potential investors, but also as part of management's task to exercise proper stewardship over the funds invested in the company and the assets in its care.

Classification of profits

It is necessary to understand the different ways in which profits can be classified as recorded in trading statements and profit and loss accounts. There are four headings: gross profit, operating or trading profit, profit before tax, net profit.

Trading statements

Trading statements or accounts show the cost of goods manufactured, the cost of sales, sales revenue and the gross profit which is transferred to the profit and loss account.

Profit and loss accounts

Profit and loss accounts provide the information required to assess a company's profitability – the primary aim and best measure of efficiency in competitive business. Profitability is a measure of the return in the shape of profits that shareholders obtain for their investment in the company. It is expressed in the following ratios: return on equity, return on capital employed, earnings per share, price/earnings (P/E) ratio, economic value added (EVA).

Financial budgeting

Budgets translate policy into financial terms. They are statements of the planned allocation and use of the company's resources.

Budgetary control

Budgetary control ensures that financial budgets are met and that any variances are identified and dealt with.

Cash management

Cash management involves forecasting and controlling cash flows (inflows and outflows of cash).

Cash budgeting

An operating cash budget deals with budgeted receipts (forecast cash flows) and budgeted payment (forecast cash outflows).

Costing

Costing techniques provide information for decision making and control. They are used to establish the total cost of a product for stock valuation, pricing and estimating purposes and to enable the company to establish that the proposed selling price will enable a profit to be made.

Overheads are charged to cost units to provide information on total costs – this process is called overhead recovery. There are four methods of doing this: absorption costing activity-based costing, marginal costing and standard costing.

References

Chartered Institute of Personnel and Development (2010) *Next Generation HR, Time for Change – Towards a next generation for HR*, London, CIPD

Ulrich, D (1997) Judge me more by my future than my past, *Human Resource Management*, **36** (1), pp 5–8

Questions

1   What is involved in being 'businesslike'?

2   What are the essential financial skills HR professionals need?

3   What is a balance sheet?

4   What is involved in balance sheet analysis?

5   What is liquidity analysis?

6   What is capital structure analysis?

7   What are the different ways of classifying profits?

8   What is a trading statement?

9   What is a profit and loss account?

10   What are the main components of a profit and loss account?

11   What is profitability?

12   What is return on equity?

13   What is return on capital employed?

14   What are earnings per share?

15   What is the price/earnings ratio?

16   What is financial budgeting?

17   What is budgetary control?

18   What does cash management involve?

19   What is an operating cash budget?

20   What does costing involve?

Postgraduate study skills

22

Key concepts and terms

- *Flash card*
- *Learning style*
- *Qualitative research*
- *Quantitative research*
- *Triangulation*

LEARNING OUTCOMES

On completing this chapter you should be able to define these key concepts. You should also know about:

- Learning styles
- Basic study skills
- Making the most of lectures
- Getting the most out of reading
- How to revise
- How to write essays and reports
- The principles of good writing
- Referencing

Introduction

Postgraduate study skills are concerned with what those studying for post-graduate degrees or for professional qualifications need to know and be able to do to learn effectively. The skills are those associated with the learning acquired from lectures and reading and those concerned with accessing, evaluating and conducting research. They are linked to essay and report writing and the skills required to revise for and take examinations. Most significantly, they are an essential aspect of continuing professional development and lifelong learning. This chapter deals with the conditions required for effective learning, the study skills involved, preparing for and taking exams and writing essays and reports.

Effective learning

Effective learning is partly dependent on the context – the quality of teaching and the educational resources available. But it is primarily a matter of what learners do – how they make use of or adapt their learning style.

Learning styles

Learners have different styles – a preference for a particular approach to learning. Kolb et al (1974) identified the following learning styles:

- Accommodators, who learn by trial and error, combining the concrete experience and experimentation stages of the cycle.
- Divergers, who prefer concrete to abstract learning situations and reflection to active involvement. Such individuals have great imaginative ability, and can view a complete situation from different viewpoints.
- Convergers, who prefer to experiment with ideas, considering them for their practical usefulness. Their main concern is whether the theory works in action, thus combining the abstract and experimental dimensions.
- Assimilators, who like to create their own theoretical models and assimilate a number of disparate observations into an overall integrated explanation. Thus they veer towards the reflective and abstract dimensions.

Another analysis of learning styles was made by Honey and Mumford (1996). They listed the following four styles:

- Activists, who involve themselves fully without bias in new experiences and revel in new challenges.
- Reflectors, who stand back and observe new experiences from different angles. They collect data, reflect on it and then come to a conclusion.
- Theorists, who adapt and apply their observations in the form of logical theories. They tend to be perfectionists.
- Pragmatists, who are keen to try out new ideas, approaches and concepts to see if they work.

However, none of these four learning styles is exclusive. It is quite possible that one person could be both a reflector and a theorist and someone else could be an activist/pragmatist, a reflector/pragmatist or even a theorist/pragmatist.

It is useful for learners to identify which style or mix of styles they prefer as this will affect the way they set about learning. But they must be prepared to flex their style in different situations.

Study skills

Study skills are concerned with absorbing, classifying, evaluating and recording ideas, concepts and information and reflecting on the meaning and significance of what has been absorbed. They cover learning from lectures and reading, and revision. More pragmatically, they prepare people to pass examinations. At professional or postgraduate level it is probable, even in a taught master's programme, that students will be left to their own devices much more than when they were taking their first degree (although undergraduates from some universities may question the extent to which they were ever taught a lot during their course). It is to be hoped that students honed their study skills at undergraduate level but they will need to exercise those skills even more effectively when they are postgraduates. And those who are studying for a professional qualification at postgraduate level such as that offered by the Chartered Institute of Personnel and Development (the CIPD), who have not attended a further or higher educational establishment, will need to give careful thought to the approach they adopt. Both categories of postgraduate student need to apply study skills such as those described below.

By the time you get to a postgraduate level of studies you should have become familiar with the best ways of getting to know your subject. But it will do no harm to be reminded of the basic principles you should adopt when pursuing your studies. These are concerned with making the best use of lectures (including note taking), your reading, and the information available on the internet, reflecting on what you have learned and revising.

Making the best use of lectures

A lecture has been defined as 'a system whereby the lecturer's notes are transferred to student's notes without passing through the minds of either' (Horn, 2009: 28). To achieve more than that during the lecture you should:

- carefully track the structure of the lecture from introduction to conclusion – follow the train of the lecturer's thoughts, which should have been made clear, although this may not always be the case and you might have to work hard during or after the lecture to make sense of it;

- listen actively – engage with the topic, relate the content of the lecture to what you already know, think about how it ties in with your experience;
- be critical – challenge in your mind any statements or assumptions made by the lecturer and if you feel strongly about them, challenge the lecturer – politely;
- follow the lecturer's PowerPoint slides and read the notes, but do not rely on them – do your own thinking and pay attention to your own note taking as suggested below.

Note taking during lectures

- Do not write too much – focus on key ideas, words and phrases. You can't get everything down.
- Avoid taking detailed notes on something you could easily get out of a textbook.
- Record the key points in brief paragraphs or notes.
- Number paragraphs for easy reference.
- Record any recommendations made on further reading or references.
- If you miss something, leave a space – it may be covered later in the lecture or in the conclusion and you can always refer to the lecturer's notes.

After a lecture

Following the lecture:

- Read through the notes.
- Tidy them up.
- Fill any gaps.
- Label and file the notes.
- Consider transcribing your notes onto a computer file – this is a good way of reinforcing the learning and will make them easier to access and read when using them as the basis for an essay or paper or revising; you can keep them in a portfolio alongside notes you make from your reading and any other information you need to record about your studies (some establishments require students to keep a portfolio).

Getting the most out of reading

The first thing to do is to decide what to read – there is plenty of choice. Your tutor should help by recommending key texts and referring to significant journal articles. Any good textbook will refer to supporting material. If you are studying human resource management it is obviously a good idea to read *People Management* and take a look at the information available on the CIPD website, which includes CIPD research reports and fact sheets. But you should also at least refer to the main British HR journals to spot relevant articles and identify useful research. These include the *British Journal of Industrial Relations*, the *British Journal of Management*, *Employee Relations*, the *Human Resource Management Journal* and the *International Journal of Human Resource Management*. If you cannot reach them in a library, they can be accessed if you are a member of the CIPD in EBSCO on the CIPD website. You can also use Google Scholar. Additional material is available from the publications of Income Data Services and Industrial Relations Services.

In reading such material, especially any that refers to current research, you should subject the contents to the tests of critical evaluation as set out in Chapter 19. Your own understanding will be increased if you analyse the positions, arguments and conclusions the author reaches to establish the extent to which they are based on sound logical reasoning.

Whatever you read, it is up to you to spot what is relevant. Lectures and general reading may help you to do this by providing the background to the subject matter. But it is ultimately up to you to extract what you think is significant in the shape of ideas, concepts, references to research, useful quotes and prescriptive material. Record these (this is the best way of concentrating the mind on complex material) or at least indicate where they can be found when wanted.

Make sure you are up to date with information which has appeared since your favourite textbook was published. This means collecting press cuttings, articles and in-company case studies and materials (from other organizations as well as your own).

Ensure that your notes are easily accessible when wanted for an essay or paper or for revision. They should be indexed and they can be sorted in a concertina file whose compartments reflect the major content themes. Alternatively, they can usefully be stored in a computer file. They can also be recorded on flash cards – A5 index cards which contain a summary (often in bullet points) of the main points concerning a topic and which can be referred to quickly, especially if they are indexed.

Revising

Revising for an exam can be a daunting task – 'Where do I start?' 'Where do I end?' 'What do I do in between?' Answers to these questions are provided in the lists of dos and don'ts listed below. There are more dos than don'ts; revision is a positive process. See Table 22.1

Taking exams

Table 22.2 sets out the dos and don'ts of taking exams.

TABLE 22.1 Dos and don'ts of revision

Dos and don'ts of revision	
Do	**Don't**
• Refer to the syllabus to identify the main subject areas.	• Leave revision to the last minute before the exam.
• Study previous exam papers to find out how examiners cover the syllabus and what are the most typical questions they ask in each area. Identify recurring questions.	• Simply keep on reading your notes – focus on the material you need to help answer exam questions.
• Define your revision priorities – draw up a list which sets out priorities, starting with the important and simple topics, continuing with the important but complex (and time-consuming) topics and finishing with the lowest-priority topics – those that are complex but not vital.	• Ignore your timetable. • Revise your timetable unnecessarily simply because you are bored with it. • Allow yourself to be diverted – set aside times for revision and do not permit interruptions.
• Select the topics you need to revise (covering the main areas in which questions are frequently asked in examinations).	• Pile up too much revision material – concentrate on the key issues, possibly recorded in flash cards.
• As a rule of thumb, know at least 50% of the content of the syllabus in detail and the rest more superficially so that if necessary you can say something sensible about any topic at all.	• Overdo it – there is a limit to what anyone can absorb, hence the need to pace yourself and avoid 'burning-the-midnight-oil' spells of revision.
• Break up what you need to revise into short, easily absorbed pieces.	
• Draw up a timetable, listing the topics you want to revise in order of priority.	

TABLE 22.1 (continued.)

Dos and don'ts of revision	
Do	**Don't**
• Set short-term goals for revision. • Identify where you can find the revision material – ideally it should all be in your notes, which you may need to reduce and reclassify for ease of reading and in accordance with priorities. It can usefully include a set of flash cards covering the most impor- tant topics, which provide a quick and easy way to revise key points. • Pace yourself – track your progress against the timetable and readjust if necessary. • Check your learning. Record the key things you have learned and refer to your revision priorities and timetable to ensure that you are up to speed. • Work out answers to a range of questions for each topic. • Practise answering sample ques- tions in each area in handwriting to check that you can produce persuasive and legible answers in the time available (this is very im- portant). Refer to your notes and if they are not sufficiently helpful, revise or expand them.	

TABLE 22.2 Dos and don'ts of taking exams

Dos and don'ts of taking exams	
Do	**Don't**

• Answer the question – this is very familiar advice but it is remarkable how, in the experience of most examiners (including this one), many candidates fail to do so.
• Pay particular attention to what you are asked to do in the question and do it. You will lose marks if you don't. Typically, you may be asked to:
  – *critically evaluate* a concept, notion or idea: this means that you are expected to show that you can use critical thinking to make informed judgements about the validity, relevance and usefulness of ideas and propositions, weighing arguments for and against them, assessing the strength of the evidence and deciding which are preferable;
  – *discuss*: write about the key aspects of the subject, critically evaluate it and assess the implications;
  – *refer to recent research* (recent usually means within the last five years but it can be stretched to 10 years for important projects): you need only summarize the main messages and give the name of the researcher and the date;
  – *refer to examples from within your own organization or one known to you*: show that you understand the practical issues by reference to actual practice;
	• Answer the question you would have liked to ask yourself (because you know all about it) rather than the one put by the examiner.
	• Spend too much time answering the questions you know about, leaving insufficient time to deal with the remaining questions.
	• Put down everything you know, rather than what the examiner asked you to do.
	• Try to get away with not providing examples or research evidence if asked to do so.
	• Present the examiner with undigested hunks of prose – set out each section clearly and ensure that they follow one another logically.
	• Produce an unstructured and confusing document – ensure that the examiner knows where you are coming from, where you are going and where you have got to.
	• Write illegibly – think of the examiner, who is only human and will tend to mark you down if your prose is virtually unreadable.
	• Rely on bullet points, simply listing headings without exploring the issue (in desperation you might use bullet points for the final answer if you are short of time but you will lose marks).

TABLE 22.2 (continued.)

Dos and don'ts of taking exams	
Do	**Don't**
– *justify*: supply evidenced reasons which support your argument; – *outline*: set out the main points or general principles relating to the topic; – *review*: explore the meaning and significance of a topic. • Develop your arguments logically. • Give practical examples wherever possible. • Seize every opportunity to display your knowledge by citing authors, sources, research, your own organization, other organizations, case study scenarios, benchmark achievements elsewhere, etc. • Structure your answers so that your material is easy to read and easy to follow. This means: following a logical progression from introduction to conclusions, underlined side headings to separate one part of your answer from the next (especially where a question has two or more sections); lists of itemized points; clear differentiation between your introduction and your conclusions. • Write legibly and articulately. Your presentation skills make a difference, especially at the margin.	• Deliver glib statements with no real explanation of what they mean in practical terms. • Forget that examiners prefer candidates who analyse the subject critically and conduct systematic reviews of the subject matter and its implications. • Pepper answers with dubious assumptions or grand overgeneralizations which result in unconvincing arguments. • Try to get away without incorporating properly identified evidence into material, to support assumptions and views. • Simply lift standard prescriptions wholesale from textbooks and apply them without any real understanding of their meaning. • Recommend so-called 'best practice' in a few words that are insufficient to convey its real content and meaning and for use in situations for which it has no apparent relevance.

Essay and report writing

As a postgraduate student you will be required to produce essays and reports on any research projects you carry out. Report writing is also an important skill for practitioners who may be involved in dealing with a problem (troubleshooting). The approaches you should use, which are applicable to essays as well as research and business reports, are given below.

1 Define the task. Decide what you are setting out to achieve (your objective) and, broadly, how you intend to achieve it. In a research report, note any basic propositions or assumptions that you are likely to put forward or adopt or any theories or concepts that you will evaluate. Decide on a provisional title and the likely scope of the essay or report.

2 Decide what information you need. This depends on the range of subject matter to be covered and whether it is a simple essay, an extended dissertation, a research project or a business troubleshooting report. Information for academic essays and reports will be obtained from your notes, additional reading of books, journals and other sources such as e-learning material and Wikipedia, blogs, or research. Troubleshooting business reports will rely on an identification of the facts required and a systematic process of getting and analysing those facts.

3 Obtain the information. If you are a postgraduate student preparing an essay or a dissertation, trawling through your lecture and reading notes should be straightforward if you have recorded and filed them properly. Reading round the subject means a little more work. Don't overdo it – trying to absorb too much information will only confuse you. Information for research reports is obtained from literature reviews, surveys, interviews and the assembly of case studies.

4 Analyse the information. Reflect on the information you have obtained. Check what you have found out and decide if you have enough. Establish the extent to which it will enable you to achieve your objective and support and clarify a convincing argument. If it doesn't, get more data.

5 Plan the structure of the essay or report. It is essential to structure an essay or report so that the reader can follow your line of reasoning readily. You have to consider, first, how you will introduce the essay or report setting out what it is about, your aim and any propositions or assumptions you are making; second, how you will present your views or evidence (which might include research findings) and develop your argument ; and finally, how you will reach a conclusion.

An essay or report should have a beginning, a middle and an end. If a report is lengthy or complex it will also need a summary of conclusions and recommendations. There may also be appendices containing detailed data and statistics. A report should be structured as follows:

- Beginning. Your introduction should state why the report has been written and why it should be read. A problem-solving report should define the problem and explain the circumstances. The sources of any evidence that will be referred to in the report should be identified and details of how that evidence was obtained should be supplied. The structure of the report should be described.
- Middle. The middle of the report should contain the facts you have assembled, your analysis of those facts and your observations on how they illuminate your proposition or support your argument. In a business problem-solving report the analysis should lead logically to a diagnosis of the causes of the problem.
- End. The conclusions and recommendations included in the final section should flow from the analysis and diagnosis. One of the most common weaknesses in reports is that the facts do not lead naturally to the conclusions; the other is for the conclusions not to be supported by the facts.
- Summarize the facts and your observations. In a problem-solving business report in which you have identified alternative courses of action, set out the pros and cons of each one, but make it quite clear which one you favour and why. Don't leave your readers in mid-air.
- The final section of a business report should set out your recommendations, stating how each of them would help to achieve the stated aims of the report or overcome any weaknesses revealed by the analytical studies. The benefits and costs of implementing the recommendations would be explained after the conclusions. A plan should be set out for implementing the proposals – the programme of work, complete with deadlines and names of people who would carry it out. The recipient(s) of the report should be told what action, such as approval of plans or authorization of expenditure, you would like them to take.
- This structure of a business report can be used when dealing with a problem case study question in an examination.

6 Draft the essay or report. When you draft your essay or report, bear in mind that the way in which you present and write it will considerably affect its impact and value. High-quality content is not enough; it must be presented well.

The reader should be able to follow your argument easily and not get bogged down in too much detail. The information you provide and your ideas should be grouped together so they can be presented in separate paragraphs. Paragraphs should be short and each one should be restricted to a single topic. Headings should be placed before sections to enable the reader to follow your ideas and arguments to your conclusion. Textbooks (like this one) and business reports tend to have more headings to guide readers than do essays, dissertations and journal articles. If you want to list or highlight a series of points, tabulate them or use bullet points but don't sacrifice meaning to clarity by omitting important material. Your arguments and proposition need substance; bullet points can make them look superficial.

Read and reread your draft to cut out any superfluous material, repetition, grammatical errors or flabby writing. Ensure that the argument is clear, convincing and flows from start to finish. Reorganize the structure of the report, including how it is paragraphed and its headings, to increase clarity.

Do not clutter up the main pages of a detailed report with masses of indigestible figures or other data. Summarize key statistics in compact, easy-to-follow tables with clear headings. Relegate supporting material to an appendix.

In a long or complex report, especially a business report, it is helpful to provide an executive summary of conclusions and recommendations. It concentrates the reader's mind and can be used as an agenda in presenting and discussing the report. The abstract at the beginning of a journal article serves the same purpose.

Good writing

Table 22.3 sets out the dos and don'ts of good writing.

Source references

In academic essays, dissertations or reports and in journal articles and textbooks it is essential when quoting someone or referring to something they have written to give the source. The normal conventions for referencing are:

- In the text of the essay or article give the name of the author or authors (if there are more than two authors, give the name of the first author followed by 'et al') and then the date in brackets. If it is a direct quotation give the page number(s), eg Gowers (1962: 37).
- If in an essay or article you refer to more than one publication by an author in the same year, attach 'a', 'b', etc to the name, eg Ulrich (1997a).
- Place references at the end of the essay or article and list them by author in alphabetical order. In a book, put them either at the end of the chapter or the end of the book.
- A reference to a book should state, in order, the family name of the author or authors, their initials, the date of publication in brackets, the title of the book in italics, the place of publication and the name of the publisher, eg Ulrich, D (1997) *Human Resource Champions*, Boston MA, Harvard Business School Press.

TABLE 22.3 Dos and don'ts of good writing

Do	Don't:
• Keep language simple and direct, eg use *begin* not *initiate, buy* not *purchase, find* not *locate, go* not *proceed, use* not *utilize.*	• Use more words than are necessary to express your meaning (avoid verbosity or padding).
• Prefer the short word to the long.	• Use jargon unless a technical term is unavoidable; in which case define it.
• Prefer the familiar word to the unusual or stylish.	
• Use words with a precise meaning rather than those that are vague.	• Use superfluous adjectives or adverbs.
• Prefer concrete words or phrases to abstract ones, eg *This material is scarce* rather than *The availability of this material is diminishing.*	• Use clichés.
	• Write long meandering sentences.
• Use active verb forms where possible rather than passive, eg *You should ensure...* rather than *It should be ensured...*	• Write *alternatively* when you mean *alternately.*
	• Write *less* when you mean *fewer.*
• 'Use the short expressive phrase even if it is conversational' (Winston Churchill, cited by Gowers, 1962: 37).	• Write *refute* when you mean *deny* or *repudiate.*
	• Write *mitigate* when you mean *militate.*
• Use short sentences to help you think clearly and gain the understanding of your reader. Express separate points or ideas in distinct sentences.	• Write *practical* when you mean *practicable.*
	• Misspell eg *accommodate, accessory, confident* (assured), *confidant* (person trusted with knowledge), *consensus, dependant* (as a noun), *dependent* (as an adjective), *desiccate, embarrass, liaise, stationary* (at rest), *stationery* (paper), *superintendent, underlie.*
• Remember that *each* demands a singular verb when it is the subject, eg *Each of the proposals has merit.*	
• Split an infinitive if it reads better.	
• Start a sentence with a conjunction, eg *and, but, or,* if it makes sense and reads well. But don't overdo it.	
• Use prepositions at the end of sentences whenever you like.	
• Say what you mean and mean what you say (after Lewis Carroll).	

- If the reference is to a chapter in an edited book it should look like this: Boxall, P F, Purcell J and Wright P (2007) Human resource management; scope, analysis and significance, in (eds) P Boxall, J Purcell and P Wright *The Oxford Handbook of Human Resource Management*, Oxford, Oxford University Press, pp 1–18.
- The page numbers of the chapter are sometimes included at the end as in the above example.
- A reference to an article should state, in order, the family name of the author or authors, their initials, the date of publication in brackets, the title of the article in plain lower case, the name of the publication in italics, the volume – which can be just the number – in bold, the issue number – often in brackets and not always included, although it is helpful when tracing the article – and the page numbers, eg: Armstrong, M (2000) The name has changed but has the game remained the same?, *Employee Relations*, **22** (6), pp 576–89.

Note that there may be some minor variations in these styles between publishers, especially in punctuation. This also applies to academic institutions. The examples given above conform to the Kogan Page house style, which minimizes punctuation.

KEY LEARNING POINTS

Postgraduate study skills are concerned with effective learning by those studying for postgraduate degrees or for professional qualifications at that level.

The skills are those associated with the learning acquired from lectures and reading and those concerned with accessing, evaluating and conducting research.

Effective learning

Effective learning is partly dependent on the context – the quality of teaching and the educational resources available. But it is primarily a matter of what learners do – how they make use of or adapt their learning style.

Study skills

Study skills are concerned with absorbing, classifying and recording ideas, concepts and information and reflecting on the meaning and significance of what has been absorbed.

To get the most out of a lecture you should:

- carefully track the structure of the lecture from introduction to conclusion;
- listen actively;
- be critical;
- follow the lecturer's slides and read the notes, but do not rely on them – do your own thinking.

Getting the most out of reading

- Decide what to read.
- Subject what the writer says to the tests of critical evaluation as set out in Chapter 19.
- Analyse the positions, arguments and conclusions the author reaches, to establish the extent to which they are based on sound logical reasoning.

Revising

The dos and don'ts of revising are given in Table 22.1.

Taking exams

The dos and don'ts of taking exams are given in Table 22.2.

Writing essays and reports

The approaches to use are:

- Define the task.
- Decide what information you need.
- Obtain the information.
- Analyse the information.
- Plan the structure of the essay or report.
- Draft the essay or report.

Good writing

The dos and don'ts of good writing are given in Table 22.3.

References

In academic essays, dissertations or reports and in journal articles and textbooks it is essential when quoting someone or referring to something they have written to give the source. The conventions are set out in the final section of this chapter.

References

Gowers, E (1962) *The Complete Plain Words*, Harmondsworth, Penguin Books

Honey, P and Mumford, A (1996) *The Manual of Learning Styles*, 3rd edn, Maidenhead, Honey Publications

Horn, R (2009) *The Business Skills Handbook*, London, CIPD

Kolb, D A, Rubin, I M and McIntyre, J M (1974) *Organizational Psychology: An experimental approach*, Englewood Cliffs NJ, Prentice Hall

Questions

1 What is the significance of the concept of learning styles?
2 What are study skills?
3 How can you make the best use of lectures?
4 What are the best approaches to taking notes?
5 What should you do to get the most out of a lecture?
6 How can you get the most out of reading?
7 What are the key 'dos' of revising?
8 What are the key 'don'ts' of revising?
9 What are the key 'dos' of taking exams?
10 What are the key 'don'ts' of taking exams?
11 How should an essay or report be structured?
12 What are the main points to be considered when drafting an essay or report?
13 What are the 'dos' of good writing?
14 What are the 'don'ts' of good writing?

APPENDIX
Alignment of text with CIPD modules

Leading, managing and developing people: indicative module content

1 Review and critically evaluate major contemporary research and debates in the fields of HRM and HRD

	Page
● Major research studies on contemporary developments in the HRM and HRD fields published in the UK and overseas, including those carried out or sponsored by the CIPD	(See index and support material)
● Evidence on links between HR practice and business outcomes	98–99
● Measuring the value of the HR function	83–84
● HRM and HRD practices in the most successful organizations	66–77
● Developing an effective interface between HR and line management through partnership working	84–85

2 Evaluate major theories relating to motivation, commitment and engagement at work and how these are put into practice by organizations

● Understand, explain and evaluate major theories relating to motivation, commitment and engagement at work and how these are put into practice by organizations	144–57 162–72 175–81
● Major motivation theories and their critics	164–72
● The significance of effective leadership, reward, performance management and career development opportunities	151

3 Debate and critically evaluate the characteristics of effective leadership and the methods used to develop leaders in organizations

- Types of leadership and management styles and their impact — 11–15
- Characteristics of successful and unsuccessful leaders — 10–11, 16
- Developing effective leaders in organizations — 16–17

4 Contribute to the promotion of flexible working and effective change management in organizations

- Understand and contribute to the promotion of flexible working — 201–06
- The growing significance of flexibility — 201
- Different types of flexibility — 202
- The contribution made by HRM and HRD specialists to the promotion of flexible working — 205–06
- Effective approaches to change management and major theories in the field — 185–97
- The central role played by people management practices in the effective management of change — 194–97

5 Critically discuss the aims and objectives of the HRM and HRD functions in organizations and how these are met in practice

- Organization and job design — 66–67
- Attracting and retaining people — 68–70
- Motivating and managing performance — 71–72
- Efficient administration of the employment relationship — 72–73
- Managing employee relations — 74
- Training and developing people — 34–40
- Rewarding people — 72

6 Assess the contribution made by HRM and HRD specialists in different types of organization

- Major contemporary developments in HRM and HRD practice in larger private sector companies, small and medium-sized enterprises, public sector organizations, voluntary sector organizations and international corporations — 101–10

7 Promote professionalism and an ethical approach to HRM and HRD practice in organizations

Developing skills for business leadership: indicative module content

1 Manage themselves more effectively at work or in another professional context

2 Manage interpersonal relationships at work more effectively

7 Demonstrate an essential people management skill set

8 Demonstrate competence in postgraduate study skills

Author Index

Subject Index